CBT for Those at Risk of a First Episode Psychosis

Can severe mental illness be prevented by early intervention?

Mental illness is highly prevalent in the general population and has its onset mostly in adolescence and young adulthood. Early intervention usually leads to improved prognosis. This book describes a newly developed, evidence-based cognitive behavioural intervention that can be used by clinicians to treat the precursor symptoms of psychosis and other severe mental illness. *CBT for Those at Risk of a First Episode Psychosis* offers a detailed new psychotherapy that has been shown to reduce the chance of transition to a first psychotic episode and to improve the chance for recovery. This encompasses:

- psycho-education about prepsychotic symptoms;
- a review of literature about psychological processes that are known to play a role in the development of psychosis;
- a comprehensive manual – illustrated by numerous clinical vignettes – that can be used to treat help-seeking subjects with an increased risk of developing psychosis;
- links to online resources and exercises to be used in therapy and education;
- a description of the multicentre randomised clinical trial investigating this new psychotherapy.

The vast collective experience and expertise of the authors of this handbook results in an invaluable text for clinicians working in mental health care, as well as students, lecturers and researchers who have an interest in the prevention of schizophrenia and other severe mental illness.

Mark van der Gaag is Professor of Clinical Psychology at the VU University, Amsterdam, and Head of Psychosis Research, Parnassia Psychiatric Institute, The Hague.

Dorien Nieman is a clinical and research psychologist in the Department of Psychiatry, Academic Medical Center, University of Amsterdam.

David van den Berg is a healthcare psychologist in the Early Detection and Intervention Team, Parnassia, The Hague.

CBT for Those at Risk of a First Episode Psychosis

Evidence-based psychotherapy for people with an 'At Risk Mental State'

Mark van der Gaag, Dorien Nieman and David van den Berg

LONDON AND NEW YORK

First published 2013
by Routledge
27 Church Road, Hove, East Sussex BN3 2FA

Simultaneously published in the USA and Canada
by Routledge
711 Third Avenue, New York, NY 10017

Routledge is an imprint of the Taylor & Francis Group, an informa business

© 2013 Mark van der Gaag, Dorien Nieman and David van den Berg

The right of Mark van der Gaag, Dorien Nieman and David van den Berg to be identified as authors of this work has been asserted by them in accordance with sections 77 and 78 of the Copyright, Designs and Patents Act 1988.

All rights reserved. No part of this book may be reprinted or reproduced or utilised in any form or by any electronic, mechanical, or other means, now known or hereafter invented, including photocopying and recording, or in any information storage or retrieval system, without permission in writing from the publishers.

Trademark notice: Product or corporate names may be trademarks or registered trademarks, and are used only for identification and explanation without intent to infringe.

British Library Cataloguing in Publication Data
A catalogue record for this book is available from the British Library

Library of Congress Cataloging in Publication Data
Gaag, Mark van der, 1953–
CBT for those at risk of a first episode psychosis: evidence-based psychotherapy for people with an "at risk mental state"/by Mark van der Gaag, Dorien Nieman, and David van den Berg.
pages cm
1. Psychoses – Treatment. 2. Cognitive therapy. 3. Evidence-based psychotherapy. I. Nieman, Dorien. II. Berg, David van den.
III. Title.
RC512.G33 2013
616.89'1425 – dc23
2012046066

ISBN: 978-0-415-53967-8 (hbk)
ISBN: 978-0-415-53968-5 (pbk)
ISBN: 978-0-203-50347-8 (ebk)

Typeset in Times New Roman and Helvetica Neue
by Florence Production Ltd, Stoodleigh, Devon, UK

Contents

List of illustrations ix
Foreword by Patrick McGorry xi
Acknowledgements xiii
Abbreviations xv

Introduction 1

PART I
Theory and evidence 3

1   What is an At Risk Mental State? 5

   What is the incidence of psychosis in ARMS? 6
   Prevalence and incidence of psychotic-like experiences 7
   Closing-in strategy 7
   What is the risk of psychosis in help-seeking ARMS subjects? 8
   Ethical issues 8

2   How to identify ARMS subjects? 9

   Importance of identifying ARMS subjects 9
   Instruments 10
   Procedure 11
   Conclusion 13
   CAARMS case examples 13
      Ibrahim   13
      Ben   14
      Agnes   15

3	**What are extraordinary experiences?**	**17**
	Several kinds of extraordinary experiences	17
	Sensory experiences 17	
	Distorted self-experiences 17	
	Ideas of reference 18	
	Speech and motor derailment 18	
4	**Which cognitive biases are associated with ARMS?**	**19**
	Perceptual bias	20
	Selective attention for threat (seeing danger anywhere) 20	
	Memory biases	23
	Source monitoring and hallucinations (remembering thoughts and phrases as originating from others) 23	
	Hindsight bias (I knew it all along)	24
	Attribution bias	26
	Self-serving bias and personalisation bias (blaming others for failure) 26	
	Covariation bias (overestimation of causality and underestimation of chance) 29	
	Reasoning biases	31
	Jumping to conclusions/data-gathering bias (hasty conclusions) 31	
	Negative expectation bias (pessimism) 36	
	Dogmatism/belief inflexibility bias (I know I am right, I need no proof) 39	
	Emotional reasoning (because if I feel anxious, there must be danger) 40	
	Confirmation bias (bias against disconfirmatory evidence) 42	
	Behavioural bias	43
	Avoidance behaviour (evading threat) 43	
5	**The nature of cognitive biases**	**45**
	Are some cognitive biases endophenotypes?	45
	Transdiagnostic biases	47
	Dopamine sensitisation, cognitive biases and extraordinary experiences	47
	Are cognitive biases open to change?	49
	Cognitive bias modification in anxiety and mood disorders 49	
	Cognitive biases, anxiety, depression and subclinical psychotic symptoms 49	
	Effects of metacognitive training in psychosis 50	
6	**Evidence for preventing or postponing a first episode psychosis**	**51**
	Introduction	51
	Goals of early detection	52

	Evidence for early intervention	53
	The Dutch Early Detection and Intervention Evaluation trial (EDIE-NL)	55
	Participants 55	
	Interventions 56	
	Results 57	
	Evidence for the protocol 58	

PART II
Practice of CBT for ultra-high risk   59

7	A manual for coping with extraordinary and remarkable experiences	61
	Rationale of the treatment	61
	THE MANUAL: 'COPING WITH EXTRAORDINARY AND REMARKABLE EXPERIENCES'	62
	(1) Introduction and (2) Pre-assessment (one session)	62
	(3) Psycho-education and normalising (one session)	74
	(4) CBT assessment and metacognitive training (six sessions)	85
	(5) Case formulation and goal setting (one session)	118
	(6) Cognitive behavioural intervention (6 to 12 sessions)	122
	(7) Post-assessment (one session)	140
	(8) Consolidation (one session)	141
	(9) Booster sessions (for instance, four sessions)	141

8	Typical vignettes of treatment cases	143
	When suspicion starts to impede functioning	143
	Introduction and assessment 143	
	Normalising information and alternative explanations 144	
	Metacognitive training 145	
	Case formulation 146	
	Cognitive behavioural therapy 146	
	Relapse prevention and end of therapy 147	
	When coincidence does not exist	148
	Introduction and assessment 148	
	Normalising information and alternative explanations 149	
	Metacognitive training 149	
	Case formulation 149	
	Cognitive behavioural therapy 150	
	Relapse prevention and end of therapy 151	
	When experiences and thoughts become intrusive	151
	Introduction and assessment 152	
	Normalising information and alternative explanations 152	
	Metacognitive training 152	

    Case formulation 153
    Cognitive behavioural therapy 153
    Relapse prevention and end of therapy 154
When ghosts are haunting   154
    Introduction and assessment 155
    Normalising information and alternative explanations 155
    Metacognitive training 156
    Case formulation 156
    Cognitive behavioural therapy 157
    Relapse prevention and end of therapy 158
Losing touch with reality   158
    Introduction and assessment 158
    Normalising information and alternative explanations 159
    Metacognitive training 159
    Case formulation 160
    Cognitive behavioural therapy 161
    Relapse prevention and end of therapy 161
Magical thinking   161
    Introduction and assessment 162
    Normalising information and alternative explanations 162
    Metacognitive training 163
    Case formulation 163
    Cognitive behavioural therapy 164
    Relapse prevention and end of therapy 165

Concluding remarks   **167**

Appendix A: Session forms 1 and 2   169–70
Appendix B: Additional ABC forms   171
Appendix C: ABC form for extraordinary experiences with alternative explanations   173
Appendix D: Case formulation form   175
Appendix E: Treatment goals form   177
Appendix F: Pie chart form   179
Appendix G: Cumulative probability form   181
Appendix H: Behavioural experiment form   183
Appendix I: Behavioural experiments and exposure assignments homework form   185
Appendix J: Multidimensional evaluation form   187
Appendix K: Reinforcing self-esteem exercise   189

References   191
Index   207

Illustrations

Figures

6.1	Survival curves in the EDIE-NL study	57
7.1	The mechanism of switching between a fast and emotional, and a conscious and well-thought, response	102
7.2	A cognitive model of depersonalisation and derealisation	111
7.3	Diagram showing the feed-forward and feed-backward systems illustrating the feeling of being controlled	113
7.4	Planning and controlling of movement by feed-forward and feed-backward systems in the brain	113
7.5	The routes involved in thinking, speaking and listening	115
7.6	Completed case formulation form	121
8.1	Case formulation: Mike	146
8.2	Case formulation: Charles	150
8.3	Case formulation: Aisha	153
8.4	Case formulation: June	157
8.5	Case formulation: Beatrice	160
8.6	Case formulation: Jennifer	163

Tables

1.1	Transition rates in ultra-high risk studies	6
5.1	Cognitive biases in schizophrenia patients, people with an At Risk Mental State for developing psychosis, and in first-degree relatives of psychotic patients	46
7.1	Some examples of frequently occurring extraordinary and remarkable experiences	69
7.2	Registration of extraordinary experiences (ABC form)	84

7.3	Cognitive biases posing a threat when judging extraordinary experiences	85
7.4	ABC form for extraordinary experiences with alternative explanations	91
7.5	Exercise with selective attention	97
7.6	Pessimistic and optimistic interpretations	100
7.7	Preventing mistakes by use of conscious re-evaluation	103
7.8	From confirmation bias to looking for counter-evidence	106
7.9	It is not the facts, but our interpretation that scares us	107
7.10	Interpreting extraordinary events and accompanying emotions	107
7.11	Examples of behavioural experiments	134–5

Foreword

Patrick McGorry

The past two decades have witnessed a dramatic wave of progress in early intervention strategies for psychotic disorders. This paradigm shift has been led by a large group of international clinicians and researchers who are committed to the development of an evidence base to guide and sustain progress and reform in mental health care in the twenty-first century. The authors of this superb monograph are among this group of leaders, and exemplify all the best features of this reform process. With deep roots in the therapeutic relationship and drawing on innovative ideas, they have used scientific and research methods to create and validate new knowledge and skills in treating people in the earliest clinical stages of psychosis, the 'At Risk Mental State' or the prodromal stage of illness.

The early visionaries of the schizophrenia field such as Harry Stack Sullivan, followed by subsequent generations of clinicians, understood that these potentially serious mental illnesses did not usually arise out of the blue; rather, they emerged imperceptibly from milder early stages, which at the time might have been difficult to distinguish from 'problems in living'. They held out the hope that if the onset of frank psychosis could be delayed or even prevented by intervening at the first signs of trouble, then this would be a key strategy to reduce the impact of these disorders. In modern parlance this represents disease modification or 'pre-emptive' psychiatry, something that is sought in all potentially serious or persistent illnesses.

The operational definition of 'At Risk Mental State' or the 'UHR' (ultra-high risk) state in the early 1990s, showing that incipient risk for psychosis could be predicted quite accurately, enabled researchers to begin to craft and study interventions to reduce the risk. Cognitive behaviour therapy, shown to be surprisingly effective for persistent psychotic symptoms in chronic schizophrenia, was an obvious candidate for testing in the earliest stages because of its safety and acceptability to patients. Several trials have shown that it does seem to be effective and the results of these studies indicate that CBT should be offered as first line therapy to UHR patients. Low dose antipsychotic medications, because of the increased risks associated with their use, are typically being withheld until and unless sustained and full threshold psychosis supervenes despite psychosocial interventions.

This valuable resource maps the landscape of this field and communicates how to go about this form of clinical intervention. It is another huge brick in the wall of an evidence-based approach to early intervention, which increases in height and strength as every year goes by. The authors have made a series of major contributions in how to formulate, engineer and safely deliver interventions during this critical stage of illness; also, in how to access enriched samples of patients in need of such care. Patients and families as well as a new generation of clinicians around the world have so many reasons to be extremely grateful for the dedication and skill of this extremely talented group of authors.

Acknowledgements

We would like to thank the many colleagues who played a role in the realisation of this book: Sven van Amstel, Hiske Becker, Petra Bervoets, Nynke Boonstra, Marion Bruns, Sara Dragt, Sarah Eussen, Saskia van Es, Sarah Eussen, Gitty de Haan, Mischa van der Helm, Ceres Horsmeijer, Martijn Huijgen, Helga Ising, Lianne Kampman, Rianne Klaassen, Don Linszen, Aaltsje Malda, Carin Meijer, Julia Meijer, Roeline Nieboer, Bianca Raijmakers, Judith Rietdijk, Marleen Rietveld, Nadia van der Spek, Annelies van Strater, Tinie van de Tang, Zhenya Tatkova, Jenny van der Werf, Swanny Wierenga, Lex Wunderink, Annemieke Zwart. Gratitude also goes to the people who we consulted on the scientific study: Paul French, Rachel Loewy, Kees Korrelboom, Tony Morrison, Niels Smits, Lucia Valmaggia and Alison Yung.

Abbreviations

ABCs	activating event, beliefs and consequences
ACC	anterior cingulated cortex
ADHD	attention deficit and hyperactivity disorder
ARMS	At Risk Mental State
BADE	bias against disconfirmatory evidence
BAI	Beck Anxiety Inventory
BDI	Beck Depression Inventory
BLIPS	brief limited intermittent psychotic symptoms
BSABS	Bonn Scale for the Assessment of Basic Symptoms
BSABS-P	Bonn Scale for the Assessment of Basic Symptoms-Prediction list
CAARMS	Comprehensive Assessment of At Risk Mental States
CBM	cognitive bias modification
CBT	cognitive behavioural therapy
DSM	*Diagnostic and Statistical Manual of Mental Disorders*
DUP	duration of untreated psychosis
EDIT	Early Detection and Intervention Team
EF	executive functioning
ESP	extrasensory perception
FEP	first episode psychosis
fMRI	functional magnetic resonance imaging
GAF	Global Assessment of Functioning
GP	general practitioner
JTC	jumping to conclusions
MANSA	Manchester Short Assessment of Quality of Life
MC	motor cortex
MCT	metacognitive training
NAcc	nucleus accumbens
NNT	number needed to treat
OCD	obsessive–compulsive disorder

OCS	obsessive–compulsive symptoms
PANSS	Positive and Negative Syndrome Scale
PFC	prefrontal cortex
PQ	Prodromal Questionnaire
PRIME	Prevention through Risk Identification, Management and Education
PSYRATS	Psychotic Rating Scales
PTSD	post-traumatic stress disorder
RCT	randomised controlled trial
SC	sensory cortex
SCAN	Schedules for Clinical Assessment in Neuropsychiatry
SIAS	Social Interaction Anxiety Scale
SIPS	Structured Interview of Prodromal Syndromes
SMA	supplemental motor areas
SMART	Specific, Measurable, Attainable, Relevant and Time bound
SOFAS	Social and Occupational Functioning Assessment Scale
TAU	treatment as usual
UHR	ultra high risk
VP	ventral pallidus
VTA	ventral tegmental area

Introduction

The authors have been working for many years with individuals with schizophrenia and have seen the devastating effect that this illness has on their lives, and on the lives of their families and friends. For the vast majority of our patients, schizophrenia remains a mental disorder with an unknown aetiology, unchanged prevalence and a disabling outcome. Various treatments, especially pharmacological ones, have been tried with the aim of improving its disabling lifetime course (Lieberman et al., 2005). However, both symptomatic and functional outcomes are still far from optimal.

Recently, instead of being classified as a neurodegenerative disorder, schizophrenia is now considered by some to be a neurodevelopmental disorder with first and recurrent psychotic episodes as a late stage of the illness (Insel, 2010). Despite this new conceptualisation, in most patients the underlying mechanisms of decreased functioning at work/school and with social relationships remain unknown. Poor social functioning in psychosis tends to emerge early, even in the prodromal period, and can become chronic (Carpenter and Strauss, 1991).

The study of young individuals with an At Risk Mental State (ARMS) for developing psychosis is a promising approach to unravel developmental mechanisms involved in the aetiology of schizophrenia. A psychosis is usually preceded by a period of months (or even years) in which the subject experiences frightening mild psychotic symptoms, such as sometimes hearing a voice or occasional attacks of paranoia. Although the risk of making a transition to a first psychosis is increased in subjects with these symptoms, psychosis is not inevitable. Research on ARMS may enable us to develop prevention strategies, which would have a significant impact in terms of mental health care. Intervention in the ARMS stage may be more effective than intervention after psychotic onset, because the individual is in a more treatment-responsive stage of illness in which the neurobiological and psychosocial damage is less extensive.

In our institutes, we have been treating ARMS subjects with cognitive behavioural therapy (CBT) and noticed that these subjects are highly responsive to psycho-education with regard to their symptoms; this often leads to normalisation and improved social functioning. Although only a small percentage of ARMS subjects eventually develops a first psychotic episode, almost all ARMS subjects are afraid that they will 'go mad' and seek help. Cognitive biases (such as jumping to conclusions, selective attention to threat and negative expectation bias) seem to negatively influence the course of ARMS symptoms and play an important role in the onset of a first psychosis (Moritz and Woodward, 2007a, 2007b). Therefore, in 2008 we initiated a randomised controlled trial to investigate the effects of a newly developed CBT for ARMS subjects, targeting cognitive biases and catastrophic interpretations of ARMS symptoms.

The basic CBT techniques described by French and Morrison formed the basis of our manual (French and Morrison, 2004). However, we have enlarged the protocol with detailed psycho-education on cognitive biases and the effects of dopamine supersensitivity on perception and reasoning. Furthermore, we have added many exercises specifically developed for the ARMS group to demonstrate the effect of cognitive biases on symptoms and behaviour.

The first section of the book (Chapters 1 to 5) covers the introductory topics. Chapter 1 describes the background of the ARMS concept. Chapter 2 contains an overview of the diagnostic process leading to inclusion in the ARMS group, and presents a brief introduction to the possibility of starting an ARMS diagnostic centre. Since ARMS is often unrecognised and mistreated, starting a diagnostic and treatment centre for ARMS subjects might prove to be of great clinical value. Chapters 3 to 5 describe the scientific and clinical background of the extraordinary experiences and cognitive biases in these ARMS patients.

The second and third sections of this book (Chapters 6 to 8) go into more detail. In Chapter 6 we describe the randomised controlled trial that demonstrates the effectiveness of the newly developed CBT. In the third section, Chapter 7 describes the manual that we used in the trial. In addition, we have included practical tips for the therapists, as well as some explanatory dialogues that will serve to clarify the manual's use in daily practice. The parts that refer to the manual (for the patient) are highlighted by a black side rule throughout. The basic manual (without these additions) can be found on the website that supports this book (www.routledge.com/9780415539685), together with the forms used in this CBT and other useful materials. Finally, Chapter 8 presents (anonymous) case examples of typical ARMS subjects treated with the manual.

We hope that this book and the related website will find its way to clinical psychologists, psychotherapists and psychiatrists working in mental health care who are in need of a safe and evidence-based treatment option for patients with ARMS.

PART I

Theory and evidence

1

What is an At Risk Mental State?

Most patients with schizophrenia go through a prodromal period in which they experience problems such as depression, sleeplessness, agitation, cognitive difficulties, and decline in social and vocational functioning. In addition, psychotic symptoms can be experienced at a subclinical level. Retrospectively, these features are recognised as prodromal to the outbreak of a first psychotic episode.

Many of the prodromal features are non-specific and cannot be used as a single predictor of an imminent psychosis. For instance, many first episodes are preceded by depression, but a depressed mood does not necessarily end in a psychotic state for most people who experience a depressed mood. For this reason, it has been very difficult to predict relapse and even more difficult to predict the transition to a first psychotic episode. To predict the transition to psychosis, the best strategy seems to be to follow up subjects at ultra-high risk for developing a first psychosis. The current international consensus differentiates ultra-high risk subjects into four groups (McGorry, Yung and Phillips, 2003; Miller *et al.*, 2003; Yung *et al.*, 2005); individuals in these groups have an ARMS:

1. a genetically endowed group with a schizotypal personality disorder or a first-degree relative with psychosis (genetic group);
2. subclinical psychotic symptoms of adequate intensity and low frequency (subthreshold frequency group);
3. subclinical psychotic symptoms of low intensity and relatively high frequency (subthreshold intensity group);
4. florid psychotic symptoms during less than seven days, which go into remission without an external intervention such as antipsychotic medication. This condition is also called brief limited intermittent psychotic symptoms (BLIPS).

In addition to the above-described criteria, there has to be impairment in social functioning as assessed with the Social and Occupational Functioning Assessment Scale (SOFAS) (Goldman, Skodol and Lave, 1992), i.e. a SOFAS score of ≤ 50 in the past 12 months or longer, and/or a drop in the SOFAS score of 30 per cent for at least one month in the past year.

What is the incidence of psychosis in ARMS?

The transition rates from ARMS into a frank psychosis have a relatively wide range. Earlier studies reported relatively high transition rates (about 40 per cent; McGorry, Yung and Phillips, 2003; Miller *et al.*, 2003), whereas more recent studies report more modest transition rates (7–20 per cent; Ruhrmann *et al.*, 2010). Over the years, the transition rates in the Australian project have been declining, which the researchers attribute to an improved health-care system that detects ARMS subjects much earlier than previously, when subjects were already in a late prodromal stage (Yung *et al.*, 2007). This offers a clinical advantage, because therapy may be more effective in an early prodromal state and can result in a reduction in the number of transitions. Another explanation for the lower transition rates might be the inclusion of a larger proportion of 'false positives' in the research sample. False positive means that the person is *suspected* of being at risk for developing a psychosis, but will never actually develop a first psychosis.

Table 1.1 shows the reported transition rates from studies (published 2002–2012). A recent meta-analysis showed 18 per cent transition after 6 months;

Table 1.1 Transition rates in ultra-high risk studies

First author and year of publication	No. of patients	Period of follow-up months	Transitions (%)	Transitions in first 12 months (%)
Miller 2002	13	6 and 12	46 and 54	54
Yung 2003	49	12	41	41
Lencz 2003	37	6	27	
Mason 2004	74	26	50	23
Yung 2004	104	12	35	
Haroun 2006	50	12	13	13
Yung 2006	119	6	10	
Lemos 2006	30	12	27	27
Lam 2006	62	6	29	
Riecher Rössler 2007	50	12	23	23
Yung 2008	292	24	16	8
Cannon 2008	291	30	35	14
Nieman 2009	72	36	25	8
Riecher Rössler 2009	64	Mean 5.4 years	34	29
Ruhrmann 2010	245	18	15	7
Demjaha 2012	122	24	15	11
Ziermans 2011	72	24	13	10
Bechdolf 2012 control group	65	24	20	17
Addington 2011 control group	24	18	13	13
Morrison 2012a control group	144	24	9	7
van der Gaag 2012 control group	99	18	22	20
Mean				19

22 per cent after 1 year; 29 per cent after 2 years and 36 per cent after 3 years (Fusar-Poli et al., 2012).

Prevalence and incidence of psychotic-like experiences

Psychotic features are not uncommon in the general population. Having one or more psychotic symptoms was found in 24.8 per cent ($n = 5877$) of the American population (Kendler, Gallagher, Abelson and Kessler, 1996), in 17.5 per cent ($n = 7076$) of the Dutch population (van Os, Hanssen, Bijl and Vollebergh, 2001) and in 17.5 per cent ($n = 2548$) of the German population (Spauwen, Krabbendam, Lieb, Wittchen and van Os, 2003). In a birth cohort, 25 per cent ($n = 761$) reported at least one psychotic symptom at age 26 years (Poulton et al., 2000). In an English–German–Italian study, in which hypnagogic and hypnopompic hallucinations were also included, the percentage increased to 38.7 per cent ($n = 13057$) (Ohayon, 2000).

It is difficult to detect a rare disease in the general population. The incidence of subclinical psychotic symptoms is about 100 times as high in the population as the incidence of a psychotic disorder (Hanssen, Bak, Bijl, Vollebergh and van Os, 2005). In a population-based survey using the Dutch NEMESIS cohort ($n = 7076$), 18.1 per cent of the subjects had one or more self-reported psychotic symptoms, while 0.4 per cent had a non-affective psychotic disorder and 1.1 per cent had an affective psychotic disorder. After three years the group with one or more psychotic symptoms was symptom free in 84 per cent of the cases. Persistent psychotic symptoms (without meeting the diagnosis of a psychotic disorder) were present in 8 per cent of the cases, whereas another 8 per cent of the subjects had developed a more serious condition and was in need of treatment because of the psychotic symptoms.

In the common pathway to psychosis, psychological appraisal processes seem to play an important role. A negative emotional appraisal of the symptoms preceded the transition into psychosis (Hanssen et al., 2005). Furthermore, subclinical hallucinations have a higher incidence of developing into frank psychosis when the person develops secondary delusional beliefs and appraisals (Krabbendam et al., 2004).

In the NEMESIS study, self-rated symptoms were validated by professional judgement. In 37 per cent of the cases, the professionals judged the symptoms to be absent. It is important to be aware that self-assessment may result in an overrating of symptoms. However, the false positives, where the professional down-rated a self-reported symptom, still had a higher rate of developing psychosis (OR = 19.2) after three years. The true positives had, of course, the highest rate (OR = 77.1) (Bak et al., 2003).

Closing-in strategy

Since subclinical symptoms are highly prevalent in the general population and most of these symptoms remit spontaneously, preventive intervention is not really an option. Too many false-positive subjects, who will never develop psychosis, will be treated unnecessarily. To reduce the number of false positives, the sample that is assessed must be enriched.

Enrichment can be achieved by combining risk factors: the closing-in strategy. For example, the risk of developing psychosis within two years when a subject experiences one psychotic symptom is only 8 per cent; the risk of developing psychosis within two years when the subject has a family history of schizophrenia is only 1 per cent; however, the combined risk of these two variables for developing psychosis within two years is 25 per cent.

This increase in risk is also present in other risk factor combinations (van Os and Delespaul, 2005):

Subclinical symptom with distress and/or help seeking	14%
Subclinical symptom with depressed mood	15%
Subclinical symptom with impaired social functioning	16%
More than one subclinical symptom	21%
More than one subclinical symptom with depressed mood	40%

A possibility is to screen a young and help-seeking population with a self-rating instrument and then perform the 'gold standard' CAARMS interview to detect the psychotic and the at-risk subpopulations. The ultra-high risk group is then composed of young people with an axis 1 disorder and psychotic-like experiences with some distress; this group will have a theoretical risk of transition within two years of 15–25 per cent.

What is the risk of psychosis in help-seeking ARMS subjects?

In a help-seeking population, 59.2 per cent of the patients remitted in one year; 13.5 per cent made the transition into frank psychosis and 27.3 per cent had persistent subclinical symptoms (Simon et al., 2009). Compared to the general population, the number of transitions has almost doubled and the number of patients with persistent subclinical positive symptoms has more than tripled. Over a two-year time frame, if an intervention could reduce the number of non-remitted patients from 40 to 20 per cent it would be regarded as a valuable intervention. When we take into account the costs of a transition, more modest results could also be cost-effective as schizophrenia is a very costly condition over a lifetime because of high admission costs and huge losses due to persistent vocational impairment and disability pensions.

Ethical issues

The main issue in preventive intervention is the number of people who are treated unnecessarily. This is especially true with non-perfect treatments (e.g. 50 per cent success rate) and adverse side effects (e.g. of antipsychotic medication). The minimum requirements are an identified risk population with a transition rate into psychosis of 25 per cent, and a 50 per cent reduction in transitions as a result of the intervention. In that case the number needed to treat is ten, which is considered to be acceptable. When the population/individual is seeking help themselves, then the objection of unnecessary treatment is no longer valid.

2

How to identify ARMS subjects?

Importance of identifying ARMS subjects

Many studies have shown the importance of the duration of untreated psychosis (DUP) for the long-term prognosis in first episode psychosis patients (Drake, Haley, Akhtar and Lewis, 2000; Large, Nielssen, Slade and Harris, 2008; Larsen et al., 2011; Melle et al., 2008). Patients with a long DUP have more severe symptoms at first presentation, and long DUP may be associated with a reduced response to antipsychotic medication (Perkins, Gu, Boteva and Lieberman, 2005).

In previous studies assessing DUP, a wide range in median and mean DUP was found. Marshall and colleagues conducted a systematic review and found a mean DUP of 103 weeks, as assessed in 26 studies (Marshall et al., 2005). A more recent review reported a median DUP of 21.6 weeks, as assessed in 24 studies (Anderson, Fuhrer and Malla, 2010).

The Northwick Park Study reported that if things are not well managed in the early stages of psychosis, then deterioration continues until finally a crisis occurs, which frequently involves the police (Johnstone, Crow, Johnson and MacMillan, 1986). Floridly psychotic subjects may be admitted involuntarily. However, there is evidence that such admissions can lead to the development of post-traumatic stress disorder (PTSD) (Frame and Morrison, 2001; McGorry et al., 1991). During psychosis, subjects are often unable to work and become socially isolated. Patients often lack insight into their illness and may alienate family and friends. In retrospect, the period before the onset of frank psychosis is called the prodromal period and can last up to five years. Prospectively, this period is called the ARMS period, because not all subjects with an ARMS for developing psychosis will make the transition to psychosis.

In the ARMS period, subjects are often aware that something is wrong. They may be afraid of losing their mind. Subjects in the ARMS phase could say: 'Sometimes I think I'm being followed – but I know this is unlikely', whereas a psychotic patient may say: 'I am being followed'. Obviously, it is easier to intervene if subjects still have illness insight and illness awareness. In addition, subjects with an ARMS may still maintain social contacts, work and/or education, although to a decreasing extent because of their symptoms. Intervening in the ARMS phase offers the opportunity to help subjects preserve their activities and thus avoid a decline in functioning. Furthermore, if subjects are already in care before their first psychotic episode and unfortunately do make the transition to psychosis, then they have a DUP of almost zero weeks.

Some argue that detecting ARMS subjects carries the risk of stigmatising these subjects and making them more worried than is necessary. In our experience, ARMS subjects do not feel stigmatised when their symptoms are discussed and when they are treated for their symptoms. Because of the closing-in strategy (see Chapter 1), subjects are seeking help and they are already worried. Offering treatment in the form of psycho-education and help with preserving their daily activities (work/schooling and social contacts) reduces catastrophic interpretations of extraordinary experiences and is usually not experienced as stigmatising.

Instruments

Over the years, several instruments have been developed to identify subjects with an ARMS for developing psychosis. The Structured Interview of Prodromal Syndromes with its rating scale, Scale of Prodromal Symptoms, was developed at Yale University (USA) by the group of McGlashan (Miller *et al.*, 2003). This instrument is comparable but slightly different from the other widely used scale: the Comprehensive Assessment of At Risk Mental States (CAARMS). This latter instrument was developed in Australia (Yung *et al.*, 2003) and is updated every few years based on latest scientific findings.

The CAARMS (version 3) is composed of seven sections:

1. Positive symptoms (four items)
2. Cognitive change attention/concentration (two items)
3. Emotional disturbance (three items)
4. Negative symptoms (three items)
5. Behavioural change (four items)
6. Motor/physical changes (four items)
7. General psychopathology (eight items).

The positive symptom items are currently the main items on the basis of which subjects are included in an ARMS sample. The four positive symptoms items are:

1.1 Unusual thought content
1.2 Non-bizarre ideas
1.3 Perceptual disturbance
1.4 Disorganised speech.

These items are scored with anchor points on intensity (0–6-point Likert scale) and frequency/duration (0–6-point Likert scale). Furthermore, dates of start and end of symptoms are annotated, as well as the level of distress (0–100) and relationship with drug use (0–2). The CAARMS can be found on the website related to this book. It is important to ascertain the combination of intensity and frequency/duration of the positive symptoms if a subject has attenuated positive symptoms, BLIPS, psychosis and/or is above or below the threshold symptoms (see case examples below).

In the 1960s Huber and Gross designed the Bonn Scale for the Assessment of Basic Symptoms (BSABS) on the basis of the primary symptoms of schizophrenia according to Bleuler (Bleuler, 1911). Basic symptoms are subtle, subjective, subclinical disturbances in cognitive, motoric and emotional functioning. Further analyses of basic symptoms resulted in a set of predictive criteria based on nine cognitive disturbances (BSABS-P) (Klosterkötter, Hellmich, Steinmeyer and Schültze-Lutter, 2001; Schültze-Lutter and Klosterkötter, 2002). The BSABS-P has predictive validity for a first psychotic episode over a period of ten years and may reflect the earliest signs and symptoms of a schizophrenic development.

More recently, the self-report Prodromal Questionnaire (PQ), was developed by Loewy and colleagues to screen for possible ARMS symptoms (Loewy, Bearden, Johnson, Raine and Cannon, 2005). If subjects score above a certain cut-off, a semi-structured interview, like the CAARMS, is recommended to ascertain whether subjects fulfil the ARMS criteria. Ising and colleagues reduced the 92 items of the PQ to 16 items with acceptable sensitivity and specificity (Ising et al., 2012). The 16-item PQ can be used to screen for possible ARMS symptoms in help-seeking subjects with psychiatric symptoms (Rietdijk, Linszen and van der Gaag, 2011).

It is important to screen for psychosis or ARMS in help-seeking subjects with psychiatric symptoms because psychosis can be overlooked if subjects receive help for symptoms other than psychotic symptoms. Several studies report a high rate of subjects who meet the criteria for a psychotic disorder who had not been detected by clinicians, suggesting that caretakers in mental health care are often unaware of the presence of psychotic symptoms in patients who seek treatment for other types of mental disorders (Boonstra et al., 2011; Marshall et al., 2005). Therefore, screening with the PQ-16 in the general help-seeking population in secondary mental health care may help in reducing DUP and identifying ultra-high risk subjects who might otherwise not be detected. Furthermore, several studies found a large percentage of patients with a psychotic disorder in a sample referred with a suspicion of a psychotic development (Broome et al., 2005a; Nelson and Yung, 2007; Nieman et al., 2009). Thus, an important function of the ARMS projects could be earlier recognition of psychosis and therefore a reduction in the duration of untreated psychosis.

Procedure

As discussed in Chapter 1, psychotic-like symptoms are too common in the general population to be able to screen for ARMS subjects in those groups (e.g. in schools). Therefore, a closing-in strategy has been adopted by almost all centres that focus on the ARMS phase. Potential ARMS subjects are either referred by primary or secondary (mental) health services or are detected by screening in a help-seeking psychiatric population. Before inclusion in an ultra-high risk group, the CAARMS or Structured Interview of Prodromal Symptoms (SIPS) is usually employed to ascertain whether subjects fulfil the ARMS criteria. An interview with another person close to the patient (e.g. parents, a sibling or husband/wife) increases the reliability of the SIPS or CAARMS scoring. All information obtained should be used during scoring. Sometimes (especially young) subjects may trivialise their symptoms or may be reluctant to reveal all their extraordinary experiences. Speaking to the parents usually provides a lot of extra information, making the scoring more reliable.

A CAARMS or SIPS interview generally takes about 1–1.5 hours. The ARMS intake usually starts with questions about why the subject has sought help. When using the CAARMS, the questions of the Social and Occupational Functioning Assessment Scale (Goldman et al., 1992) are subsequently asked. This scale is comparable to the Global Assessment of Functioning (GAF) scale but without the inclusion of symptomatology. Subjects receive a score (range 0 to 100) related to their social and occupational functioning. In the CAARMS, all inclusion groups require a SOFAS score of ≤ 50 or a reduction of at least 30 per cent in the SOFAS score for at least one month, compared to premorbid functioning in the past year. This criterion was added to the CAARMS because many ARMS studies reported a significantly lower mean baseline SOFAS or GAF score in the ARMS group that later makes the transition to psychosis, compared with the ARMS group that does not make the transition (Yung et al., 2003). In clinical practice, subjects with mild positive symptoms with no decrease in functioning usually do not make the transition to psychosis. Furthermore, drug use in the past and present is recorded, as are physical illnesses and (psychiatric) medication history.

It is recommended that parents also be interviewed, especially when subjects are relatively young. When parents are interviewed, this takes place at the same time that the patient is seen for the CAARMS. Generally, the parents are pleased to cooperate, because they are worried, having noticed the symptoms of their child. In addition, parents can report symptoms that may not be mentioned by the patient because he/she is ashamed to describe them (e.g. hallucinations), or he/she is not aware of them (e.g. disorganisation). In the interview with the parents, the development of their child is discussed from pregnancy to present. Development is important to screen for pervasive development disorders. It is important to know whether subjects fulfil the DSM-IV criteria (APA, 2001) for pervasive development disorder, because this diagnosis influences treatment. If symptoms are present for more than five years without an increase in intensity, frequency or duration, subjects are not included in the ARMS group.

After the interviews with the parents and patients, the professionals involved discuss their findings. All information is written down in a report and the CAARMS is scored on the basis of all information. Subsequently, the patient is discussed in a consensus meeting with psychiatrists, psychologists, nurses, psychiatry residents and psychology students. It is sometimes difficult to decide whether a subject falls into the ARMS group or has crossed the border into frank psychosis because, for example, the subject has difficulty describing the frequency of the symptoms. In all centres using the CAARMS, these difficulties occur because the border between ARMS and frank psychosis is not clear cut. It can be compared with the process of day becoming night. When is the exact moment to call it night instead of day? Several case examples describing the CAARMS assessment are presented at the end of this chapter.

It may also be difficult to decide whether a subject fulfils the ARMS criteria or has below-threshold symptoms. In this situation a general rule is: if in doubt, better in than out. Thus, it is safer to offer a subject with possible ARMS symptoms a benign therapy such as cognitive behavioural therapy than to send a subject home with no follow-up contact. Another possibility is to schedule a CAARMS interview after six months and thereby monitor the symptoms. In any case, it is recommended that subjects be discussed in a consensus meeting with experienced CAARMS interviewers present in order to come to a joint decision. Before being able to use the CAARMS, professionals should attend a CAARMS course followed by clinical training supervised by an experienced CAARMS interviewer.

An appointment is scheduled shortly after the consensus meeting to discuss the findings with the patient and his/her parents. First, the reports are summarised, giving an overview of what has been said during both interviews (with the patient and parents). Then, the conclusion and advice for treatment is given. Offering treatment or monitoring is usually comforting for the parents and the patient. In several centres where only adult patients are treated, the parents are not invited. Trained psychologists conduct the CAARMS interview and discuss their findings in a weekly meeting with an experienced psychologist.

Conclusion

Detecting and treating subjects at ultra-high risk is important because intervention in the ARMS phase may reduce the chance of transition to psychosis and improve the prognosis. In addition, screening for ARMS symptoms helps to detect unrecognised psychosis. When setting up an ARMS screening and treatment centre, it is important that professionals are well trained in the CAARMS – both theoretically and in clinical practice. In addition, decisions about diagnosis should be made in a consensus meeting.

CAARMS case examples

Ibrahim

Ibrahim is a 28-year-old entrepreneur whose business went bankrupt eight months ago. One month after the bankruptcy his wife left him. Ibrahim moved into a small and unfurnished apartment where he sleeps on a couch. The bankruptcy has loaded Ibrahim with considerable financial problems. He has a large debt and can no longer pay the mortgage on his house. His wife divorced him. She blames Ibrahim for ruining their lives and for putting her and their children in such a problematic situation. Ibrahim feels responsible and is full of self-blame. Although Ibrahim asked some friends for help, he did not receive structural assistance. Also, his brothers are too poor to help him out financially. Ibrahim is heavily disappointed in other people, especially since he always helped others when business was going well for him.

Five months ago he developed severe depressive symptoms and increasingly withdrew from social life. He did not enjoy activities and felt depressed most of the time. He sat in the apartment a lot, barely ate and only went out once or twice a week to look for work.

Three months ago Ibrahim started to hear a voice. For over three weeks Ibrahim heard this voice every day for more than one hour each day. Usually the voice came when he sat on his couch ruminating on his problems. Ibrahim heard the voice speaking clearly to him but he did not recognise the voice. The voice was very critical and insulted Ibrahim. The voice also ordered Ibrahim to hurt himself – Ibrahim did not comply with these commands. The voice made Ibrahim feel very anxious and depressed.

Ibrahim became fully convinced that the voice he was hearing was, in fact, the devil. He felt that he was being punished for doing bad things in his life, such as drinking alcohol and having girlfriends as a teenager. Ibrahim felt that the voice was completely right when it denigrated him. During this period Ibrahim only left the house once a week. He says that he was totally occupied with the voice; for instance, he would argue with it for hours.

After a month, in which he had distanced himself from his family, his two brothers came and took Ibrahim in. They also took him to the local community health centre. One brother arranged a part-time job for Ibrahim in a friend's construction company. This brought some structure back into Ibrahim's life. He still heard the voice, but the frequency and intensity of it diminished. Ibrahim noticed that concentrating his mind on things other than his problems had a positive influence on him.

During assessment with the Early Detection and Intervention Team, Ibrahim reports that he sometimes still hears the voice. This occurs less than once a week and lasts only a few seconds. He indicates that he also feels less severely depressed, and that the voice and the depressive symptoms are intertwined. He now doubts whether the voice is actually the devil or an intrapsychic phenomenon that is part of his depression. Ibrahim still has some problems and feels that he is on his own in life. He seeks help to get his life back on track, to become less depressed and to ward off insanity.

Assessment with CAARMS

On the CAARMS, Ibrahim's symptoms meet the psychotic disorder criteria on both the unusual thought content and the perceptual abnormalities subscales. Although he is clearly not suffering from psychosis at this moment, he experienced frank hallucinations for more than three weeks in the past year. He clearly heard a voice; this occurred every day and lasted for more than one hour each day. He also developed unusual thoughts about the source of the voice that meet the psychotic disorder criteria. He was fully convinced that it was the devil that spoke to him and that his behaviour was heavily influenced by it. There was also a definite drop in the level of functioning during the past year. Although the described symptoms resolved spontaneously, they were present for more than one week; therefore the symptoms exceed the criteria for BLIPS.

Ben

Ben is a 26-year-old administrative assistant, who married a year ago. Ben married his girlfriend after she accidentally became pregnant. Ben loves his wife and his two-month-old son, but also indicates that he sometimes feels trapped in this new situation. He feels he did not have enough time to adapt. Six months ago Ben started to have anxiety attacks. He frequently calls in sick at work and he stopped playing soccer. Ben also sees his friends less frequently and started to increase his cannabis usage.

Every night Ben is anxious when he lies in bed. He wonders whether there is something (for instance a ghost) in the room that wants to harm him. He focuses on sounds he hears and tries to see whether there is anything unusual in the dark. Sometimes he sees shadows out of the corner of his eye; at those moments he is afraid. He often curls up to his wife and pulls the covers over his head. About twice a week he gets out of bed to search for the source of a sound or to see whether there is actually something there. At those moments Ben is almost certain that a ghost is there. In the daytime, or when asked at assessment, Ben says that he is 50 per cent certain that something supernatural is out there to get him. He mentions that he knows that these thoughts are strange and unrealistic. Every day it takes Ben about two hours to fall asleep. He is often tired in the mornings. At work he has been blaming the baby, but actually it is the fear of ghosts that is keeping him awake. He feels guilty that he is hiding behind excuses and he feels ashamed towards his wife about being so anxious.

The last two months Ben hears someone calling his name about three times a week. This occurs most often when he is in a crowded place (such as on the bus going to work) or when he has his headphones on. He turns round to see who is calling him, but does not see anyone he knows. He wonders who or what might be calling him. Sometimes he thinks that it is the same ghost(s) that he fears at night. At other times he attributes it to being tired because he is not getting enough sleep. About twice a week Ben hears his son crying. However, when he goes to check on him he sees that his son is asleep. Because Ben's wife mentions that she also has this experience, this does not frighten Ben.

Assessment with CAARMS

Ben's functioning is negatively influenced by his extraordinary and remarkable experiences. His symptoms meet the ARMS criteria on the CAARMS unusual thought content and perceptual abnormalities subscales. Ben sees shadows and/or hears sounds that frighten him every day. Moreover, he hears someone calling his name about three times a week. These are mild to moderate perceptual abnormalities. Because Ben doubts the origin of these experiences, the intensity does not exceed the ARMS criteria. He interprets these experiences in an unusual way, that is, that there are ghosts that want to harm him; this is a highly unlikely thought. Although it influences his behaviour to some extent, he also doubts this interpretation, especially when he is away from the triggering situation.

Agnes

Agnes is a 23-year-old student who recently moved out of her parent's house into a student dormitory. Agnes is quite anxious and reports several unusual experiences. She often thinks that people believe she is a 'stupid cow'. Agnes' weight is above average and she thinks people will reject her because she is overweight. In school she often has the fleeting idea that people are laughing at her behind her back. On the other hand, she realises that she cannot really know what they are actually talking about, and that people have better things to do than talk about her. She thinks it might just be her negative self-esteem that is triggered in these situations. Agnes ignores her negative thoughts as much as possible and does not really act upon them.

About twice a week Agnes hears sounds that frighten her. Usually these occur when she is at home alone. Then she often thinks that there is a burglar or 'something'. She has no concrete ideas about what this 'something' might be and what it might be up to. Agnes is startled by these sounds. However, after a minute or so she gets a grip on herself and rationally states that it was probably just a sound coming from the neighbours. Then she can take her mind off it and continue with what she was doing.

Also, about three times a week, Agnes experiences either a feeling of déjà vu or some strange coincidence. For instance, last week a friend that she just happened to think about suddenly sent her a text message. She feels comforted when things like this happen and interprets it as a sign that she is on the right track in her life. Agnes does not actively search for these signs. Twice a month Agnes has a strange experience when she is falling asleep. It sometimes feels as though someone is sitting on her chest. She awakes and is startled but sees that no one is there and falls asleep again.

About once a month Agnes cannot find the right words to say something. Sometimes she finds it difficult to remember things that she has learned and should know. However, during the last year she has never received any comment about her speech.

Agnes recently joined a cycling club and also started work as a library assistant. Agnes has a few good friends and spends time with her new roommates. She is content with her personal life.

Assessment with CAARMS

Although Agnes experiences some extraordinary and remarkable experiences, her symptoms do not meet the ARMS criteria or the psychosis criteria on the CAARMS. She sometimes thinks that others will reject her. This appears to be a socially anxious interpretation linked to her low self-esteem. Others do not appear to be of malicious intent. Moreover, she clearly questions these thoughts and does not change her behaviour. The sounds that frighten Agnes only occur twice a week and affect her for only a few minutes. Therefore, they do not meet the frequency criteria. Feelings of déjà vu and coincidence are relatively common. Agnes gives normalising and positive meanings to these experiences. She is startled but not burdened by them. Agnes has hypnagogic experiences. These only occur with a low frequency and she has not developed unusual ideas about this. She observes it and falls asleep again. That Agnes sometimes cannot find the word to say something and that she forgets things are normal phenomena and do not meet the intensity or frequency criteria for ARMS.

In summary, although Agnes experiences some extraordinary experiences, these occur at low intensity or low frequency and do not negatively influence her functioning as a friend, co-worker or student.

3

What are extraordinary experiences?

Extraordinary experiences usually have a quality that has never been experienced before, causing subjects to search for an explanation. Because these experiences generally cannot be explained by 'common sense' and are not comparable to previous experiences, many people come up with extraordinary explanations. For example, when a person hears whispering when no one is present, they may start to wonder about ghosts, spirits or aliens.

Several kinds of extraordinary experiences

Sensory experiences

One group of extraordinary experiences is composed of sensory experiences that are not shared by others present. It concerns hearing sounds (e.g. voices, noises), unexplained visual experiences (e.g. visions, seeing ghosts), unusual bodily experiences (e.g. feeling touched), or smells that nobody else seems to smell. Although these experiences are often of a hallucinatory nature, people often come up with a supernatural explanation.

Distorted self-experiences

Other extraordinary experiences are the result of a distorted sense of 'self'. This can be described as a 'loss of the usual common-sense orientation to reality, unquestioned sense of obviousness, and unproblematic background quality that normally enables a person to take for granted so many aspects of the social and practical world' (Sass and Parnas, 2003). Nelson and colleagues listed the following basic self-disturbances (Nelson, Thompson and Yung, 2012; Nelson, Yung, Bechdolf and McGorry, 2008):

- a diminished sense of basic self, such as sense of inner void, lack of identity, being different from others, etc.;

- distorted first-person perspective, such as decreased or temporally delayed sense of mineness to experience, pervasive sense of distance between the self and experience, and spatialisation of the self. These are varieties of depersonalisation;
- a decreased ability to be affected by objects, people, events, states of affairs, as though the person is no longer fully participating or entirely present in the world;
- derealisation: an impression that the surrounding world has somehow transformed, is unreal, or is strange;
- intense reflectivity: tendency to take oneself or parts of oneself or aspects of the environment as objects of intense reflection, e.g. thinking about one's own thinking;
- loss of 'common sense' and perplexity: difficulty automatically grasping the meaning of everyday events; the 'naturalness' of the world and other people is lacking.

Ideas of reference

Sometimes subjects feel as if external forces or other people influence them. These subjects can, for example, describe thoughts that seem not to be originating from themselves. These experiences may lead to delusional experiences of thought insertion. In other instances, subjects may start perceiving hidden messages, such as on the television or in the newspapers. In the ultra-high risk period subjects are usually able to convince themselves that they are imagining things, but when the transition to florid psychosis is made these perceptions become convincing.

Speech and motor derailment

Another category of extraordinary experiences is associated with a loss of control over speech and movements. Subjects may experience difficulty with finding the right words to express what they want to say. Subjects may also experience reduced motor control; namely, movements are sometimes clumsy and/or less coordinated than before.

4

Which cognitive biases are associated with ARMS?

A multitude of studies have reported on the role of cognitive biases in schizophrenia (Moritz and Woodward, 2007b). These biases are thought to underpin the emergence and/or maintenance of the disorder, particularly delusions (for reviews, see Bell *et al.*, 2006; Blackwood *et al.*, 2001; Garety and Freeman, 1999). Cognitive biases relate to attribution style, decision-making style and data gathering. There is increasing evidence that patients are not cognisant with these biases. Freeman and colleagues have reported that despite a marked data-gathering bias in experimental studies, patients view themselves as rather hesitant decision-makers who are open to other views and sufficiently weigh the pros and cons of different positions (Freeman *et al.*, 2006). This is compatible with other findings (Mckay *et al.*, 2006). Recent research conducted with the Beck Cognitive Insight Scale, which taps into the awareness of cognitive biases, supports this inference (Warman and Martin, 2006a). The amelioration of this fundamental dissociation of objective and subjective performance by making patients aware of these cognitive biases and providing direct experience of their caveats, lies at the core of a metacognitive training for schizophrenia patients as developed by Moritz and Woodward (Moritz and Woodward, 2007a).

Research shows that cognitive biases are also present in ARMS subjects. Broome and colleagues examined whether there is a data-gathering bias in people at high risk of developing psychosis. Individuals with an ARMS ($n = 35$) were compared with a matched group of healthy volunteers ($n = 23$) (Broome *et al.*, 2007). Participants were tested using a modified version of the 'beads' reasoning task with different levels of task difficulty. When task demands were high, the at risk group made judgements on the basis of less information than the control group ($p<0.05$). Within both groups, jumping to conclusions was directly correlated with the severity of abnormal beliefs and intolerance of uncertainty ($p<0.05$). This may underlie a tendency to develop abnormal beliefs and a vulnerability to psychosis.

Cognitive biases that play a role in the onset of psychosis, and probably also in the onset and maintenance of subclinical psychotic symptoms, are described below.

Perceptual bias

Selective attention for threat (seeing danger anywhere)

A normative function of the mechanisms underlying fear is to facilitate detection of danger in the environment and to help the organism respond effectively to threatening situations. Biases in processing threat-related information have been assigned a prominent role in the aetiology and maintenance of anxiety disorders (Beck, 1976; Eldar *et al.*, 2012; Eysenck, 1992; Mathews, 1990; Mathews and MacLeod, 2002; Williams, Watts, MacLeod and Mathews, 1988). Specifically, several authors have suggested that the attention system of anxious individuals may be distinctively sensitive to and biased in favour of threat-related stimuli in the environment. Over the last two decades, this notion has fostered intensive research on attention biases in anxiety using different experimental tasks both in clinical populations displaying a variety of anxiety disorders and in non-clinical individuals reporting high levels of anxiety. A meta-analysis concluded that the threat-related bias is a robust phenomenon in anxious individuals, which does not exist in non-anxious individuals (Bar-Haim *et al.*, 2007). Although the threat-related bias in anxious individuals holds under a variety of experimental conditions and in different types of anxious populations, this consistent phenomenon is of low-to-medium effect size. Anxiety is a common symptom in ARMS subjects. Many ARMS subjects are anxious because of their extraordinary experiences and they are often focused on threat-related stimuli in the environment.

When we experience anxiety, our attention is drawn to cues linked to the objects or events that are the focus of our concerns. This attentional capture by threat-related stimuli is particularly characteristic of patients with anxiety disorders and has been the subject of much investigation within the clinical-cognitive literature (Bishop, 2008; Mathews and MacLeod, 1994; Mogg and Bradley, 1998). Recently, the advent of neuroimaging has enabled investigation of the neural mechanisms underlying selective attention to threat. Both subcortical regions implicated in threat detection (specifically the amygdala and prefrontal cortical regions implicated in top-down attentional control) are activated in response to task-irrelevant threat stimuli (Bishop, 2008).

Building on findings from the basic neuroscience literature (Armony and Ledoux, 1999; Ledoux, 2000), it has been suggested that a direct subcortical thalamo-amygdala pathway may facilitate the 'automatic' preattentive processing of threat-related stimuli (Dolan and Vuilleumier, 2003; Vuilleumier, Armony, Driver and Dolan, 2001).

These findings raise the possibility that anxiety may not only modulate output from an amygdala-based threat-detection mechanism, but may also be associated with impoverished recruitment of prefrontal control mechanisms to support the further processing of task-relevant stimuli and/or to inhibit the further processing of threat-related distractors. In line with this proposal, anxiety has been associated with lower levels of self-reported attentional control (Bishop, Jenkins and Lawrence, 2007; Derryberry and Reed, 2002), impaired executive function

(Eysenck 1992), disrupted inhibition of threat-related stimuli (Fox, 1994) and reduced activation of prefrontal mechanisms in response to the presentation of threat-related stimuli (Cannistraro and Rauch, 2003; Shin, Rauch and Pitman, 2006).

A literature review suggests that neural mechanisms underlying bottom-up sensory and top-down control processes interact to determine the extent of processing received by threat-related stimuli (Bishop, 2008). Manipulations of attentional focus, primary-task perceptual load, and stimulus presentation parameters (duration, backward masking, etc.) have differing influences upon amygdala and prefrontal activation to such stimuli. Under high perceptual load, competition for perceptual resources appears to curtail the processing of threat distractors at an early stage, eliminating the amygdala response to these stimuli (Pessoa, Padmala and Morland, 2005; Bishop *et al.*, 2007). In contrast, under low perceptual load, feed-forward or bottom-up activity can be sufficient for such distractors to lead to amygdala activity. Under these conditions, it is argued that salient distractors compete for further processing resources, such as entry to working memory and guidance of response selection. In line with this, under low perceptual load, prefrontal cortical regions implicated in top-down attentional control are selectively activated in response to the occurrence of threat-related distractors (Bishop *et al.*, 2007).

In ARMS subjects, altered age-related variation in amygdala and ventrolateral prefrontal cortex activation has been reported, relative to controls. Controls displayed decreased amygdala and increased ventrolateral prefrontal cortex activation with age, while ARMS patients exhibited the opposite pattern (increased amygdala and decreased ventrolateral prefrontal cortex activation), suggesting a failure of the prefrontal cortex to regulate amygdala reactivity. Moreover, a psychophysiological interaction analysis revealed decreased amygdala-prefrontal functional connectivity among ARMS adolescents, consistent with disrupted brain connectivity as a vulnerability factor in schizophrenia. These results suggest that the at risk syndrome is marked by abnormal development and functional connectivity of neural systems subserving emotion regulation (Gee *et al.*, 2012).

Contemporary researchers in neuropsychology, cognitive neuroscience, and clinical psychology have proposed that it is likely that intact executive functioning (EF) facilitates the successful use of cognitive behavioural techniques (Hariri, Bookheimer and Mazziotta, 2000; Martin, Oren and Boone, 1991; Posner and Rothbart, 1998). EF encompasses a heterogeneous set of cognitive abilities (e.g. allocation of attention, inhibitory control, hypothesis generation) governed by the prefrontal cortex (PFC). Even in a non-patient sample, Derryberry and Rothbart found that adults who reported having good ability to focus and shift attention (both of which require sound EF) also reported less negative affect than those who reported poor command over attentional skills (Derryberry and Rothbart, 1988). The PFC and executive skills contribute to the regulation and management of emotional responses (Posner and Rothbart, 1998) and the attainment of motivationally significant goals (Levenson, 1994; Frijda, 1994). Some have speculated that the PFC may be specifically involved in the mitigation of worry in generalised anxiety disorder through cognitive restructuring (Stein,

Westenberg, and Liebowitz, 2002). Wells and Mathews' self-regulatory EF model of emotional dysfunction also highlights the role played by metacognitive skills and attentional focus in emotional distress and relapse following treatment (Wells and Matthews, 1996). The exact neural substrates of CBT have yet to be identified; however, Mayberg has proposed a circuit involving the anterior cingulate cortex and other medial prefrontal areas (Mayberg, 2003).

Several papers assert that, whereas the action of anti-anxiety drugs is to directly suppress fear-driven outputs from the amygdala, CBT works by strengthening descending cortical projections from the PFC to the amygdala, allowing the assertion of reason over automatic fear responses (Gorman, Kent, Sullivan and Coplan, 2000; LeDoux, 1996). Consistent with these assumptions, recent functional magnetic resonance imaging (fMRI) data implicate the PFC in the intentional regulation and management of emotion (Beauregard, Lévesque and Bourgouin, 2001; Hariri *et al.*, 2000; Pelletier *et al.*, 2003). Decreased metabolic activity in left prefrontal areas, as indicated by PET, is associated with increased metabolic activity in the amygdala (Abercrombie *et al.*, 1996). Amaral and colleagues have argued for the existence of a descending inhibitory pathway between the medial PFC and the amygdala, and Davidson's integrated model asserts that the left medial PFC is one of the major inhibitors of amygdalar outputs, although this may only be the case in non-dispositional episodes of negative affect (Amaral, Price, Ptikanen and Carmichael, 1992; Davidson, 2002).

CBT in ARMS subjects may be effective by strengthening functions of the PFC. We hypothesise that the efficacy of CBT is partly dependent on patients' use of EF, which is likely to be involved in most CBT exercises. For instance, the treatment manual and homework assignments require the on-going use of thought restructuring exercises that teach patients to challenge cognitive biases and catastrophic thoughts with contradictory evidence, and subsequently generate new adaptive thoughts based on the evidence. Behavioural plans are formulated and implemented, and anxiety-driven behaviours (e.g. avoidance, defensiveness) are replaced by adaptive responses. Patients are also asked to engage in daily self-monitoring of cognitive, behavioural and physiological symptoms, and provide numerical ratings of mood. All of these skills are likely to involve the PFC and executive system (Mateer 1999; Norman and Shalice, 1986). In essence, CBT teaches patients to increase and refine the use of EF to better manage symptoms of distress (Mohlman and Gorman, 2005).

Case example: Matthew

Matthew is a 25-year-old computer technician. A few years ago he was in therapy for a cannabis addiction. Matthew is worried that his contract, which is ending in five months, will not be prolonged. His concern started after his manager told him not to worry about his contract, while the owner of the company told him he had to push his performance up a notch. Matthew says this contradictory information made him think that they wanted to cheat him. Sometimes Matthew thinks his colleagues are involved as well and wonders whether they are talking about him behind his back. A few times a week Matthew keeps an eye on his colleagues when they are conversing. He tries to make out what they are up to and whether they are looking at him. This distracts him from his work, negatively influencing his performance, which in its turn increases his distress about his contract not being extended. Matthew explains that he is not sure whether he is suffering from delusional ideas. He has not spoken to anyone about his thoughts. He fears that they will think he is crazy.

Matthew has become very socially sensitive. He thoroughly scans every environment he is in and has noticed people on the streets are often looking at him. He has no idea why people would be watching him. Besides this, Matthew constantly checks the streets for hidden signs. About once a week he picks up a piece of paper from the street, because he feels it might contain a message directed at him. He knows this is an unrealistic thought. He has no idea why someone would send him a message and why this person would do this in such an awkward way. His selective attention for other people and potential messages means that he pays less attention to the traffic. A few weeks ago he was almost run over by a car. This near-miss made him think there might be maniacs driving around who purposely run into people. When Matthew crosses the street he now checks approaching cars to ensure they are reducing speed and are not deviating from their course. All this is causing Matthew a lot of stress and he has increased his cannabis use to calm himself. He feels he is losing control and explains that his behaviour resembles that of his uncle who has schizophrenia.

Memory biases

Source monitoring and hallucinations (remembering thoughts and phrases as originating from others)

Source monitoring bias was described for the first time about three decades ago. In the original experiment, psychiatric patients with a history of hallucinations were less capable of identifying the words, meaning and grammatical style of their own expressed thoughts following about a one-week lapse in time than non-hallucinating psychiatric patients. Both groups did not differ in the ability to remember verbal material, the stability of their opinions or communication skills (Heilbrun, 1980).

In another study, delusional patients were compared with hallucinating patients. The subjects had to give answers to easy and difficult questions. After a week the subjects had to sort a pile of cards with the answers they gave the week before. They had to decide on three piles of cards: self-generated, experimenter-generated, new answers. The patients made more mistakes than the experimenter. Hallucinating patients had a bias to attribute the answers to difficult questions to the experimenter (Bentall, Baker and Havers, 1991). This external attribution also takes place when listening to their voice during distortion (Allen et al., 2004).

A meta-analysis of 23 studies found this cognitive bias (to attribute self-generated thoughts and answers to other people) present in schizophrenia patients with hallucinations (Waters and Babcock, 2010). This bias is increased when attention is directed to the self (Ensum and Morrison, 2003) and when subjects are in an emotional state (Morrison and Haddock, 1997). The source monitoring bias may be a causal factor in auditory hallucinations. The hallucinating person attributes his auditory experience to an external origin. This bias is endophenotypical, as it has been found in prodromal state, in remitted patients, and also in siblings of schizophrenia patients (Brunelin *et al.*, 2007).

Case example: George

George is 18 years old and in his final year of high school. He lives with his parents and has a girlfriend who he meets a few times a week. He does not do drugs and only occasionally drinks alcohol. Over the last few months he has had some odd experiences. About once a week he hears bells ringing when he lies in bed. He hears them a couple of times within a period of five to ten minutes. Three times a week he hears voices in music, or in noises such as the spinning of the washing machine. These experiences last for less than an hour and only cause moderate concern.

The last six weeks he has started to experience intrusive thoughts and images that are aggressive and racist in nature. He sometimes hears these racist comments aloud in his head; this has made him question the origin of these comments. He is inclined to attribute these experiences externally. They cannot be his own since he is not a racist at all and therefore does not identify with them. He has no idea what the source of these experiences might be. George has a few good friends who are black and feels rather ashamed by his thoughts. He has not spoken about his experiences to anyone. He has tried to suppress the intrusive thoughts, to discuss with them and even tried to agree with them. All attempts at coping were futile. This makes him feel powerless. He has started to avoid black people in the streets, because they might become aware that he has these thoughts. A few weeks ago he told his parents about his problems. They encouraged him to seek help. At the initial assessment George explains that he is not sure about what he is experiencing. Most of the time he is sure that the aggressive and racist intrusive experiences are his own unwanted thoughts. At other times he strongly feels that they are not. He wonders if he is a bad person or if he is losing his mind.

Hindsight bias (I knew it all along)

Another memory bias is the hindsight bias. Hindsight bias indicates the phenomenon that once one knows the answer, one tends to think that one knew it all along, even when the original answer (that was given previously) was false. This bias may be stronger in psychotic patients than healthy subjects. It contributes to the formation of delusions. Psychotic people accept an improbable conclusion more easily. The correcting ability of past memories is weakened because of hindsight bias. Instead, the reconstructed hindsight memories seem to support the conclusion (Woodward, Moritz, Cuttler and Whitman, 2006b).

In a typical hindsight study, subjects are presented information about a chance event, which has two or more possible outcomes. They are then informed about which outcome actually occurred and are asked to indicate the likelihood of that outcome occurring had they not been told what happened. This hindsight probability estimate is compared to a 'foresight' estimate obtained from subjects given the same information, but who were not told which outcome actually occurred. The greater the difference between probability estimates, the greater the effect of the hindsight bias. When the hindsight bias is operating, events that occurred are retrospectively seen as having been more likely to occur and events that did not occur are retrospectively seen as having been less likely to occur (Christensen-Szalanski and Willham, 1991).

The results of a meta-analysis revealed that the overall effect size ($y = 0.17$; corrected $r = 0.25$) of the hindsight bias is not large (Christensen-Szalanski and Willham, 1991). This does not mean that the bias should be ignored since, depending upon the costs and benefits of making a correct and incorrect decision, effect sizes much smaller than this can still be of practical significance (Elstein, 1989; Rosenthal and Rubin, 1982). At the same time, given the small observed effect size of the hindsight bias, its effect will more likely be washed out by the random error inherent in the real world than would have occurred had the effect size been larger. Consequently, before issuing warnings to correct for the hindsight bias one needs to examine closely its potential impact for the specific situation of concern. A study also showed that people who retrospectively claim that they 'knew all along' what would occur are not necessarily exhibiting the hindsight bias. Many people faced with a dichotomous choice (e.g. act, not act), who retrospectively claim to have known all along that the observed outcome would occur, might have acted the same way even in foresight.

Belief in the paranormal or claims of paranormal experiences may be, at least in part, associated with cognitive biases. A total of 48 undergraduate college students were engaged in an exercise in telepathy in which the colour of cards was 'sent' to them by the experimenter under two conditions. In a Hindsight-possible condition, participants recorded whether their choice was correct following the revelation of the colour. In the Control condition participants committed to a particular response by writing it down before receiving feedback, thus eliminating the ability to alter retrospectively what 'was known all along'. Consistent with a hindsight bias, participants performed significantly better under the Hindsight-possible condition. Moreover, a significant correlation was found between paranormal beliefs assessed on Tobacyk's 1988 Revised Paranormal Belief Scale in the Hindsight-possible but not in the Control condition, suggesting a confirmation bias (Rudski, 2002). ARMS subjects frequently report paranormal experiences. Sometimes ARMS subjects become more and more convinced of the reality of their paranormal experiences caused by the confirmation and hindsight biases.

Case example: Kathleen

Kathleen is a 23-year-old woman studying to become a nurse. For the past six months she has had dreams during the night that seem to come true during the day. The moment the event takes place, she has vivid memories of the dream. For example, she dreamed that a girl she knew in high school was going to call her and that very same day, this girl rang her up. Kathleen is starting to think that she has psychic abilities. She is thinking about dropping out of school and focusing solely on the further development of her innate psychic powers. Sometimes she thinks she can make a real difference in the world by predicting future events. It feels like a burden to her to have such a responsibility. Her therapist suggests writing down her dreams on awakening. From that moment on, Kathleen noticed that her dreams were not predictive of actual events any more. In retrospect, she concludes that her mind may have tricked her into believing that she had predictive dreams about future events. She is both disappointed as well as relieved and is reconsidering dropping out of school.

Attribution bias

Self-serving bias and personalisation bias (blaming others for failure)

Attribution style is associated with depression. A number of studies showed that individuals with depression tend to excessively use internal attributions for negative events (Alloy, Abrahamson and Whistehouse, 1999; Joiner 2001; Moore and Fresco, 2007), whereas healthy individuals avoid such self-blame and make more internal attributions for positive events, an attribution style that is known as self-serving bias (Kaney, Bowen-Jones, Dewey and Bentall, 1997). Thus, they tend to take credit for success (internal attribution of positive events) and to deny responsibility for failure (external attribution of negative events). More recently, a consistent body of literature has shown that both paranoid deluded individuals, as well as those with manic symptoms (Lyon, Startup and Bentall, 1999), show a tendency for the personalising bias (Bentall, Kaney and Dewey, 1991; Candido and Romney, 1990; Fear, Sharp and Healy, 1996; Kaney and Bentall, 1989; Kinderman and Bentall, 1997; Lyon, Kaney and Bentall, 1994; Sharp, Fear and Healy, 1997). In tasks assessing hypothetical situations, they excessively attribute positive events to internal causes (self) and negative events to external causes (circumstances or other people).

Kinderman demonstrated that relative to normal and depressive controls, paranoid patients made more external personal attributions for negative events, showing a characterised personalising bias (Kinderman and Bentall, 1997). Other researchers reported similar results (Kinderman and Bentall, 2000), but findings were less consistent when subjects with and without persecutory delusions were compared (Sharp et al., 1997; Silverman and Peterson, 1993). For example, studies have also shown a potential association with hallucinations and with externalising bias (Janssen et al., 2006).

Two definitions of personalisation are in use in the literature about schizophrenia. Both definitions will be discussed and relevant literature will be summarised. The relationship of personalisation and theory-of-mind dysfunction will be examined. Theory-of-mind dysfunction refers to a difficulty with accurate attribution of mental states in order to explain and predict other people's behaviour. There is considerable evidence of theory-of-mind dysfunctions in schizophrenia (Brüne, 2005; Harrington, Siegert and McClure, 2005).

Since personalisation plays an important role in schizophrenia, it could be assumed that in the prodromal phase this bias also influences the course of clinical symptomatology. A case illustration is given at the end of the paragraph. Personalisation or self-referential bias is defined as attaching personal meaning to irrelevant external events (Beck, Grant and Perivoliotis, 2009). During delusional periods, patients are often locked into an egocentric perspective. They see themselves as at centre stage in a drama in which all events are relevant to them. Coughing, television commercials, muffled conversations can take on a special, threatening meaning: for example, conveying overt or hidden messages directed specifically to the deluded patient.

Personalising bias is defined as a bias to blame others rather than circumstances (Langdon, Corner, McLaren, Ward and Coltheart, 2006). Paranoid delusional patients in particular were shown to have an attribution bias to excessively externalise the blame for negative events, typically to other people rather than circumstances (Bentall and Kaney, 1996; Kinderman and Bentall, 1997).

Personalising bias may constitute a vulnerability to develop persecutory delusions and may reflect cognitive deficits, including theory-of-mind impairment. Langdon and colleagues investigated this hypothesis in 34 schizophrenia patients with a history of persecutory delusions and 21 healthy controls (Langdon *et al.*, 2006). Counter to predictions, theory-of-mind impairment did not increase personalising bias, which was marked in all participants, whether clinical or nonclinical; instead, theory-of-mind impairment was correlated with poor insight. Their findings indicate multiple pathways to poor insight, one of which is a theory-of-mind difficulty, impairing the capacity to simulate other perspectives for the purpose of critically evaluating one's own beliefs and circumstances.

Brakoulias and colleagues report on an 8–11 week CBT programme that targeted delusions (Brakoulias *et al.*, 2008). Probabilistic reasoning, attribution bias (personalisation as defined by Langdon *et al.*, 2006) and theory-of-mind were assessed pre- and post-treatment in 40 medication-resistant psychotic patients. Delusional conviction, preoccupation and distress were rated each session. At baseline, 11 patients showed some form of abnormal probabilistic reasoning, 13 excessive attribution biases and 13 defective theory-of-mind compared to norms. Fourteen patients completed the CBT programme and showed significant reductions in delusional conviction and preoccupation. Despite some inconsistent evidence of improvement in verbal theory-of-mind tasks, reasoning styles (attribution bias) in these 14 patients were largely unchanged by CBT. The authors conclude that reasoning abnormalities associated with delusions in the sample mark a vulnerability that persists and is independent of the effectiveness of CBT in psychotic patients (Brakoulias *et al.*, 2008).

Bentall and colleagues argue that in the absence of a well-developed theory-of-mind skills, the paranoid individual is unable to attribute the negative actions of others to situational factors. This inability leads to an external locus of control (Bentall and Fernyhough, 2008). A genetic high-risk study has reported that, in adolescents at high genetic risk of psychosis, an external locus of control predicted the later development of illness (Frenkel, Kugelmass, Nathan and Ingraham, 1995). An external locus of control will, in turn, lead to a tendency to anticipate social threats and hence paranoid beliefs. Processes underlying the stage of threat anticipation in this model may be implemented by striatal dopamine neurons (Moutoussis, Williams, Dayan and Bentall, 2007; Moutoussis, Bentall and Williams, 2008). A jumping-to-conclusions style of reasoning will prevent reality testing and will therefore serve to maintain paranoid beliefs once established.

Thus, personalisation as defined by Langdon and Beck influences the course of symptoms in schizophrenia patients. Brakoulias and colleagues reported no influence of CBT on personalisation bias (Brakoulias et al., 2008). Studies in anxiety disorders do show an effect of CBT on abnormal reasoning styles. A fundamental assumption of the cognitive model of anxiety disorders is that activation of maladaptive cognitive structures, or schemata, directly influence the content of an individual's perceptions, interpretations, memories and attention allocation, leading to the production and maintenance of anxious states (Beck, Emery and Greenberg, 1985). Idiosyncratic biases favouring processing of threat-related information have been demonstrated across the anxiety disorders, and numerous studies have shown the preferential encoding of information that is consistent with the threat-related concerns of the individual (Williams, Watts, MacLeod and Matthews, 1997). For instance, patients with panic disorder are hyper vigilant to threat cues pertaining to body sensations (Ehlers, Margraf, Davies and Roth, 1988), whereas patients with social phobia are overly attentive to social threat cues (Hope, Rapee, Heimberg and Dombeck, 1990; Mattia, Heimberg and Hope, 1993).

Just as information-processing biases (e.g., hyper vigilance to threat cues) have been shown to create vulnerability and maintain anxious states, the presumed mechanism of change in CBT is the degree to which dysfunctional beliefs and information-processing biases are successfully targeted and corrected (Beck et al., 1985). For instance, studies in the treatment of social phobia (Mattia et al., 1993) and generalised anxiety disorder (Mathews, Mogg, Kentish and Eysenck, 1995) have shown that idiosyncratic processing biases are present (and significantly different from controls) at pre-treatment, but then are significantly reduced (and equal to controls) following successful treatment with cognitive therapy. In contrast, treatment non-responders continue to demonstrate processing biases (to a greater extent than controls).

To the best of our knowledge, personalisation has not been investigated in ARMS subjects, nor has the influence of CBT on personalisation in people with ARMS been investigated. It could be hypothesised that ARMS subjects show more improvement in abnormal thinking styles than psychotic patients because ARMS subjects usually have better insight.

Case example: John

John tells at intake that in the last few months certain sounds have started to convey a meaning to him. Sometimes he thinks that when someone coughs, that person means he is dissatisfied with John's posture and that John has to sit up straight. John can usually dismiss these thoughts as strange and impossible but the feeling remains that the coughing expresses a hidden message. Furthermore, the thought sometimes comes to his mind that the hand with which someone gives him a drink conveys a message about his social status. He does not know yet whether the right or the left hand means that he is viewed as a person of lower social status. Usually John can ignore these thoughts but recently they have been starting to bother him more and more.

John has lived alone since he started to study bookkeeping a year ago. John failed some classes and reports difficulties with his concentration. He cannot take in material he reads, and he needs to read chapters over and over again in order to grasp the meaning. Instead of blaming his failing concentration for the difficulties he has with his studies, he began to think that fellow students disliked him and intentionally send him messages expressing their disapproval. Their hidden messages, coughing and making other sounds, make it difficult for John to focus his attention. In the last few months he often failed to attend his classes. He spends a lot of time alone in his room playing computer games or surfing the Internet. John reports sleeping problems and feelings of irritability. He has not spoken to anyone about his odd experiences. He is afraid people will think he is crazy. He himself also labels his thoughts as strange and is very afraid of going mad.

Covariation bias (overestimation of causality and underestimation of chance)

Covariation detection is the ability to detect that two events tend to co-occur in a regular and consistent way. Detecting covariance is important for understanding and predicting the world – for example, by learning what cues signal forthcoming reward or punishment. However, it is important to distinguish between temporal contiguity, when two events occur within a short space of time independently of each other, and covariation, when two events predominantly occur together and do not tend to occur independently, and thus may be dependent on each other (Harvey, Watkins, Mansell and Shafran, 2004). Several studies have shown that phobic fear is accompanied by a covariation bias, that is, phobic subjects tend to overassociate fear-relevant stimuli and aversive outcomes. Such a covariation bias seems a fairly direct and powerful way to confirm danger expectations and enhance fear (de Jong, van den Hout and Merkelbach, 1995). The covariation bias occurs when people find an illusory correlation between two categories of events that, in reality, are correlated to a lesser extent or even correlated in the opposite direction (Alloy and Tabachnik, 1984; Chapman and Chapman, 1967).

A total of 22 believers and 20 sceptics of extrasensory perception (ESP) participated in a telepathy experiment. Subjects were asked to judge the covariation between transmitted symbols and the corresponding feedback given by a receiver. Believers overestimated the number of successful transmissions ('hits'). Sceptics were characterised by accurate hit judgements. For believers, positive correlations between hit responses, their heart rates and their experienced arousal were found. In addition, subjective arousal was positively associated with the hit estimates given at the end of the experiment. This response pattern was absent in the group of sceptics. It was concluded that covariation bias as a psychophysiological concept plays an important role in the maintenance of paranormal belief (Schienle, Vaitl and Stark, 1996).

Believers in the paranormal show a general tendency to underestimate the likelihood of coincidence. As a consequence of this type of probability misjudgement, believers are often positively surprised about a chance outcome, which they then interpret as a paranormal experience. In another study, believers estimated that they had attained fewer hits on a computer-simulated coin-tossing task than disbelievers, although there was no difference in performance between the two groups. Interestingly, believers felt that they had exerted greater control over the outcomes of the coin tosses than sceptics. The believers' perception of the outcome was accompanied by a severe underestimation of the number of chance hits attainable in the task (Blackmore and Troscianko, 1985).

For the majority of believers, the personal contact with a paranormal phenomenon, which most commonly includes experiences with telepathy, was stated as the reason for their conviction. Within a group of 1,236 adult Americans, a quarter declared that they had been involved in a telepathic experience (Gallup and Newport, 1991); the same percentage was found in a British survey (Blackmore, 1984).

Connolly and colleagues were the first to examine covariation biases in contamination fear, as is reported by about half of the patients with obsessive–compulsive symptoms (OCS) (Connolly, Lohr, Olatunji, Hahn and Williams, 2009; Rasmussen and Eisen, 1989). Contamination fear is defined as the persistent fear of being tainted or impure through real or perceived contact with a contaminated object such as a dirty person or place (Rachman, 2004). The study revealed that subjects who had a high fear of contamination showed a specific covariation bias, leading participants to overestimate the contingency between contamination stimuli and fear outcomes that was not present in subjects with a low fear of contamination. A recent model of OCS suggests that an aetiological pathway to contamination fear is the perceived covariation between contamination stimuli and aversive outcomes. Accordingly, inaccurate contingency perception may contribute to the aetiology and maintenance of OCS-contamination fears through reinforcing danger expectancies and strengthening associative learning contingencies (e.g. Mineka and Sutton, 1992). Covariation biases are hypothesised to function as maintenance and pathogenic factors for anxiety disorders by reinforcing harm expectations and strengthening learning contingencies (e.g. Mineka and Sutton, 1992). A number of studies have rendered support for this prediction (e.g. Tomarken, Mineka and Cook, 1989; de Jong, van den Hout and Merkelbach, 1995; de Jong, Merckelbach and Arntz, 1995). The typical covariation methodology requires the presentation of several types of stimuli (e.g., snake, knife, landscape pictures) immediately followed by several types of paired outcomes (e.g., electric shock, tone). Each picture/outcome pairing occurs in equal frequency. Following repeated stimulus/outcome presentations, the participants are asked to estimate the overall percentage of trials in which each stimulus was presented with each outcome. Results characteristically yield an overestimated covariation bias for fear-aversive stimulus–outcome pairings compared to fear-neutral pairings. Furthermore, a number of studies indicate that fearful individuals provide more biased covariation estimates compared to less fearful individuals (Kennedy, Rapee and Mazurski, 1997; de Jong, van den Hout and Merckelbach, 1995; de Jong, Merckelbach and Arntz, 1995).

Thus, the covariation bias plays an important role in paranormal experiences and obsessive–compulsive symptoms, both of which are often reported by ARMS subjects. If ARMS subjects do not receive information about the covariation bias, this bias may reinforce these experiences, resulting sometimes in delusional convictions.

Case example: Husain

Husain is a 21-year-old student who lives with his parents. He has been experiencing negative intrusive thoughts for as long as he can remember. Lately these thoughts have been increasingly disturbing. He started to pick up signs that others might actually know what he is thinking. He has no idea how, but assumes that others may be able to read his mind. He concludes that maybe his mind has somehow 'gone open'. This is a dreadful idea, since it would mean that he has no privacy. He asked friends, but they deny that they can know what he thinks. Husain has, however, observed reactions in others when he had aggressive or sexual thoughts. For instance, a classmate would suddenly look at him or laugh directly after he had a shameful thought. A few times Husain experienced that a friend said something that he had just thought or something that was clearly related to his negative thoughts. He noticed these reactions most often in one professor in the university and started to avoid her as much as possible; this made him miss classes. When he saw her he tried to think 'good things'. However, suppressing the negative thoughts had an adverse effect, and they increased in frequency and intensity. Lately, Husain has started wondering whether people really can read his mind, or whether they are all lying to him. He has no idea why they would lie about their ability. He is worried about his own mental health and has made an appointment with his general practitioner.

Reasoning biases

Jumping to conclusions/data-gathering bias (hasty conclusions)

Jumping to conclusions has been proposed as an etiological factor involved in the formation of delusions from the earliest stages. Garety and colleagues postulate a critical role for the tendency of deluded individuals to hastily adopt beliefs despite insufficient data collection, comprising one part of the so-called jumping to conclusions (JTC) bias (Garety, Bebbington, Fowler, Freeman and Kuipers, 2007). This propensity may be analogous to the manner whereby delusional beliefs are developed and maintained on the basis of too little evidence. Delusions are consensually defined as fixed false beliefs not amenable to contrary evidence, and are hallmark symptoms of schizophrenia spectrum disorders. Although it was initially proposed that delusional ideation cannot be explained by a pathology of reasoning (Maher, 1988), several studies have revealed a number of aberrations in reasoning in individuals with schizophrenia with current or past delusional ideas (Bell *et al.*, 2006; Bentall, Corcoran, Howard, Blackwood and Kinderman, 2001; Davies, Coltheart, Langdon and Breen, 2001; Garety and Freeman, 1999; Young and Bentall, 1997).

JTC paradigms typically involve the beads task, where the subject is presented with jars containing beads of two colours (e.g., black-and-white beads divided 60/40 in one jar and 40/60 in the other) and is asked from which jar beads are being drawn when the jars have been hidden from view. Individuals with schizophrenia tend to request fewer beads before deciding which jar is the source of the beads (draws-to-decision procedure). The main interpretation of this finding is that individuals with schizophrenia display a data-gathering bias, in that they seek less information before reaching a decision (Garety and Freeman, 1999). In many clinical studies in which individuals with delusions were compared with non-clinical controls on the number of draws to decision in probabilistic reasoning tasks, data gathering turned out to be hastier in the delusion group (Conway *et al.*, 2002; Dudley, John, Young and Over, 1997a, 1997b; Fear and Healy, 1997; Garety, Hemsley and Wessely, 1991; Garety *et al.*, 2005; Huq, Garety and Hemsley, 1988; Mortimer *et al.*, 1996; Moritz and Woodward, 2005; Peters and Garety, 2006; van Dael *et al.*, 2006). Such replication of a finding is rare in psychosis research and is firm evidence for the presence of a JTC bias in individuals with delusions. About 50–60 per cent of individuals with delusions jump to conclusions (defined as making a decision after two or fewer beads).

Studies investigating the specificity of the JTC bias showed that JTC (as measured by the beads task) could not be explained by memory deficit (Broome *et al.*, 2007; Menon, Pomarol-Clotet, McKenna and McCarthy, 2006), impulsivity (Dudley *et al.*, 1997a; Menon, Mizrai and Kapur, 2008; Young and Bentall, 1997), or general cognitive functioning (Mortimer *et al.*, 1996). The beads task is considered a specific and reliable measure of the JTC bias.

The JTC bias has also been found in people who score high on delusional ideation scales (Colbert and Peters, 2002; Linney, Peters and Ayton, 1998; Moritz and Woodward, 2005; van Dael *et al.*, 2006; Warman and Martin, 2006a, 2006b), and in people who have remitted from delusions (Moritz and Woodward, 2005; Peters and Garety, 2006). Broome and colleagues compared 35 individuals with an ARMS for developing psychosis with a matched group of healthy volunteers ($n = 23$) (Broome *et al.*, 2007). Participants were tested using a modified version of the 'beads' reasoning task with different levels of task difficulty. As in the classical version of the paradigm, participants in this study were informed that a series of beads would be drawn from one of two jars containing beads of two colours in the ratios 85:15 and 15:85. They were instructed to monitor the colours of successively drawn beads until they were as certain as they could be as to which of the jars the beads were being drawn from. A pseudo-random predetermined list was used to determine the colour of the bead shown. Beads were presented on a computer screen, with participants responding via a button press. The modified version involved three conditions: (a) two jars with bead ratios of 85:15, (b) two jars with 60:40, and (c) three jars with 44:28:28. Participants were asked to indicate which jar the beads were being drawn from when they were 'as certain as possible'. Real jars of beads in the appropriate ratios and colours were shown to the subjects when the task was being explained beforehand. Working memory was assessed using an adaptation of the digit span task that used a string of different coloured beads (between 5 and 9, as in the beads task) rather than numbers. Participants were presented with five different length strings of coloured beads, two trials of each, using a laptop. Beads were presented at one-second intervals and after presentation participants were asked to recall the order of the colour in which beads were presented. Longest span of beads and total errors were recorded.

Tolerance of uncertainty was evaluated using the Freeston Intolerance of Uncertainty scale (Freeston, Rheaume, Letarte, Dugas and Ladouceur, 1994). This questionnaire is a 27-item Likert scale that was designed to generate a single summary score and cover a wide range of concepts; however, factor analyses of the scale identified constructs covering 'behavioural attempts to control the future and avoid uncertainty, inhibition of action, emotional reactions such as frustration and stress, and cognitive interpretations that being uncertain reflects badly on a person' (Freeston *et al.*, 1994). Intolerance of uncertainty is conceptualised as a manifestation of basic dysfunctional (trait) schema that may in turn guide information processing and appraisal. It can generate and maintain anxiety in ambiguous situations both through facilitating the perception of difficulties where none exist and, where difficulties do exist, lead to inefficient responses to them.

When task demands were high, the at-risk group made judgements on the basis of less information than the control group. Within both groups, jumping to conclusions was directly correlated with the severity of abnormal beliefs and intolerance of uncertainty. In the at risk group it was also associated with impaired working memory whereas in the control group poor working memory was associated with a more conservative response style. Thus, people with an ARMS also display a jumping to conclusions reasoning style, associated with impaired working memory and intolerance of uncertainty. This may underlie a tendency to develop abnormal beliefs and a vulnerability to psychosis.

Van Dael and colleagues studied JTC in individuals with psychosis and their relatives, and in individuals in the general population high or low in non-clinical psychotic symptoms (i.e. four groups differing in levels of delusional ideation and vulnerability to psychosis). Hasty data gathering was associated with both delusional ideation and psychosis liability. As the authors argue, JTC may be both partly a trait factor reflecting liability for psychosis and partly a state factor as it covaries with level of delusional ideation. In other words, JTC could contribute to both delusion formation and maintenance (van Dael *et al.*, 2006). Consistent with this work, two studies did not find statistical differences in JTC between deluded and remitted patients (Moritz and Woodward, 2005; Peters and Garety, 2006), although the last study found a tendency to normalisation of JTC. Colbert and Peters found evidence of JTC in non-clinical individuals with high delusional ideation compared with individuals with low clinical delusional ideation (Colbert and Peters, 2002). Van Dael and colleagues did not replicate this. Furthermore, in a non-clinical study examining an association of JTC and paranoid thinking, there was no evidence for such a link (Freeman *et al.*, 2005).

In a study by White and Mansell, 17 delusion-prone and 22 control students completed four versions of the beads-in-a-jar paradigm (including multiple jar variants) to test recent claims regarding JTC's specificity to less ambiguous paradigms with a limited number of jars. Additional measures were administered to tease out a potential mechanism underlying JTC. The delusion-prone group showed a higher JTC bias that proved relatively robust across variants. Task performance was related to degree of self-reported rushing. It is concluded that delusion-prone individuals exhibit JTC, even when confronted with more ambiguous scenarios, potentially as a consequence of feeling rushed. Thus, delusion-prone individuals also show JTC (White and Mansell, 2009).

In addition to the exact relationship of JTC and the development of delusions, the cause of hasty data gathering itself remains to be determined. There have been a number of speculations: some authors note the need to consider the goal of reasoning (Dudley and Over, 2003); others raise the issue of the level of the threshold at which an explanation is accepted. The belief confirmation bias (Freeman *et al.*, 2005) or a bias against disconfirmatory evidence (Moritz and Woodward, 2006) may be related to JTC; and data gathering is likely to be influenced by the availability of alternative explanations for experiences (Freeman *et al.*, 2004). However, previous suggestions that JTC reflects a generalised need for closure have been discounted (Freeman *et al.*, 2006).

Longitudinal studies on psychosis and reasoning

Several studies have investigated the changes in reasoning in patients with psychosis, using a longitudinal observational design. In these studies, psychotic symptoms and reasoning were measured when patients were acutely psychotic, and when remitted, or according to a fixed follow-up schedule.

Woodward and colleagues investigated a variation of the beads task (involving fishing from a lake instead of drawing beads from a jar) (Woodward, Munz, Leclerc and Lecomte, 2009). Twenty-six subjects with schizophrenia were tested at two time points 12 weeks apart. Patients were taking part in a longitudinal randomised controlled trial on group CBT for early psychosis (Lecomte *et al.*, 2008). The results revealed a significant negative correlation between change in task performance (number of requested pieces of information) and change in delusion scores over time. This evidence is consistent with the contention that the JCT task is sensitive to the cognitive systems underlying delusions in schizophrenia spectrum disorders. Thus, CBT may have a positive effect on JTC.

In contrast, Peters and Garety reported that symptomatic improvement after treatment with antipsychotic medication was not associated with improvement in JTC bias. Using the beads task, they tested 17 patients, all on antipsychotic medication, while they were actively deluded and when they were remitted (on average after 17.4 weeks). On remission of psychosis, the JTC bias persisted despite an improvement in probability judgements. The authors suggested that the JTC bias is relatively stable and, thus, may be involved in the formation and persistence of delusion but does not respond to antipsychotic treatment (Peters and Garety, 2006).

Menon and colleagues measured JTC, using the beads task and an emotionally salient version of this task (where comments about a person instead of beads were presented), when 19 psychotic patients began antipsychotic treatment, and at week 2 and week 4. They found that, although psychotic symptoms continued to improve at week 2 and week 4, JTC improved (indicated by an increase in draws to decision) within two weeks of treatment and then remained the same at week 4. The improvement was found in the emotionally salient version, but not the neutral version, of the task. Although baseline draws to decision predicted subsequent change in positive symptoms, there was no significant correlation between symptom changes and changes in draws to decision (Menon *et al.*, 2008).

Relationship between symptom severity and JTC

There is a wealth of literature on JTC and psychosis, but only a few studies have systematically analysed the relationship between severity of symptoms and JTC using a cross-sectional design. With a large sample of 100 patients with active delusions, Garety and colleagues found that JTC correlated significantly with delusional conviction, and that there was a trend for JTC to be associated with higher positive and delusion symptom scores. JTC was not associated with negative or general symptomatology. This study suggests that JTC is related to severity of positive symptoms and, in particular, to delusions (Garety *et al.*, 2005).

In a large sample consisting of currently deluded, remitted deluded, deluded and depressed, and non-psychotic depressed individuals, Corcoran and colleagues did not find any significant relationship between performance on the bead tasks and severity of delusions, but current deluded status significantly predicted performance on one version of the beads task (Corcoran *et al.*, 2008).

Conclusion

Together with data from longitudinal studies (Peters and Garety, 2006; Menon *et al.*, 2008) and from studies of subjects with an ARMS (Broome *et al.*, 2007) or delusion-prone individuals (Colbert and Peters, 2002) who show an attenuated JTC, the current literature suggests that JTC may be a trait factor associated with propensity for delusions that is exacerbated in acute states of psychotic delusions. This is consistent with van Dael and colleagues, who found a dose-response relationship between JTC and level of psychosis liability (trait), in interaction with a dose-response relationship between JTC and delusional ideation (state) (van Dael *et al.*, 2006). The finding that jumping to conclusions bias is present in those at high risk of psychosis is consistent with cognitive models that suggest that the faulty appraisal of anomalous experiences plays a fundamental role in the development of the disorder (Broome *et al.*, 2005b; Garety *et al.*, 2005; Garety *et al.*, 2007). While 'jumping to conclusions' has consistently been found in patients with established psychosis (Garety and Freeman, 1999), its presence in individuals at very high risk of the disorder suggests that the presence of this impairment may influence whether an individual who is experiencing psychotic symptoms progresses to frank psychosis. Van Dael and colleagues suggest that the jumping to conclusions bias, as well as being a trait vulnerability, may have a state component, and one would expect such a bias to increase and be detectable at lower levels of task demand, as ARMS participants made the transition to psychosis. Conversely, those in whom the ARMS remitted may demonstrate an attenuation of the jumping to conclusions bias. This could be tested in a longitudinal study of subjects with an ARMS. In addition, to the best of our knowledge, it has not yet been investigated whether CBT in subjects with an ARMS targeting JTC can reduce JTC and therewith the risk of transition to a frank psychotic episode.

Case example: Samara

Samara is a 25-year-old caterer. She has her own small catering business, which is doing quite well. She has applied for help for anxiety. She explains that she has started to isolate herself socially. In the last year there have been several incidents in which she felt that people were 'out to get her'. Once she leaves the situation and takes a few days to recuperate, her anxiety decreases. She knows that others are not actually out to harm her. However, in the previous year she became very anxious in certain situations. Samara would like to learn how to prevent herself from jumping to negative conclusions that make her anxious.

Three incidences have especially made her become suspicious. During the weekends Samara often uses cannabis with friends. About a year ago she was smoking with two friends. She asked whether her friends thought that drugs might sometimes purposefully be poisoned with chemicals. Her friends did not take her seriously. Later that evening one friend complained about a sore throat. Her friends also left remarkably early that evening. Samara concluded that her friends probably thought that she had poisoned the cannabis since she had bought it. She concluded that they might want to take revenge on her. Although she rationalised her primary interpretation in the days afterwards, she still avoided her friends for some weeks.

A few weeks later she saw these friends at a party. At the time, Samara did not tell them about her suspicion. Instead, she told them that she had been ill and had therefore not been in contact. Later that evening she drank a soft drink. She noticed that it tasted strange and concluded that it might have been poisoned. She thought of an excuse and left the party.

Two weeks later the tension had subsided again. One of her friends helped her cater at a party. She drove her friend home. The next day she found her friend's mobile telephone in her car. Samara directly concluded that her friend had purposefully left her telephone in the car to eavesdrop on her. Samara confronted her friend. This friend denied that she spied on Samara or was trying to harm her in any way. Her friend also expressed her worries about Samara and advised her to seek help for her anxiety.

Negative expectation bias (pessimism)

Negative symptoms, e.g. a reduced ability to converse because nothing comes up to say, a feeling of emptiness and reduced motivation to start new things, often debilitate people who suffer from schizophrenia. Furthermore, when these patients experience cognitive deficits such as limited sustained attention, memory problems and reduced ability to plan, they can lose faith in themselves. Negative expectations about the capacity to handle problems and to enjoy social events induce feelings of depression. Not only depression, but also paranoia is associated with a pessimistic reasoning style (Strunk and Adler, 2009). The association between pessimistic reasoning style and depression on one hand, and paranoia on the other, remain when cognitive performance is controlled for (Bentall *et al.*, 2009). Grant and Beck have looked into the associations among defeatist beliefs, cognitive impairment, negative symptoms and social functioning (Beck, Rector, Stolar and Grant, 2009; Grant and Beck, 2009). Memory tasks, abstraction, attention, speed of processing, psychopathology, social functioning and endorsing defeatist beliefs were assessed in people with schizophrenia, schizo-affective disorder and normal control subjects. Greater cognitive impairments were associated with more defeatist beliefs, negative symptoms, and worse social and vocational functioning. Statistical modelling showed that defeatist beliefs were mediators in the relationship between cognitive impairments and negative symptoms, and in the relationship between cognitive impairments and social functioning. These effects were independent of depression and positive symptoms.

The defeatist beliefs are a target in CBT. Also in ARMS subjects, it has been shown that negative performance beliefs are endorsed to a greater extent than in healthy control subjects. These beliefs were associated with more negative symptoms. The association was independent of depression and positive symptoms (Perivoliotis, Morrison, Grant, French and Beck, 2009). Furthermore, social disinterest combined with defeatist beliefs has been shown to be a mediator between neurocognitive deficits and social functioning (Granholm, Ben-Zeev and Link, 2009).

More evidence comes from other research groups. Avery and colleagues demonstrated that neurocognitive deficits were only associated through executive functioning with affective flattening, while psychological variables such as effort, coping and negative expectancy appraisals made unique contributions to distinct negative symptoms as well as to the negative symptom total score (Avery, Startup and Calabria, 2009). A Swiss research group from Bern took the outcome of rehabilitation as the dependent variable. A poor rehabilitation outcome was predicted by a high degree of external locus of control, pessimistic outcome expectancies, negative symptoms and depressive resigned coping strategies (Hoffmann, Kupper and Kunz, 2000). These latter strategies are comparable to the defeatist beliefs as described by Grant and Beck. Hopelessness and giving up can determine disease outcome and social functioning to a high degree, independent of negative symptoms.

The Beck group from Pennsylvania University has developed a cognitive model of defeatist beliefs, which are a target in CBT for demoralised schizophrenia patients (Beck *et al.*, 2009). The association between neurocognitive impairment and negative symptoms is mediated by dysfunctional, defeatist beliefs. Six of these beliefs are defined as follows:

1 Social aversion: 'I attach very little importance to having close friends.'
2 Negative expectancies about performance: 'If you cannot do something well, there is little point in doing it at all.'
3 Low expectancies for pleasure: 'It is more work than it's worth.'
4 Low expectancies for success: 'I'm not going to be good enough.'
5 Low expectancies owing to stigma: 'What do you expect? I'm mentally ill.'
6 Beliefs about limited resources: 'I don't have enough energy.'

These beliefs essentially perpetuate disengagement as a protective safety behaviour and lead to a worse outcome, and diminished social and vocational functioning. The therapy for these patients is goal-oriented and the positive symptoms are not addressed unless they interfere with the accomplishment of the goals (Grant and Beck, 2009; Grant, Huh, Perivoliotis, Stolar and Beck, 2012). The therapy has to accommodate the neurocognitive impairments. The use of whiteboards and written materials is necessary to compensate for attention and memory deficits. Activity scheduling is a part of the treatment to develop more activities and to strengthen the feeling of accomplishment, satisfaction and joy. Behavioural experiments can be used to test the effect of negative expectancies on performance, enjoyment and social acceptance. The involvement of family members can be very helpful in these patients to help transfer behaviour outside in real-life contexts, to help with homework assignments, and to prevent unnecessary tension and conflicts.

Case example: Sharon

Sharon was born and raised in a troubled and neglecting family. Her father was an aggressive alcoholic and her mother suffered from recurrent depressions. Being the eldest, Sharon took on the upbringing of her younger brother and sister. She changed her brother's diapers from as early as she can remember and she cooked meals for the entire family from the age of nine. Her parents often fought and Sharon frequently functioned as a lightning rod. Father sometimes disappeared for a while and mother made consecutive suicide attempts. As a result of her upbringing, Sharon has developed very negative basic and intermediate assumptions. She feels that she is a bad person and that she will never succeed in anything she does. She thinks others cannot be trusted, and that others think she is weird and will reject her. Sharon has been referred for the treatment of a depression. She is now 26 years old and studying philosophy. Her mother died about a year ago due to cancer and since then things have started going downhill. Sharon has started to miss classes and is withdrawing herself from her social life. Lately, she has started to think that her boyfriend and dogs do not want her any more. She noticed that they pay less attention to her and concluded that they were conspiring to get her to leave. At those moments she is quite sure of her negative thoughts; later she can rationalise them. She tries extra hard to be a lovable person. She buys the best dog food available and cooks extensive dinners for her boyfriend.

In the past few months Sharon has sometimes had the idea that others do not exist, especially when she gets emails from friends; she then wonders whether that friend actually exists. She suspects a computer might be producing automatic replies or that someone else, pretending to be her friend, is in fact sending these messages. Sharon has no ideas about the purpose of this presumed trickery and is also not 100 per cent sure that it is actually going on. After seeing her face change in the mirror two months ago, she also started questioning her own existence. She talks extensively about a priori knowledge and the fact that you cannot know if the world still exists when you do not observe it. Sharon explains that she knows her mind is running away with her on these existential questions. Moreover, she stresses she always thinks and expects the worst to happen. Last week, for instance, she read about a robbery in the local newspaper. After this she became anxious when she went outside. She expects to get mugged because it will be just her luck to be the robber's next victim. Sharon has very little trust in her own capabilities and feels she is not able to cope with all her problems.

Dogmatism/belief inflexibility bias (I know I am right, I need no proof)

One of the clinical characteristics of most delusional patients is their reluctance to examine the validity of their delusions. They just know that what they think is true. Their answer to the question how do they know they are right is: 'I just know I am right.' Devout believers in God may also give this answer, referred to as religious dogmatism by some. However, this assumption cannot be tested for trueness or falseness. One just has to believe that God exists. Philosophers call this reinforced dogmatism. What is the difference compared with paranoia? In reinforced dogmatism, this is of a primary epistemological nature. In paranoia this seems to be a secondary epistemological flaw, indicating a lack of alternative hypotheses to select from and test (Rudnick, 2003).

Davies investigated the role of dogmatism in the persistence of beliefs after evidential discrediting. When people high in dogmatism form a belief on the basis of apparently bona fide evidence and this evidence is subsequently revealed to be false, it is found that they persist with their original but erroneous beliefs. During the formation of the initial belief, the original evidence is embellished and bolstered by processes such as explanation and selective recall so that indirect collateral evidence is generated that sustains it, even when the original evidence is discredited. In two experiments, Davies found support for the hypothesis that highly dogmatic individuals show greater belief persistence because the revision of their initial belief is insufficient in the light of discrediting information, whereas individuals low in dogmatism would show less belief persistence because their more open belief system allows them to reconcile their initial belief with the discrediting information (Davies 1993; Davies 1998). Moreover, it was found that individuals high in dogmatism generated fewer reasons contradicting their belief than individuals low in dogmatism.

Case example: William

William is a 26-year-old married cook. He has attention deficit and hyperactivity disorder (ADHD) and had a BLIPS in the last year. He grew up in an abusive and harsh environment. His alcoholic father physically abused him. William became extremely paranoid at an underground house party eight months ago. It was a stressful period at work and William used drugs on a weekly basis to get his mind off unpleasant things. After a previous party someone was found dead in a canal; this person had been stabbed several times with a knife. William started to pick up signals that there might be a secret conspiracy going on in which some partygoers ritually slaughtered people for fun. The flyer for the next party mentioned that this was going to be an even bigger party. William interpreted this as a warning signal; this time more people would get murdered. He concluded that he was one of the next victims. Nevertheless, he went to the party because his friends pressured him. He told them that he was feeling a bit paranoid. They did not take him seriously and made jokes about his suspiciousness on the way to the party. At the party William saw all kinds of proof for his negative expectation. One of his friends had brought a colleague to the party. When this colleague used a knife to cut the XTC pills William snapped. He fled the party and ran for miles, convinced that 'they' were after him. He took a train home and did not go to work for days. His wife calmed him down and after a few days William's anxiety lessened. He started to go to work again and stopped using drugs and going to parties.

William is now functioning well and still sees his friends. He sometimes has mild paranoid thoughts, but can reduce or ignore these quite easily. Nevertheless, he is still 70 per cent convinced that he really escaped a slaughter at the party eight months ago. William and his therapist list all the events that William sees as proof for his negative expectation. His therapist asks William to think of alternative explanations for these events; William cannot. He emphasises that he is still quite sure that these events actually referred to him and that it really meant he was in danger. He understands that his thoughts are highly unlikely and that his 'proof' is rather thin. He is able to think of alternative interpretations if they involve someone else in another situation. However, he has a strong feeling that he is right about this experience. Somehow he just 'knows' he's right.

Emotional reasoning (because if I feel anxious, there must be danger)

Emotional reasoning occurs when conclusions are drawn about a situation on the basis of a subjective emotional response. Beck and colleagues noted that anxious patients might strongly believe in the proposition 'If I feel anxious, there must be danger.' However, when danger is expected on the basis of an anxiety response and not on the basis of objective danger, false alarms are frequent and irrational fears will tend to persist (Beck *et al.*, 1985). To our knowledge, emotional reasoning has mostly been examined in anxiety disorders and in healthy adults and children. Since many ARMS subjects experience anxiety, the emotional reasoning bias is relevant to treatment of this group. Schwarz and Clore demonstrated that current mood influenced judgements of one's current life situation (e.g. someone judges his life as less satisfactory when in a sad mood) and that this effect of mood on judgements was eliminated when participants were induced to attribute their current mood to situational factors (e.g. bad weather) (Schwarz and Clore, 1983, 1988).

Arntz, Rauner and van den Hout (1995) investigated whether anxiety patients infer danger on the basis of their anxious response, whereas normal controls infer danger only on the basis of objective information. Four groups of anxiety patients (52 spider phobia patients, 41 panic patients, 38 social phobia and 31 other anxiety patients) and 24 healthy controls made ratings of the danger they perceived in scripts in which information about objective safety vs. objective danger, and anxiety response vs. non-anxiety response information were systematically varied. As hypothesised, anxiety patients were not only influenced by objective danger information, but also by anxiety response information, whereas healthy controls were not. The effect was neither situation-specific, nor specific for panic patients. This tendency to infer danger on the basis of subjective anxiety plays a role in the development and maintenance of anxiety disorders.

Muris and colleagues examined whether this so-called emotional reasoning phenomenon also occurs in children. Normal primary school children ($n = 101$) first completed scales tapping anxiety disorder symptoms, anxiety sensitivity and trait anxiety. Next, they were asked to rate danger levels of scripts in which objective danger versus objective safety and anxiety response (e.g. you start to sweat) versus no anxiety response were systematically varied. Evidence was found for a general emotional reasoning effect. That is, children's danger ratings were not only a function of objective danger information, but also, in the case of objective safety scripts, of anxiety response information. Levels of anxiety sensitivity and trait anxiety predicted this emotional reasoning effect. More specifically, high levels of anxiety sensitivity and trait anxiety were accompanied by a greater tendency to use anxiety-response information as a heuristic for assessing dangerousness of safety scripts (Muris, Merckelbach and van Spauwen, 2003).

Another study by Muris and colleagues examined the relation between childhood anxiety and threat-perception abnormalities using vignettes in which external (i.e., exposure to potential threat cues) and internal (i.e., experience of anxiety responses) information was systematically varied. Non-clinical children ($n = 156$) aged 8 to 13 years completed anxiety questionnaires and were then exposed to three types of stories: ambiguous stories, ambiguous + anxiety-response stories and non-threatening stories. From children's responses to these stories, a number of threat-perception indexes were derived. Results showed that both external and internal information inflated children's perception of threat. Further, high levels of anxiety were accompanied by enhanced threat perception in response to external threat cues. Finally, little evidence was found that high levels of anxiety, and in particular of anxiety sensitivity, were associated with a greater tendency to use internal information (i.e., emotional reasoning) (Muris, Merckelbach, Schepers and Meesters, 2003).

Case example: Joanne

Joanne's general practitioner refers her to the community mental health centre because Joanne is afraid that she might fall ill or die. As a result of such thoughts she frequently has panic attacks. Joanne is a 23-year-old medical student who is about to start her internships; however, at this moment she is not studying. Her anxiety started six months ago when both an aunt and a friend died due to a stroke. She is afraid that she might have weak veins and fears a cerebral vascular accident. She has been extensively examined and is in perfect health. Joanne is unhappy in her relationship and feels that she and her boyfriend are living separate lives.

In the last two months she has felt that she is becoming paranoid. She started to notice that she feels uneasy at home. She feels tensed, as though something is wrong. She is becoming increasingly afraid that her food or drinks might be poisoned or drugged. The first time she had such a thought was with her boyfriend's water kettle. She suddenly felt a great anxiety and tension and concluded something was wrong. She started wondering whether someone could have put poison or drugs in the kettle and stopped drinking water from it. She only drinks from the kettle after someone else has just drunk from it, so that she knows it is safe. She does not think someone is intentionally trying to harm her, but is cautious because 'these things happen' and she feels that she might be an accidental victim.

Lately, Joanne has started to think that her boyfriend might be slowly poisoning her, as in the Hollywood film *Seven*. She works late and he always cooks. She rationalises these thoughts and forces herself to eat. She used to take her contraceptive pill in the evenings, but recently started wondering whether these might have been poisoned as well since she felt strange after taking them. She is now taking her contraceptive pill in the mornings. This way she will notice if something is wrong with her and avoid dying in her sleep. Joanne tells us that she knows that her thoughts are ridiculous; but that the anxiety is so strong she feels that it must mean something. She is preoccupied with the fear of losing control over her mind and is afraid she will end up in a closed ward.

Confirmation bias (bias against disconfirmatory evidence)

When people seek new information, the information search processes are often biased in favour of the information seeker's previously held beliefs, expectations or desired conclusions. For example, people have been shown to favour information that supports their social stereotypes (Johnston, 1996), attitudes (Lundgren and Prisley, 1998), expectations in negotiations (Pinkley, Griffith and Northcraft, 1995) and self-serving conclusions (Holton and Pyszczynski, 1989). These biased information search processes lead to the maintenance of the information seeker's position, even if this position is not justified on the basis of all available information (Johnston, 1996; Pinkley *et al.*, 1995). This bias is called confirmation bias. Such processes are of particular relevance in non-routine decision-making. According to authors such as Janis or Nemeth and Rogers, an information search that is clearly biased in favour of a preferred alternative may be dangerous, because potential risks and warning signals may be overlooked and, thus, wrong decisions may be the consequence (Janis, 1982). If the decision-maker fails to consider disconfirming pieces of information, it is difficult for him or her to correct a faulty decision (Brockner and Rubin, 1985; Nemeth and Rogers, 1996).

Empirical studies on biased information search in decision-making have mainly been carried out within the framework of dissonance theory (Festinger, 1957). According to this theory, once committed to an alternative, people prefer supportive (consonant) information compared with opposing (dissonant) information to avoid or reduce post-decisional conflicts. This effect has been labelled selective exposure to information.

The confirmation bias is also called bias against disconfirmatory evidence (BADE). Delusional and non-delusional psychotic patients were more accepting of implausible interpretations than were normal controls. The patients with delusions displayed more BADE than the non-delusional patients did (Woodward, 2006a) or compared to obsessive–compulsive patients and normal controls (Woodward *et al.*, 2008). If an interpretation becomes more likely, then patients and non-patients upgrade their confidence in the correct answer, but if an interpretation becomes less likely by presenting disconfirmatory evidence, patients do not down-rate their confidence, while normal controls do (Moritz and Woodward, 2006; Woodward, Moritz, Cuttler and Whitman, 2006b).

BADE is also associated with delusion proneness and schizotypy (Buchy, Woodward and Liotti, 2007; Woodward, Buchy, Moritz and Liotti, 2007).

Also, in healthy controls from the general population, BADE is associated with delusional ideation (Zawadzki et al., 2012).

Behavioural bias

Avoidance behaviour (evading threat)

Avoidance behaviour is a crucial component of fear and is importantly involved in the maintenance of anxiety disorders. Presumably, fear conditioning leads to avoidance of the feared object or context (Glotzbach, Andreatta, Pauli and Muhlberger, 2012). Marks (1987) suggested a distinction between fear and anxiety. Fear is linked to a specific threat, whereas anxiety is a more diffuse state not related to a specific object or stimulus. People often either avoid situations they fear before they enter them or they escape and leave such a situation. One of the reasons why avoidance behaviour is problematic is that such behaviour removes the opportunity to disconfirm fear-inducing beliefs (Salkovskis, 1991). For example, a schizophrenia patient often heard a voice in his head yelling 'watch out'. He always fled the situation because he believed the voice warned him about imminent danger. Because of this avoidance behaviour, the patient was unable to find out that nothing happened if he stayed in the situation. The habituation model of anxiety (Lader and Wing, 1966) implies that decreases in anxiety will occur only after prolonged exposure, and relatively brief exposure periods may actually serve to sensitise patients to their feared stimuli and prove detrimental (Marshall, 1988). Needless to say, avoidance prevents prolonged exposure by definition. Furthermore, avoidance behaviour is intrinsically problematic insofar as it interferes with functioning (Harvey et al., 2004).

During CBT, avoidance of fear-evoking situations is gradually reduced. The rationale for this originated from the learning model of fear and avoidance (Mowrer, 1960). According to this theory, avoidance behaviour is reinforced when it is followed by a reduction in anxiety. However, if the feared stimulus is avoided, extinction cannot occur. In essence, the avoidance persists because it works (it reduces anxiety). This has been confirmed experimentally in humans. If participants were given the possibility of avoiding the feared stimulus during extinction training, their fear responses to this stimulus decreased less compared to participants who were not able to avoid the stimulus during extinction. Thus, the avoidance response prevented extinction learning (Lovibond, Mitchell, Minard, Brady and Menzies, 2009). To reduce the avoidance behaviour, patients are instructed to remain in the fear-evoking situation until their anxiety has decreased. Prolonged exposure may be necessary to allow cognitive reappraisals of feared situations.

ARMS subjects often show avoidance behaviour. Some ARMS subjects have a comorbid axis-1 disorder of social phobia. The DSM-IV diagnostic criteria for social phobia encompass the avoidance of feared social situations (APA, 2001). Examples of safety behaviours employed by patients with social phobia include avoiding eye contact, monitoring one's speech and mentally rehearsing sentences. It is not difficult to imagine how such behaviours unintentionally increase the chance of the person experiencing poor social interactions and being evaluated negatively. In a study of socially anxious students, more negative responses from other people were elicited when safety behaviours were used than when no such safety behaviours were used (Alden and Bieling, 1998). Such negative responses are likely to confirm the patient's belief that they are disliked and are poor at socialising. There is increasing evidence for the importance of addressing safety behaviours in the treatment of social phobia.

In a study of Freeman and colleagues, avoidance and safety behaviours in 25 patients with persecutory delusions were investigated. Avoidance was the most common safety behaviour and higher levels of anxiety were associated with the greater use of safety behaviours. Of the 25 subjects, 14 reported avoiding meeting people or attending social gatherings, 13 reported avoiding walking on the street, 11 avoided pubs and being far from home, and 9 reported avoiding public transport and enclosed spaces. *In situ* safety behaviours included: 'protection', e.g. not answering the front door, and 'invisibility', e.g. wearing a hat or a helmet, walking quickly and keeping the eyes on the ground (Freeman, Garety and Kuipers, 2001). ARMS subjects sometimes show mild persecutory ideas and already use these avoidance and safety behaviours. For example, the case description of Mike in Chapter 8 ('jumping to conclusions') shows that this patient used a range of avoidance and safety behaviours; for example, he avoided going out alone, using public transport and sharing personal experiences with other people. By helping Mike with slowly reducing safety and avoidance behaviours, disconfirmatory experiences helped him to reduce anxiety and improve functioning.

Case example: Lisa

Lisa is 18 years old and has just finished secondary school. Next year she starts her university studies. Lisa has a history of obsessive–compulsive disorder (OCD), for which she was effectively treated in the past. In the last few months the obsessive–compulsive complaints have returned. At first she thought it was just a relapse of OCD, but she started to experience strange things and has begun to believe the devil is trying to influence her. She fears the devil will take possession of her body or will make bad things happen to the people around her. Lisa rates this thought as quite credible (70–80 per cent). Even though Lisa was raised as an atheist she has always been afraid of the devil. She experiences several strange things and is preoccupied with avoiding adversities. When she feels tingling sensations on her body she has the idea that the devil is touching her. She then rubs her skin and walks to another room. Lisa stopped playing the violin, something she used to do every day, because she is afraid the devil will manipulate her playing in such a way that it might cause others harm. Lisa explains that she has no proof for her negative thoughts and that she understands that her ideas are ridiculous. Last week she was making a sandwich when she suddenly saw a shadow out of the corner of her eye. She threw away the sandwich to prevent the devil entering her body through it. Sometimes she picks up strange smells, she then holds her breath out of fear of the same thing. Lisa explains that she is less than 50 per cent convinced that it is actually the devil and that she is probably just scaring herself with the negative thoughts. However, the expected outcome if it really were the devil is so terrifying to her that she feels it is 'better safe than sorry'.

5

The nature of cognitive biases

Are some cognitive biases endophenotypes?

Psychosis is hereditary – to a certain extent. Modern research into genetics focuses on gene × environment interaction. For genes to come to expression, they have to be turned on. When a gene is activated, it produces proteins. The proteins act within our bodies and can be beneficial in most cases, but malignant in others. As the search for schizophrenia genes related to the clinical phenotype (i.e. observable symptoms of schizophrenia) has yielded inconsistent results, the focus of schizophrenia research has shifted to the endophenotypes (i.e. intermediate markers between high-level symptom presentation and low-level genetic variability) (Greenwood, Rangrej and Sun, 2007). Endophenotypes reflect the vulnerability of an individual for the development of a certain disorder. As endophenotypes are relatively simple, well defined and measurable, it is assumed that fewer genes than the complex phenotype of schizophrenia determine them. Hereby, these endophenotypes can help to unravel the complex phenomenology of schizophrenia. Importantly, in contrast to terms such as 'biological marker' or 'vulnerability marker', endophenotypes imply a genetic connection.

Several criteria must be fulfilled in order for a biomarker to be called an endophenotype. First, the endophenotype is associated with illness in the general population. Second, it should be heritable. Third, it should be a trait marker (temporal stability) and not a state marker (fluctuating with symptom changes). Fourth, it should be present in clinically unaffected subjects with an increased risk for the disease, for instance patients with (traits of) a schizotypal personality disorder or relatives of schizophrenia patients (Gottesman and Gould, 2003).

Are the cognitive biases that we have discussed endophenotypical in nature? For this they must have been documented in patients, but also in ARMS and in first-degree relatives (see Table 5.1). This has been found for the data-gathering bias and the source monitoring bias. The data-gathering bias is found to be present in all groups of subjects with delusions, irrespective of the diagnosis. The same

Table 5.1 Cognitive biases in schizophrenia patients, people with an At Risk Mental State for developing psychosis, and in first-degree relatives of psychotic patients

Cognitive bias	Schizophrenia patients	At Risk Mental State	First-degree relatives
Source monitoring bias	Heilbrun 1980; Bentall, Baker and Havers 1991; Morrison and Haddock 1997; Keefe, Arnold, Bayen and Harvey 1999; Brébion, Gorman, Amador, Malaspina and Sharif 2002; Ensum and Morrison 2003; Moritz, Woodward and Ruff 2003; Keefe, Poe, McEvoy and Vaughan 2003; Nienow and Docherty 2004; Henquet, Krabbendam, Dautzenberg, Jolles and Merckelbach 2005; Johns, Gregg, Allen and McGuire 2006; Woodward, Menon and Whitman 2007; Brunelin et al. 2007; Costafreda, Brébion, Allen, McGuire and Fu 2008; Startup, Startup and Sedgman 2008	Laroi, van der Linden and Marczewski 2004; Levine, Jonas and Serper 2004; Brunelin et al. 2007 (remitted); Costafreda et al. 2008 (remitted); Johns et al. 2010	Brunelin et al. 2007
Jumping to conclusions	Huq, Garety and Hemsley 1988; Garety, Hemsley and Wessely 1991; John and Dodgson 1994; Dudley, John, Young and Over 1997a; Fear and Healy 1997; Young and Bentall 1997; Moritz and Woodward 2005; Moritz et al. 2009; Garety et al. 2005; van Dael et al. 2006; Menon, Pomarol-Clotet, McKenna and McCarthy 2006; Menon, Mizrahi and Kapur 2008; Moritz, Woodward and Hausmann 2006; Moritz and Woodward 2007b; Warman, Lysaker, Martin, Davis and Haudenschield 2007; Merrin, Kinderman and Bentall 2007; So, Freeman and Garety 2008; Peters, Thornton, Siksou, Linney and MacCabe 2008; Startup, Freeman and Garety 2008; White and Mansell 2009; Lincoln, Ziegler, Mehl and Rief 2010; Lincoln, Peter, Schäfer and Moritz 2010; Langdon, Ward and Coltheart 2010; Averbeck, Evans, Chouhan, Bristow and Shergill 2011	Linney, Peters and Ayton 1998; Peters, Colbert, Linney, Lawrence and Garety 2003; McKay, Langdon and Coltheart 2006; Warman and Martin 2006b; van Dael et al. 2006; Broome et al. 2007; Warman et al. 2007	van Dael et al. 2006
Covariation bias	Brennan and Hemsley 1984; DíezAlegría, Vázquez and Hernández-Lloreda 2008	Schienle, Vaitl and Stark 1996 (ESP believers)	
Confirmation bias	Woodward, Moritz, Cuttler and Whitman 2006a; Moritz and Woodward 2006; Woodward et al. 2006a; Woodward, Moritz, Menon and Klinge 2008	Woodward, Buchy, Moritz and Liotti 2007; Buchy, Woodward and Liotti 2007 (schizotypy)	

is true for the source monitoring bias, which is associated with hallucinations, irrespective of the diagnosis.

Covariation bias and confirmation bias are candidates. They have been found present in people at risk for developing psychosis, but first-degree relatives have not yet been studied.

The fact that some cognitive biases are trait factors associated with genetic endowment may imply that they will be hard to change using psychological methods. To influence its effect, subjects should be made aware of the bias and consciously compensate. For example, people who jump to conclusions can be taught that whenever they become suspicious they should not act on the first explanation that comes to mind. They will have to come up with at least three different explanations. If they cannot think of alternative explanations, they should consider the possible explanations that are brought up by others; of course, the best way to test your hypothesis is to find out what really is going on.

Transdiagnostic biases

Transdiagnostic processes characterise most of the psychiatric disorders (Harvey et al., 2004). Selective attention is a cognitive bias that is present in all disorders. In eating disorder there is a bias to perceive food; in addiction there is selective attention for paraphernalia such as aluminium foil; in dog phobia the environment is scanned for the presence of dogs. Paranoid people scan the environment for suspicious-looking people. Selective attention for threat makes one detect more possible threats than actually exist, leading to increased anxiety. An anxious state of mind makes the person more alert, which can induce a circular process with increasing levels of anxiety.

Another transdiagnostic process is avoidance behaviour. All anxiety disorders are characterised by avoidance behaviour to evade threat and to acquire safety. Paranoid subjects often avoid other people and various situations. They tend to stay home and take certain precautions, such as keeping the curtains closed 24 hours a day and installing extra locks.

Research in psychiatry seems to be on the verge of a paradigm shift from categorisation with the DSM-IV to a more dimensional approach (Miller, 2010), mainly because it is increasingly apparent that psychiatric disorders are not distinct categories but have considerable overlap between them. In the ARMS group, subjects experience anxiety, depression, PTSD symptoms, as well as mild psychotic symptoms. They also suffer from several transdiagnostic biases.

Dopamine sensitisation, cognitive biases and extraordinary experiences

In a review of the literature, Laruelle suggests that frontal dopamine activation can inhibit dopamine sensitisation in the medial brain (Laruelle, 2000). Sensitisation refers to the process by which a cellular receptor becomes more likely to respond to a stimulus. Thus, dopamine sensitisation means that the dopamine system responds fiercely to the release of dopamine (the stimulus).

Neurodevelopmental abnormalities of prefrontal dopaminergic systems might result in a state of enhanced vulnerability to sensitisation during late adolescence and early adulthood. In that paper, Laruelle also proposed that D2 receptor blockade, if sustained, might allow for an extinction of this sensitisation process, with possible re-emergence upon treatment discontinuation (Laruelle, 2000).

A biological substrate of the salience network may be the anterior cingulate cortex and the anterior insula. Reduced activation in these areas is shown to be related to reality distortion (Palaniyappan, Mallikarjun, Joseph, White and Liddle, 2010).

Attenuated psychotic symptoms are psychotic symptoms with below-threshold frequency or duration (Yung et al., 2008). It is widely accepted that psychosis involves dopamine deregulation, as described by Howes and Kapur (2009). They propose that the locus of dopamine deregulation is primarily at the presynaptic dopaminergic control level and that this deregulation is the '*final common pathway*' to psychosis. The abnormal firing of dopamine neurons and the abnormal release of dopamine lead to an aberrant assignment of salience to innocuous stimuli. It is argued that psychotic symptoms, especially delusions and hallucinations, emerge over time as the individual's own explanation for the experience of aberrant salience. Psychosis is, therefore, aberrant salience driven by dopamine and filtered through the individual's existing cognitive and sociocultural schemas – thus allowing the same chemical (dopamine) to have different clinical manifestations in different cultures and different individuals (Howes and Kapur, 2009). Therefore, altering the existing cognitive schemas with CBT in a patient with dopamine deregulation can have beneficial effects on psychosis or UHR symptoms.

Salience behaves as a highlighter in the perceptual field. Certain stimuli emerge in the centre of the perceptual field and are experienced as extremely important.

They make the stimulus:

- in need of an appraisal;
- of personal significance;
- in need of a response.

The salience process arrests other on-going behaviour. For instance, when the person watches television and the woman presenting the weather report becomes saliently present in perception, the person might think she is speaking to them personally. The reason why and the things she says have to be interpreted. She warns drivers about icy conditions; is this a coded message telling them not to go outside because it is dangerous?

Many people with a heightened dopamine system have the impression that things being said on radio or television have a connection to their own thoughts and concerns, and convey a personal message.

This personalisation bias can make subjects think that when two people are talking, they must be talking about them, or when two people laugh, they must be laughing about them. The heightened levels of dopamine can also increase the number of intrusions into consciousness and induce delusional ideas.

Are cognitive biases open to change?

Cognitive bias modification in anxiety and mood disorders

In the field of anxiety research, the effect of cognitive bias modification (CBM) on targeting negative interpretation bias has been explored. In analogue studies, normal people from the general population have been trained to interpret social situations in a positive or negative way. This training affects their cognitive biases and their mood. Clinical efficacy has been demonstrated in social phobia, generalised anxiety disorders and paediatric anxiety disorders (Beard, 2011; Eldar *et al.* 2012).

The cognitive model of depression also found support. Optimistic/pessimistic biases are related to depressive symptoms. However, there is no evidence that depressive symptoms are associated with greater accuracy in judgements (Strunk and Adler, 2009).

A meta-analysis of 45 studies (2,591 participants) assessed the effect of CBM on cognitive biases and on anxiety and depression. CBM had a medium effect on biases ($g = 0.49$) that was stronger for interpretation ($g = 0.81$) than for attention ($g = 0.29$) biases. In addition, CBM had a small effect on anxiety and depression ($g = 0.13$), although this effect was reliable only when symptoms were assessed after participants experienced a stressor ($g = 0.23$). When anxiety and depression were examined separately, CBM significantly modified anxiety but not depression. There was a trend towards a larger effect for studies including multiple training sessions. These findings are broadly consistent with cognitive theories of anxiety and depression that propose an interactive effect of cognitive biases and stressors on these symptoms. However, the small effect sizes observed may warrant further research before clinical applications are ready to be implemented (Hallion and Ruscio, 2011).

Cognitive biases, anxiety, depression and subclinical psychotic symptoms

Positive beliefs about paranoia are positively associated with increased suspiciousness, and negative beliefs about paranoia are significantly higher in patients with a diagnosis of schizophrenia meeting criteria for persecutory delusions in comparison to those without. Patients scored higher than non-patients on both positive and negative beliefs about paranoia (Morrison *et al.*, 2011a). If the level of anxiety was manipulated, then participants with higher baseline vulnerability were more likely to show an increase in paranoia as a reaction to an increase in anxiety. This association of anxiety and paranoia was mediated by the increased tendency to jump to conclusions. Thus, there is an interaction between anxiety and reasoning biases in the development of paranoid beliefs (Lincoln, Ziegler, Mehl and Rief, 2010).

People cope with unpleasant thoughts in different ways. Reappraisal (concentrating on the unwanted thought in order to assess validity) is associated with trait paranoia, whereas 'punishment' (either thinking negatively about, or behaving negatively towards oneself in reaction to the unwanted thought) and 'worry' (replacing the thought with another anxiety-provoking thought) are accounted for by anxiety (Taylor, Graves and Stopa, 2009). Depression and paranoia could be differentiated by the nature of their future-oriented pessimistic thinking styles. Depression was associated with the tendency to underestimate the likelihood of future positive and neutral events, whereas subclinical paranoia was independently associated with overestimations of the likelihood of future threatening events (Bennett and Corcoran, 2010). A combination of metacognitive training directed at reasoning biases and promoting emotion regulation skills might prove beneficial in preventing symptoms.

Effects of metacognitive training in psychosis

A metacognitive training (MCT) programme targeting cognitive biases was developed by Moritz and Woodward and tested on feasibility. The training was positively evaluated and there were very few dropouts (Moritz and Woodward, 2007a). The MCT was tested in a small trial with 2 × 18 schizophrenia-spectrum patients. The MCT condition showed a (non-significant) improvement in hallucinations and delusions as assessed with the Psychotic Rating Scales (PSYRATS) (Drake, Haddock, Tarrier, Bentall and Lewis, 2007). Two items appeared to be most responsive: severity of distress and the intensity of distress caused by delusions. The tendency to jump to conclusions also showed a (non-significant) improvement ($p = 0.13$). Delayed memory improved in the MCT group (Moritz et al., 2011). MCT plus CBT was tested against COGPACK (a cognitive remediation package) with 2 × 24 patients and reported in a review. Patients receiving MCT+CBT improved on delusions severity as assessed with the Positive and Negative Syndrome Scale (PANSS) (Kay, Fiszbein and Opler, 1987), especially ideas of grandiosity. Furthermore, there was a tendency towards a decline in delusion conviction as assessed with the PSYRATS. The training significantly improved jumping to conclusions (Moritz, Vitzthum, Randjbar, Veckenstedt and Woodward, 2010). Another underpowered study reported a (non-significant) improvement on the PANSS positive symptoms and a (non-significant) reduction in jumping to conclusions (Aghotor, Pfueller, Moritz, Weisbrod and Roesch-Ely, 2010).

Other researchers have studied aspects of the MCT. Ross and colleagues extended the module on jumping to conclusions and found in a trial with 2 × 34 patients that the trained group showed a significant increase in data gathering (less jumping to conclusions) and a non-significant improvement in cognitive flexibility and delusion conviction. Although the data gathering improved, patients with the most severe symptoms were resistant to change (Ross, Freeman, Dunn and Garety, 2011).

Brakoulias reported an interesting study. In a small uncontrolled cohort with 16 patients, he tested the effects of CBT. He found significant within-group improvement in delusional conviction and preoccupation, but jumping to conclusions, theory of mind ability and attribution style were unaffected (Brakoulias et al., 2008).

To conclude, cognitive biases can be changed by therapy, although this does not necessarily lead to remission of symptoms. Although the cognitive biases cause (in part) the symptoms, the effect size of treatment on biases is medium, whereas the effect size on symptoms is relatively small.

6

Evidence for preventing or postponing a first episode psychosis

This chapter is an adaptation of: van der Gaag, M., Nieman, D. H., Rietdijk, J., Dragt, S., Ising, H. K., Klaassen, R. M., Koeter, M., Cuijpers, P., Wunderink, L. and Linszen, D. H. (2012). Cognitive behavioral therapy for subjects at ultrahigh risk for developing psychosis: A randomized controlled clinical trial. Schizophrenia Bulletin, 38(6), 1180–8.

Introduction

Not all people with psychosis will actively seek help, and professionals such as general practitioners (GPs) are not very well equipped to detect people with a first episode of psychosis or a developing psychosis. Most first episode psychoses (FEP) are characterised by a long duration of untreated psychosis (DUP). In the last two decades, early psychosis programmes have been developed in Australia, the UK and also in Europe and the USA. These early intervention programmes have also led to the detection of people with subclinical psychotic symptoms that do not meet the criteria for a psychotic disorder. Australian researchers in Melbourne were the first to develop criteria for the detection of people who have an ARMS (Yung et al., 1998, 2005). The criteria cover young people (14–35 years of age) in a social decline, with either a genetic risk, or attenuated psychotic symptoms, or a brief limited period of psychotic symptoms in the past year. These criteria have been tested over the last 15 years and have been found to predict the onset of a first episode of psychosis at rates several hundred fold above those in the general population (Cannon et al., 2008; Yung, Phillips, Yuen and McGorry, 2004; Yung et al., 2003).

While most of the disabling and sometimes fatal diseases (e.g. cancer, heart attacks and type II diabetes) are illnesses of old age, psychiatric diseases are predominantly found among young people. About 75 per cent of adult disorders start before the age of 25 years, and about 50 per cent of the onsets occur before age 15 years. Furthermore, 60 per cent of health-related disability in 15–34-year-olds is due to mental illness or substance abuse (Hickie, 2011). In view of the low mortality rates associated with psychiatric diseases, their costs to society are extremely high per case. The patients often suffer more than four decades during which their contributions to the economy are minimal, while they make demands on many health-care services and disability pensions. Furthermore, rates of mental illness in young people have increased in recent decades (Eckersley, 2011). The decline in social functioning in people with an ARMS for developing a psychosis is comparable to people with an FEP. In ARMS patients the social decline is associated with depression and social anxiety, but not so much with negative symptoms as is the case in FEP patients (Chudleigh *et al.*, 2011).

The early UHR studies were mostly performed by tertiary specialised clinics for detection and research of FEP and UHR patients. Only recently has early detection entered the field of routine psychiatric care. It is important to note, however, that young people are generally not included in mental health-care services. This brings in its wake a high risk of untreated cases and enormous economic loss. A reform of services is urgently needed to reach the large numbers of young people who need help, and to offer help to prevent social exclusion and chronic disease in young patients with a debut in psychosis (Hickie, 2011).

Goals of early detection

The goals of early detection are multiple. First, the goal is to postpone or prevent the transition to frank psychosis. In ARMS patients about 80 per cent will recover from the ARMS status even without any treatment (Hanssen *et al.*, 2005). Early treatment can prevent about half of the transitions, although the evidence is preliminary and inconclusive. In FEP patients only 20 per cent will suffer from a single episode and about 70–80 per cent will have a relapsing and chronic course with lifelong vulnerability and a high proportion of social exclusion (Alvarez-Jiménez *et al.*, 2011; Wiersma, Nienhuis, Slooff and Giel, 1998).

Second, early detection can improve treatment adherence as compared with FEP services because people with psychosis in early detection services are socialised in a different way. Because psychosis is explained and discussed before a psychotic breakthrough, and engagement with services is already established, most people who make a transition are also willing to adhere to antipsychotic medication treatment. This is dramatically different from the scenario in first-episode patients who enter services during a first episode of psychosis. Most psychotic patients are non-adherent to services and/or to medication (Leucht and Heres, 2006).

Third, the early detection programmes can improve access to adequate mental health services. A major cause of DUP is the secondary mental health services. Once an individual is treated for anxiety disorder or depression, the therapist is not sensitive to a frank psychosis and about 40 per cent of the DUP is caused by this inability to recognise psychosis (Boonstra *et al.*, 2011; Brunet, Birchwood, Lester and Thornhill, 2007).

Fourth, early detection may be more efficacious because the ARMS patients have a better prognosis, are more eager to undergo therapy and are more open to change. Many subjects with ARMS have intact illness awareness and are afraid of developing psychosis. Mentioning psychosis and schizophrenia too early may scare ARMS patients away. The diagnosis of schizophrenia is too stigmatised and too much a lifelong verdict. Most of them have consulted schizophrenia websites, have read their generally pessimistic content, and are horrified by such a scenario that leads to permanent disability. Not mentioning psychosis or schizophrenia in the early stages helps people to engage in the services. After two or three sessions with the therapist discussing odd and remarkable experiences, most subjects say that they are glad that attention is paid to these experiences and that although they suffer from, e.g. a panic disorder, they are most frightened by the idea that they are going mad!

Fifth, early detection is extremely important in preventing social decline and exclusion. Most FEP patients are unemployed (Wunderink, Nienhuis, Sytema and Wiersma, 2006), while the ARMS subjects are often still in jobs or school at the moment of detection (Rietdijk *et al.*, 2012). The criterion of social decline means that they are experiencing problems in at least two of four social functioning domains. For example, they no longer meet friends and distrust their colleagues, or they miss classes at school and are constantly arguing with parents and family members. Most FEP patients have lost their friends, jobs and school before the first episode, and there is evidence that the isolation after social withdrawal results in a lack of feedback on odd or paranoid ideas. Therefore, it is important that someone with an ARMS stays socially included and is exposed to realistic and delusion-breaking opinions of others.

Sixth, early detection programmes help to foster awareness in professionals in secondary mental health services about people with an imminent risk of developing psychosis. This will help to shorten DUP.

The first goal is the main goal, because early detection is of little use without an effective intervention. Several pioneering studies have been performed with the aim of preventing the transition to frank psychosis. The interventions were antipsychotic medication, cognitive behavioural therapy, omega-3 fish oil, or a combination of medical and psychosocial therapies. It was found that the efficacy of the interventions is encouraging, but as yet inconclusive (de Koning *et al.*, 2009; McGorry *et al.*, 2009; Yung and Nelson, 2011).

Evidence for early intervention

The first randomised controlled trial (RCT) was conducted between 1996 and 1999 in the PACE clinic in Melbourne, Australia (McGorry *et al.*, 2002; Phillips *et al.*, 2007). The control group ($n = 28$) received 'needs-based therapy' targeting social problems that the patients experienced. The treatment group received a combined treatment of 2 mg risperidone and a form of CBT consisting of psycho-education, skills training in handling the psychotic experiences, stress management and treatment of comorbid disorders. At the end of treatment after six months, the treated group had made fewer transitions to psychosis compared to the control group, although this effect was no longer significant at the 12-month follow-up.

Another study by this group compared CBT + placebo ($n = 44$) with CBT + risperidone ($n = 43$) and with supportive therapy + placebo ($n = 28$). After six months there were only 7 per cent of transitions and no differences between the groups (Yung et al., 2011). The 12-month outcome seems to be more differentiated (Yung, personal communication); however, at the moment of writing this book the final data have not yet been published.

The 'Prevention through Risk Identification, Management and Education' (PRIME) study was conducted in the USA from 1997 to 2003 and is a blinded RCT that compared olanzapine (5–15 mg per day; $n = 31$) with placebo ($n = 29$) (McGlashan et al., 2003, 2006). Treatment was during 12 months and follow-up was at 18 months. The drop-out rate was large in both the olanzapine group (35 per cent) and the placebo group (28 per cent). In the olanzapine group fewer patients transitioned to psychosis (5 versus 11), but this difference had disappeared at follow-up. The study was underpowered for statistical testing. Patients in the olanzapine group showed a significant increase in body weight: 8.8kg versus 0.3kg in the placebo group.

The 'Early Detection and Intervention Evaluation' study was performed in Manchester (UK) (Morrison et al., 2004). A total of 50 patients were randomised to CBT ($n = 37$) or monitoring ($n = 23$) during six months. At 12-months' follow-up there was a significant difference favouring CBT in the progression to psychosis, the prescription of antipsychotic medication, and meeting the criteria of a DSM-IV psychotic disorder. However, the difference became non-significant at 36-months' follow-up (Morrison et al., 2007).

The OPUS trial was conducted in Denmark (Nordentoft et al., 2006). Schizotypal patients were randomised to integrated therapy ($n = 42$) or treatment as usual ($n = 37$). Integrated therapy was conducted during two years and consisted of assertive community treatment, skills training and psycho-education in multiple-family groups. At 12 months, 3.2 per cent versus 16.9 per cent had made the transition to psychosis favouring the integrated condition. At 24-months, the number of transitions increased to 25 per cent and 48.3 per cent, respectively. Medication was not controlled; more than 60 per cent of the patients had been prescribed antipsychotic medication.

A remarkable study was performed in Vienna (Austria). Long-chain omega-3 fatty acids were compared with placebo. The patients were treated during 12 weeks. At the 12-months' follow-up, two of 41 patients in the fish oil condition had transitioned to psychosis compared with 11 of 40 patients in the placebo condition (Amminger et al., 2010). A large replication is now running in six European countries and in Australia, Singapore and Hong Kong. The study aims to include 320 UHR subjects (McGorry, n.d.).

A small underpowered study was performed in Canada (Addington et al., 2011). The study compared CBT ($n = 27$) with supportive therapy ($n = 24$). At the end of treatment at six months, three patients in the supportive condition had transitioned to psychosis and none in the CBT group. This difference did not change at follow-up at 12 and 18 months. Both groups improved on symptoms and social functioning, but the CBT group showed faster improvement.

The German Research Network on Schizophrenia compared CBT with supportive counselling (Bechdolf et al., 2012). The study distinguished between early prodromals with basic cognitive symptoms and late prodromals with subclinical psychotic symptoms. Of 65 patients, 11 made the transition from early to late prodromal in the supportive counselling condition and two of 63 subjects in the CBT condition. The number of subjects who converted to psychosis was zero in CBT and nine in supportive counselling – a significant result.

Most studies are small and underpowered. The EDIE-2 trial was meant to have sufficient statistical power to demonstrate the effectiveness of CBT over monitoring (Morrison *et al.*, 2011b, 2012). Of 144 subjects, ten made a transition in the CBT condition and 13 of 144 in the control condition. The effect is non-significant. Although this is a large study, it still lacked statistical power because the overall transition rate was only 8 per cent.

The Dutch Early Detection and Intervention Evaluation trial (EDIE-NL)

The Dutch Early Detection and Intervention Evaluation trial (EDIE-NL) is an RCT that compared cognitive behavioural therapy for ultra-high risk patients (CBTuhr) in addition to treatment as usual (TAU), with TAU alone, in a group of help-seeking people in mental health services. The participating secondary mental health services deal with patients seeking help for a non-psychotic axis 1 or 2 disorder. The patients also fulfil the criteria for an ARMS according to the criteria of the CAARMS (Yung *et al.*, 2005). In these criteria marked social decline is a prerequisite for inclusion in the attenuated symptoms group and also in the group with brief limited intermittent psychotic symptoms (BLIPS). The tertiary mental health service at the university clinic provides treatment for people seeking help for subclinical psychotic symptoms. We note that most of these patients also exhibit a comorbid axis 1 or 2 disorder.

Participants

Patients were eligible for inclusion if the following criteria were met: (a) age 14 to 35 years; (b) a genetic risk or CAARMS scores in the range of ARMS; (c) an impairment in social functioning, that is, a score on the SOFAS (Goldman *et al.*, 1992) of 50 or less and/or a decline of 30 per cent on the SOFAS for a month in the past year.

Patients were excluded if they met any of the following criteria: (a) current or previous use of antipsychotic medication with more than 15 mg cumulative haloperidol equivalent; (b) severe learning impairment; (c) problems due to organic condition; (d) insufficient competence in the Dutch language; (e) history of psychosis.

The self-rating of subclinical psychotic symptoms on the PQ was followed by an interview-based rating with the CAARMS – the gold standard for diagnosing psychosis and ARMS. If patients fulfilled every criterion, they were asked to participate in the study and informed consent was obtained. The patients were told that the treatment of the disorder they were seeking help for would continue regardless. In addition, they were informed that they showed a risk profile for developing future mental problems and could be offered a preventive intervention.

Interventions

Patients seeking help at the mental health services were treated with TAU for their axis 1 or axis 2 disorders. They were diagnosed by the routine psychiatric diagnostic services of the secondary mental health services. The diagnoses were anxiety disorders (53), depression (52), mixed anxiety and depression (10), personality disorders (15), ADHD (13), addiction problems (12), eating disorders (11), PTSD (10), oppositional defiant disorder (6), Asperger syndrome (5), relationship problems (DSM IV-code) (5), other problems (9). Most treatments offered were CBT, pharmacotherapy, and group and couples therapy. About half the patients were randomised to an additional preventive cognitive behavioural therapy (CBTuhr) targeting risky thinking styles and behaviour. The trial specifically aims to prevent or postpone the transition to psychosis during an 18-month period.

Both the experimental and control group were treated with evidence-based active treatment for the axis 1 or 2 disorder from which they were suffering. The experimental group was given an add-on treatment that focused on subclinical psychosis. The protocol by French and Morrison (as a generic CBT protocol) (French and Morrison, 2004) has much in common with the active treatments, as CBT is the treatment recommended for many axis 1 disorders. For this reason we enriched the protocol with education on dopamine supersensitivity, explaining how this affects perception (hyper-salience for trivial stimuli) and thinking (more intrusions, more causal reasoning over coincidences, stronger data-gathering bias, etc.). Furthermore, exercises were added to experience cognitive biases; becoming aware of cognitive biases may lead to corrected secondary appraisals.

The biases addressed (among others) are:

- data-gathering bias, mainly characterised by jumping to conclusions;
- selective attention to threatening stimuli;
- confirmatory bias, moderating delusion formation;
- negative expectation bias, leading to increased distress levels as well as underrating of one's capacities;
- covariance bias, in which the chance of a causal relationship between independent events is overrated.

CBTuhr had a maximum provision of 26 weekly sessions. The mean number of sessions was 9.5 (s.d. = 7.7) with a range of 0–25. Behavioural goals are to reduce cannabis use, consolidate school and work attendance, and foster interaction with friends and relatives (see Chapter 7 of this book for the treatment manual).

The primary outcome of this study was the transition to psychosis. The transition is defined by the CAARMS criteria (Yung *et al.*, 2005) and verified by the Schedules for Clinical Assessment in Neuropsychiatry (SCAN) (World Health Organization, 1999).

The secondary outcomes were depression (Beck Depression Inventory; BDI-2) (Beck, Steer and Brown, 1996), anxiety (Social Interaction Anxiety Scale; SIAS) (Mattick and Clarke, 1998), quality of life (Manchester Short Assessment of Quality of Life; MANSA) (Priebe, Huxley, Knight and Evans, 1999); social functioning (SOFAS) (Goldman *et al.*, 1992); and personal beliefs about illness (PBIQ-R) (Birchwood, Mason, MacMillan and Healy, 1993).

Results

A total of 5,705 patients were screened with the PQ (Loewy et al., 2005). Of these, 864 patients with a score of 18 or over on subclinical positive symptoms were interviewed with the CAARMS. The CAARMS interview revealed 104 patients to be psychotic, even though their condition was not recognised during intake at the mental health institutions, or by the general practitioners at referral. A total of 302 patients fulfilled the criteria of being at risk. Of these patients, 201 patients were included in the study; 98 were randomised to the CBTuhr + TAU condition and 103 were randomised to the TAU alone condition.

In the survival analyses, the people lost to follow-up were conservatively considered as non-transitions. The Kaplan–Meyer curves showed a significant difference between the CBTuhr and control patients (logrank test χ^2 (1) = 5.575, $p = 0.032$) (Figure 6.1). In the CBTuhr condition ten patients (10.5 per cent) and in the TAU condition 22 patients (21.8 per cent) made the transition to psychosis. Overall, 16.3 per cent of the patients developed a psychotic episode.

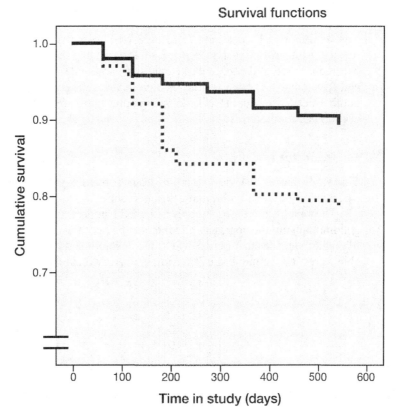

Figure 6.1 Survival curves in the EDIE-NL study. Survival of patients in the experimental condition (CBTuhr) and control condition (TAU) during 18-months' follow-up (solid line = CBTuhr group; dotted line = TAU group). Logrank test χ^2 (1) = 5.575, $p = 0.03$.

The patients who developed a psychotic episode were diagnosed using SCAN. The diagnoses for the psychotic group were: schizophrenia paranoid type (19), schizophrenia, disorganised type (2), psychotic disorder not otherwise classified (3), brief psychotic disorder (1), schizo-affective disorder (1), depression with psychotic features (4) and bipolar disorder (2).

All patients who transitioned fulfilled the PANSS criteria for psychosis (14 had one positive symptom score of intensity 4; 12 had an intensity score of 5; five had an intensity score of 6; one person had missing data). The scores on the PSYRATS revealed that 14 patients suffered from delusions, five from hallucinations, and 12 from both delusions and hallucinations.

Remission status at 18-months' follow-up

Patients in both conditions tended to show marked improvement. At the end of treatment at six months, 35 per cent were in remission; at the 12-month follow-up, 48 per cent were remitted; and at the 18-month follow-up, 63 per cent were remitted.

The CBTuhr group had a higher remission rate (70.4 per cent remission; 17.3 per cent ARMS; 12.3 per cent psychosis) than the TAU group (57.0 per cent remission; 19.4 per cent ARMS; 23.7 per cent psychosis). The chi-square linear-by-linear analysis was done to test whether the CBTuhr group was overrepresented at the good end (remission) and underrepresented at the worse end (psychosis). The association is significant: $\chi^2(1) = 4.266$, $p = 0.039$. The number needed to treat (NNT) for preventing transition is 8.8 and the NNT to accomplish remission is 7.5.

Evidence for the protocol

This study shows that the number of transitions to psychosis could be reduced by about 50 per cent with a targeted intervention.

The conclusion of this study is that a CBT intervention specifically targeting and normalising the appraisal of subclinical symptoms, and teaching awareness of cognitive biases that play a role in the development of delusional ideation, is able to reduce the number of transitions in ARMS subjects.

PART II

Practice of CBT for ultra-high risk

7

A manual for coping with extraordinary and remarkable experiences

This is a treatment protocol to use with patients with an ARMS for developing a first episode of psychosis. ARMS can be diagnosed with the use of the CAARMS (Yung and McGorry, 1996; Yung et al., 2005) or the SIPS (Miller et al., 2002).

Rationale of the treatment

The main goal of this treatment is to reduce the current distress caused by the extraordinary and remarkable experiences because they burden people with ARMS. This also reduces the chance that the person will develop a psychiatric disorder such as psychosis.

The treatment protocol has three components. First, extensive psychoeducation is given. People with ARMS are nearly always worried about their extraordinary experiences. Disease awareness is high and patients fear that they are losing control over their minds. Receiving an explanatory model of extraordinary experiences and learning that there is an adequate treatment for their fears is a hopeful and comforting message for most ARMS subjects. In many patients, this reduces distress and the preoccupation with extraordinary experiences.

Second, a metacognitive training aims to increase the insight of the patient into the effect of cognitive biases on experience, perception and reasoning. The protocol enhances monitoring by the patient of the effects of cognitive biases and helps to correct their negative impact on thoughts and behaviour.

Third, cognitive behavioural interventions are used. Cognitive interventions focus on testing and challenging dysfunctional thoughts of the patient. Behavioural interventions are focused on letting go of avoidance or safety behaviours and exposure to stimuli that are perceived as dangerous.

In most patients, the distress caused by the extraordinary experiences often decreases quickly. The experience is that patients become less anxious and depressed during therapy and start to pay less attention to the extraordinary experiences. In many patients the extraordinary experiences eventually disappear into the background. In some patients they do not. However, this is not a necessity for a successful therapy. The main goal of this treatment is to reduce dysfunctional emotional and behavioural consequences and, in doing so, reduce the chance that the patient will develop a severe psychiatric disorder in the future.

THE MANUAL: 'COPING WITH EXTRAORDINARY AND REMARKABLE EXPERIENCES'

Nine stages:

1. Introduction
2. Pre-assessment
3. Psycho-education and normalising
4. CBT assessment and metacognitive training
5. Case formulation and goal setting
6. Cognitive behavioural intervention
7. Post-assessment
8. Consolidation
9. Booster sessions

In *stage 1* the treatment is introduced. The therapist checks whether the patient is motivated for treatment and whether he can and is willing to meet the terms of the treatment. *Stage 2* is the pre-assessment with several instruments. These two stages take one session to complete. During *stage 3* normalising psycho-education is given and discussed. In *stage 4* the ABC (activating event, beliefs and consequenses) model is used to help patients to find the activating event, beliefs and consequences in experiences, and to learn how activating events can induce their beliefs and what consequences their beliefs have. The ABCs are also used to explore which activating events, beliefs and consequences cause emotional and behaviour problems. During this stage the patient also receives a metacognitive training focused on becoming aware of certain cognitive biases and learning to manage them. This stage includes about six sessions. In *stage 5* the therapist and patient jointly develop a case formulation based on the information obtained in the previous stage. They also formulate clear treatment goals. The case formulation and formulated goals steer the cognitive behavioural interventions in *stage 6*. The intervention stage covers between 6 and 12 sessions. In *stage 7* the post-assessment is performed. *Stage 8* involves making explicit what has been learned and how to retain this for future situations. Finally, in *stage 9* booster sessions are performed if necessary.

(1) Introduction and (2) Pre-assessment (one session)

Preparation

Inform yourself about the patient. We assume that an ARMS was established using the CAARMS or SIPS. The CAARMS (or SIPS) interview is the most important diagnostic and outcome measurement. Read the information in the patient file and examine the CAARMS (or SIPS) scores.

Print a copy of the workbook 'A manual for coping with extraordinary and remarkable experiences' for the patient. Also hand out a notebook or folder in which the patient can keep their therapy forms. Lastly, gather several session forms (Appendix A), the DACOBS, BDI2 (Beck *et al.*, 1996). Anxiety is assessed with the Beck Anxiety Inventory (BAI) (Beck and Steer, 1993). The workbook, session forms and DACOBS can be obtained from www.routledge.com/9780415539685. The BAI, and BDI2 are present in most mental health-care institutions.

Session forms

Introduce yourself and become acquainted with the patient. Explain that an agenda will be made every session and that all sessions will be evaluated. It is also important to stress that the therapist and patient will work together to find out what problems need attention and how problems can be addressed. Therapy means an active role of the patient. The therapy can partly be regarded as a course, and courses require homework and training. An advantage of following a course is learning new skills and being able to use these skills in the future to overcome problems without the help of a therapist. Hand over the first part of the manual in a folder in which the patient can also keep their therapy forms. Fill in session Form 1 ('start') and set the agenda. Note the reviewing of the outcome of the CAARMS or SIPS, discussing the rationale and content of the treatment, and the pre-assessment on the agenda. The session forms are filled in twice, both by the patient and the therapist. Let the patient store the forms in the homework folder. Every session ends with filling in session Form 2 ('end').

Psycho-education and normalising

Start with discussing the outcome on the CAARMS or SIPS. Clarify what extraordinary experiences need to be targeted in the treatment.

> *Therapist:* The first point on the agenda is discussing the experiences and symptoms that made you seek help. You were interviewed recently and that showed that you are distressed by several extraordinary experiences. Shall we look into these experiences?
> *Patient:* All right.
> *Therapist:* I see that five months ago you started to think that your colleagues are plotting against you to get you to quit your job. I can see that you indicate that you're 50 per cent convinced of these thoughts and that they cause considerable distress.
> *Patient:* Yes. That's still the case. I'm the only part-timer and quite a bit younger than the others. Sometimes I feel they're talking about me behind my back and are secretly discussing how they can get rid of me. Last week it flared up when I saw that I was the only one that wasn't mentioned on the holiday schedule.

Therapist: Okay, that's unpleasant. I see that this situation is disrupting your functioning ...

Patient: That's correct. I'm constantly on guard, trying to catch my colleagues talking about me. Moreover, I pressure myself to perfect my work, so that they can't use bad functioning as an excuse to fire me.

Therapist: So you are still going to work?

Patient: I am, but some days I cannot get myself to go there and then I call in sick.

Therapist: Good. I also see that you've regularly been hearing your own thoughts out loud for the past three months. This distresses you quite a bit, but it doesn't disturb your functioning that much.

Patient: Yes, that's correct. It's not like I can't continue with what I was doing. I think I'm starting to get used to it. But I do worry about it quite a bit. I googled 'thought hearing' and ended up at a forum for people with psychoses. Since that moment I've feared that I'm losing it.

Therapist: I can imagine. Especially when you experience such extraordinary things and read such things on the Internet. I don't think that you're 'losing it'. I do believe that it was a good step for you to seek help. I'll explain more about that later.

Patient: Okay.

Therapist: I also see that you sometimes hear someone calling your name, while you are alone. This doesn't really disrupt your functioning, but it does cause some distress.

Patient: Yes. It's actually quite similar to the experience of hearing my own thoughts out loud. It does startle me, though, when I suddenly hear my name. Usually I feel tense for an hour or so after it happens.

Therapist: That's clear. Do you have any other extraordinary or remarkable experiences that we haven't talked about?

Patient: No, this is it, I guess.

Therapist: All right. In summary, we see that lately you've been worrying about your colleagues. You sometimes feel that they're conspiring against you. In addition, you've been hearing your own thoughts out loud for the last few months. And you've also heard your name called several times, which startled you. You indicated that these experiences have made you wonder whether you are losing control over your mind. Is this an adequate summary? Am I forgetting any other extraordinary experiences?

Patient: No, I don't think so.

Next, give information about the aim and the rationale of the treatment. This is also extensively described in the manual, which the patient is going to read as homework.

> **TIP:** Be conscious of the fact that disease awareness is high in most ARMS subjects. Losing disease awareness is the last step in developing a frank psychosis. Almost every ARMS patient fears loss of control over his psyche. Emphasise that the patient is not crazy and generate hope for recovery.

> **TIP:** Do not spend too much time on psycho-education in this session. This will follow in the next stage of the protocol. Do ensure that you convey the most important messages.

- You are not crazy at this moment.
- Extraordinary experiences are normal experiences in most cases.
- You are burdened by the extraordinary experiences because you worry about them a lot and therefore react quite strongly to them.
- The aim of this treatment is to reduce the distress that the extraordinary experiences cause in the present and by doing so decrease the chance that these experiences will start dominating your life in the future, leading to more severe problems.

EXAMPLE

'You're burdened by extraordinary experiences and are afraid that you're losing control over your mind. I can assure you, you're not crazy at this very moment. You are distressed by what we call extraordinary and remarkable experiences. These are quite normal phenomena that are highly prevalent in the general population. One in every ten people has a period in their lives in which they hear sounds or voices while there is no one near them. About one in every ten people feels that others consciously and continuously hinder them. The vast majority of these people do not suffer from any mental disorder. The content of their experiences or thoughts are not that negative or frightening. Therefore, they don't pay a lot of attention to these experiences or thoughts. This often has the effect that these experiences slowly disappear.

The meaning one gives to events has a crucial role in this process. Imagine that you hear a sound in your house at night after you've just gone to bed. If you interpret this as an intruder with bad intentions, you will probably be very scared and might even call the police or hide yourself. When you attribute the sound to your cat or maybe your neighbours, you will probably feel relaxed, turn over and fall asleep. Psychologists have known for some time that it is not the facts in life, but rather the meanings we give them, that determine how much they burden us. That's a good thing, because your thoughts about the extraordinary experiences can be examined, tested and possibly changed!

This treatment has been scientifically researched and found to be effective. It will probably reduce the distress that the extraordinary experiences are causing at the moment. As a consequence you will also start to pay less attention to the extraordinary experiences. By doing this we decrease the chance that the extraordinary experiences will start to dominate your life in the future.'

> **TIP:** If you find it useful, you can use the acronym EXTREME (EXTraordinary and REMarkable Experiences).

Basic information

Discuss what the practice of CBT is all about. Tell the patient that they should actively participate in the therapy process. The real changes in life and health are predominantly achieved in between the sessions by registering, practising and experimenting. The whole treatment will probably take between 10 and 16 weekly sessions. Ensure that this is acceptable for the patient and that the patient commits to the therapy.

Administering measurements

Introduce the questionnaires. The DACOBS has seven subscales and measures four cognitive biases: jumping to conclusions, dogmatism, selective attention for threat, and self-as-target bias. It measures two cognitive limitations: theory of mind problems, and cognitive limitations in attention and memory. Lastly, it also measures avoidance behaviour. The psychometrics, reliability and validity are good (van der Gaag *et al.*, 2013). The severity of depression symptoms is assessed with the BDI 2 (Beck *et al.*, 1996). Anxiety is assessed with the BAI (Beck and Steer, 1993).

Homework

Give the patient the following homework for the next session:

- Read the following sections from the manual.
- Normal and abnormal extraordinary experiences.
- The method of this module.
- Dopamine as misleader.
- How can you enter the danger zone after an extraordinary experience?
- Fill in the DACOBS, BAI and BDI2 at home and bring them to the next session.

> **TIP:** Disease awareness is very high in most people with a UHR. Most patients are also very motivated for therapy and for consuming information. It has sometimes happened that a patient reads the entire manual before the second session; this can be undesirable. Therefore, we recommend that you give the patient only those parts that they need in order to do the homework that week. In this way they gradually acquire the entire manual. The complete manual can be found online (www.routledge.com/9780415539685).

Extraordinary and remarkable experiences should not interfere with your mood and daily functioning. This manual will help you to keep your extraordinary experiences manageable in daily life, although your extraordinary experiences may be annoying and intruding at times. You can work through this manual with your therapist. Together you can look into your personal problems and explore how they are connected to extraordinary experiences. Solutions will be sought for your problems. The described method consists of a combination of cognitive behavioural therapy and an educational course.

Introduction of this module

Normal and abnormal extraordinary experiences

You have sought help because of anxiety, depression, difficulties with focusing and attention, or other problems. In addition, you have indicated to occasionally suffer from strange or extraordinary experiences. You and your therapist will go through this manual together, which deals with these strange and extraordinary experiences.

Strange and extraordinary experiences are frequent in the general population and are usually harmless. Some examples of strange and extraordinary experiences are given in Table 7.1. Almost everybody experiences moments in which a surrounding feels different from before, that the familiarity seems lost. Something seems changed – but what?

About half of the general population believes in telepathy, and many people have had the experience that, when you think about someone, the phone rings and it is that very person calling you at that specific moment. Or that you think about a name, say John, and at the same moment this name is pronounced on the radio. Sometimes these experiences occur a few times in the week and it seems as though this can no longer be a mere coincidence.

Everybody is suspicious from time to time and that is not necessarily a bad thing. People that are too trusting are prone to be the victim of abuse. Healthy suspiciousness keeps us from harm. In groups, usually one subject is the 'black sheep', and bullying and harassment are very common at school and at work.

More than one in ten people feels constantly hindered, and about one in 30 feels threatened by others.

Hearing, seeing, feeling or smelling things that others do not, and without a clear source in the external world, is called an extraordinary experience, a hallucination and (sometimes) a vision. About one in six people experiences a period in their lives in which voices or sounds are heard, but without anyone nearby. In the past two weeks, about 2 per cent of the Dutch population heard voices or sounds without a clear source. This is roughly equivalent to over 320,000 people; so it is a relatively common experience.

In some periods of development (such as puberty, adolescence and young adulthood), it is difficult to get used to new social roles and to changing expectations of the environment. Many people experience feelings of depression, indifference and want to be left alone. Some think about death as a solution for their problems.

All of the above-mentioned experiences are normal experiences that are familiar to many people and often disappear naturally. However, a small group of people becomes increasingly troubled by these extraordinary experiences, and these experiences may start to interfere with their everyday life. Some people become so suspicious that they hide away all day; they watch everything and hardly ever go out. Other people start to hear voices frequently and they assume that the voices belong to powerful people or other creatures, and they feel intimidated and start to submissively obey the voices. A third group gradually withdraws from daily life. Contact with other people costs them too much energy and results in negative feelings. They become 'hermits' who are occupied with the Internet or their hobby all day long. Others feel that they receive messages or that they are controlled, and spend a lot of time thinking about their experiences.

The treatment and the course that lie before you are intended to prevent those strange and extraordinary experiences from becoming a burden, and from starting to interfere with your daily life. So, how will you deal with this together with your therapist?

The method of this module

First, we can discuss your extraordinary and remarkable experiences. Many people think something supernatural is causing them, but that is not the case. We have solid scientific explanations for many of the strange mental and/or physical experiences. Take lightning, for example. Once we understood about electricity, the idea of the god Wodan travelling in his carriage and throwing lightning to the earth from the sky was abandoned.

In addition, we know that the progression of normal remarkable experiences to a severe and disturbing matter is related, among other things, to how we initially interpreted the extraordinary strange experience.

Someone who notices that his thoughts sometimes stop altogether can interpret this in several ways; for example:

1 My thinking is bumpy lately. Perhaps I'm too tired and need to take a rest for a while.

Table 7.1 Some examples of frequently occurring extraordinary and remarkable experiences

Alienating experiences

- The surroundings seem strange, new and not familiar
- Time seems to pass quicker, and then slower
- You lose contact with yourself and it seems as though you are not in everyday reality

Experiences of being influenced

- Feelings and thoughts do not seem to be under control of your own will; they seem to have been taken over or inserted
- Experiences that remind you of and evoke thoughts about telepathy
- Thoughts about messages that are meant specifically for you, sent by others sometimes via, e.g. the radio or television

Experiences of threat

- The frightening assumption that people are conspiring against you
- The experience that others are 'out to get you'

Sensory perceptions that only you have

- The experience of sounds, whispering, a voice in or outside your head, or hearing your own thoughts spoken out loud
- Strange visual perceptions and visions
- Unusual bodily perceptions without a clear external cause

Confusion and difficulties with concentrating

- Difficulty with regulating one's thoughts and choosing the right words.
- Others say they cannot understand you properly

Changed experiences in the contact with other people

- Experiencing little pleasure from the company of others
- Nervousness in the proximity of others
- People say that they think you do not express your feelings enough
- People say that you act strangely or that you have strange habits
- Everyday problems and stressors become heavier to bear
- Problems in the interactions with people at work or school

2 I've lost control over my thinking. This may signify that something or somebody has taken control and that person is interfering with me. It annoys me. How on earth can they do that to me and interfere with me that way?
3 Someone else has control over my thoughts. I cannot fight it. The other person is stronger than me. Soon he may force me to do things I don't want to do.

Different interpretations lead to different feelings. Which of the above interpretations leads to anger, which to fear and which to weaker emotions?

We will look at different interpretations of strange experiences and how to deal with them. We will distinguish several risky thinking styles (also known as cognitive biases) that can cause interpretations that can make you a victim of the extraordinary experiences. We will teach you how to recognise these risky thinking styles and how to handle them.

You will list the extraordinary experiences together with your therapist. Between the sessions you will be asked to read parts of this manual that describe extraordinary experiences, how a substance (a neurotransmitter) in your brain is often responsible for these strange and extraordinary experiences, how your very own thoughts about the source and meaning of your extraordinary experiences can make you frightened and can cause loneliness. In addition, you will become acquainted with risky thinking styles that can cause your problems. If you recognise these thinking styles and correct them, the chances increase that you will get better.

Besides these matters that have to do with your extraordinary and strange experiences, other items of your personal life can be dealt with. The better you have your personal life in order, the less the chance that the extraordinary experiences will gain hold of you. So, we will also focus on how your life is going and how your life experiences are associated with the strange experiences you sometimes have. By improving your understanding of the experiences, they will acquire a new meaning for you and this will allow you to cope with them better.

Finally, we will focus on the most important subject, that is, how you can keep your life on course in this period of your life. The aim is to achieve goals that are important for you. Therefore, this part of the treatment is very 'down to earth' and deals with tangible activities and actions to get ahead in life. This manual has several course elements. In addition, this manual includes individual cognitive behavioural elements to offer you tailored help in dealing with strange experiences and problems that you encounter in your life.

During the sessions we will work with an agenda. Both you and your therapist can add points to the agenda that need to be discussed. Your therapist will give you a manual about dealing effectively with extraordinary and strange experiences (this manual), and a register book. At the start of every session you will fill in a Session Form and you will compile the agenda together. At the end of every session you will again fill in a Session Form, and we will try to agree on possible homework items. Please bring this manual and register book with you to every therapy session. The register book contains other forms that we will use during the sessions, or sometimes as homework.

The sessions last 45 minutes, are held once a week, and we will have 10 to 20 sessions in the coming six months.

Together with your therapist you will learn how to examine your own thinking styles. Because some thinking styles carry the risk that normal extraordinary experiences can escalate into a nasty/scary conviction, you will learn how to prevent risky thinking styles deceiving you. Furthermore, it is important that you learn how you can better deal with everyday problems, and how you can avoid withdrawing from everyday life. Friends, school or work, social contacts and good family relationships are very important for your well-being.

After we have made a list of your extraordinary experiences, we will formulate them in a clear manner so you can understand how your negative feelings and problem behaviours are associated with your extraordinary experiences, and what you have encountered so far. Subsequently, we expect a period of change to start in which you will hopefully feel better and better, and can again become the family member, friend, classmate, colleague, sports team member, etc., that you want to be.

Finally, we will look at how your ideas about yourself, others and the world around you influence your thoughts, the outcome of your treatment and this course. You will make an inventory, together with your therapist, as to how these matters are associated with each other, and what your personal problem list is concerning fears, depression, activity level and other disturbing problems. Because this part is individually tailored, it is less suitable for the type of course such as the one you are familiar with through this manual. Perhaps you have already started to formulate your problems and to analyse them. In addition to the problem list, you will also make a goal list, containing goals that you want to achieve in the coming period. These matters will also be dealt with in your individual sessions.

Dopamine as misleader

Prolonged stress can lead to an imbalance of substances in your brain. In case of depression the imbalance involves serotonin. The production of this neurotransmitter is too low in the brain of depressed people.

If the level of dopamine (a substance similar to serotonin) in the brain is disrupted, this can lead to strange experiences, such as hearing voices and experiencing the feeling that something important is about to happen, or thinking strange thoughts that seem to belong to someone else. Furthermore, details in your surrounding can become the focus of attention and give you the feeling that they contain a meaning or message that is of vital importance to you. The accompanying feelings of great excitement, or fear, can make you afraid that something terrible is about to happen. Because dopamine also regulates daily motivation, imbalance of this neurotransmitter can also lead to a specific passion. On the other hand, when levels are reduced, this can lead to a loss of interest in hobbies, sexuality, sports and friends.

Dopamine is usually released in the brain if a new phenomenon comes into our field of perception. For example, if the door opens behind you and a motorcycle cop with flashing light and siren appears, the nerve endings of your brain (the synapses) will release dopamine in the synaptic cleft between the previous and next nerve fibre.

At the level of experience, you will go (more or less) through the following steps:

- You stop what you are doing.
- You fixate your eyes and attention on the motorcycle cop.
- You try to apprehend what is happening.
- You prepare to flee (if you have a bad conscience) or you approach (if the policeman is your best friend).

After you have apprehended the situation, dopamine drops to normal levels and you usually go back to what you were doing. Scientists assume that, in people experiencing strange and extraordinary experiences, dopamine is sometimes released without a proper cause. Because people are used to the release of dopamine in new and important events, they will react in a similar way to these random moments. If you are, for example, watching the news and the brain suddenly releases dopamine, you will get the feeling that what the newsreader is saying is very important for you personally; it may appear as if the newsreader is speaking to you directly and that the message is of vital importance. Because the feeling is so strong and real, most people will not doubt this feeling. You may associate the news message about forgery in the elections with yourself, and may think the newsreader is warning you that some people want to deceive you.

The release of dopamine at the wrong moment can mislead you in a nasty way. Unexpected things happen and you have the strong conviction that something or someone has taken control of your thoughts and feelings. We can reassure you: ghosts do not exist, the dead rest, and, despite an intensive search, extra-terrestrial life has never been found. The most likely explanation of your strange experiences is the release of dopamine at the wrong moment in your brain.

How can dopamine disrupt?

A specific small group in the population probably has an inherited vulnerability in the dopamine system. In this group, prolonged daily stressors do not induce habituation; on the contrary, they induce sensitisation. This means that the brain leaves more receptors for dopamine in a 'high state' and therefore becomes more receptive and sensitive to dopamine. If dopamine high state increases, a stronger reaction is expected to the release of dopamine than in people with fewer 'high state' dopamine receptors. The noticeable consequence is that daily problems have more influence and become a bigger burden.

Dopamine is also responsible for general motivation. This means that without dopamine, you may have no achievements in school or elsewhere. Dopamine also plays an important motivating role in emotional or exciting events. It is important to know in certain situations whether you have to 'flee or fight'. Therefore, a situation is judged as a personal threat, until proven otherwise.

Most people with extraordinary experiences just experience them only from time to time, and the experiences sometimes disappear, or remain present unobtrusively. They do not determine the person's life. However, a small group of people develop a severe case of dopamine supersensitivity that we call 'psychosis'. These people start to suffer from their extraordinary experiences, suggesting that voices are trying to gain power over them. In others, healthy suspiciousness develops into pathological paranoia, which is validated (in their eyes) all day long by small events.

What can you do about it?

If dopamine is disrupted to such an extent that the midbrain is soaked in it, then that person is no longer in touch with reality. We then speak of psychosis. At this moment, antipsychotic medication can be of help. In general, psychotic symptoms such as confusion, delusions and hallucinations disappear with this kind of medication. A disadvantage of this medication is that it does not heal, but it only suppresses the symptoms. For many people suffering from (recurrent) psychoses, long-term use of this medication is necessary and sometimes even lifelong. However, these medications are not suitable to be prescribed in case of extraordinary experiences. They cannot suppress them and they cannot prevent a possible future psychosis.

There is substantial scientific evidence indicating that the interpretation you give of your extraordinary experiences is of great importance. It determines whether you can live with it, or start to suffer from it. Besides the extraordinary experiences, if you also experience other complaints (such as anxiety or depression) and your working or school life and social life with friends and family crumbles, you can enter into a danger zone.

How can you enter the danger zone after an extraordinary experience?

An extraordinary experience becomes dangerous if you are occupied too much by it and if it prevents you from staying in contact with other people in everyday life. We will go through several examples with you.

John, like many others, sometimes feels he is mentally in contact with other people. His parents are getting old and, when visiting them last weekend, he noticed how terrible they were looking. On Wednesday he constantly thought about his mother; when he called her that evening he found out that she had a high fever that day and was feeling very ill. John thought he had sensed that through thought transfer. On television he sees a programme in which someone claims there is 'more between heaven and earth', and again he thinks about the number of times he has sensed things in advance. John realises it might be possible that he can read minds, but he does not understand how the transfer of thoughts takes place. Thoughts are not the same as radio waves. There are many people with the same experience as John. They do not understand it either, but they just go on living.

How can John now enter the danger zone? This will happen if John becomes truly convinced of having a remarkable psychic gift, that is, being able to communicate with others through feelings, and that he is sometimes able to predict the future. If John speaks to his parents about it, they are unlikely to believe him. They will think he is strange and hope that it will pass. If John decides not to talk to other people about it, withdraws into books about paranormal perception and seeks contact with movements with similar convictions, there is a considerable chance that he will lose contact with friends, relatives and even possibly colleagues. People, who are not embedded in a group of people, sometimes eventually lose contact with the reality of those people.

Another example: Mary occasionally hears her name being called, despite nobody being there. Sometimes she experiences that her thoughts are repeated by a voice. Sometimes a voice in her head tells her what to do, for example, 'Go get the groceries' or 'Don't trust that neighbour'. At any given moment about one in 50 people experiences hearing a voice while nobody is speaking. The best course of action is not to take the voice too seriously, and just keep on doing whatever you were doing. Sometimes the brain plays tricks with strange experiences, especially before going to sleep.

Mary could enter the danger zone if she interprets the voice as coming from someone powerful, such as the secret service, a conspiracy of Satanists, the devil himself, etc. If the voice is interpreted like this and Mary feels threatened, or humiliated by her obedience and thinks there is no escape from the voice, she will probably become anxious and depressed and sleep poorly. She will probably try to soothe the voice by being obedient and try to keep it a secret because the voice demands that from her, then she will go outside less, report ill from work, etc. The interpretation of the voice as being powerful and evil, and the related obedience, isolates Mary; she starts leading a life others have no knowledge of.

Robert was bullied a lot at school. He found out that other people could turn against you in an instant and try to make your life miserable. He learns it is better to distrust people because, before you know it, they do not return your pen, or mock you, etc. Now he is an adult, but he is cautious at work too. Others can get along with each other much better and he often sees others laughing. He usually thinks they are talking and laughing about him for being a fool.

Robert can enter the danger zone by avoiding certain situations and places, and being alert all day to the possibility of dangerous people. For example, if today you decide to pay attention to dogs, by the end of the day you will have seen more dogs than during the entire previous week. The same applies to paying special attention to suspicious-looking people. Whoever does that all day long will have become a frightened person by the end of that day. If Robert starts avoiding places that have a lot of people (e.g. the station, or supermarket), he will quickly become isolated. Also, people around Robert will certainly not agree with him that many people are out to get him, so he will become even more isolated.

From these examples, it can be seen that extraordinary experiences are common and remain innocent if you can put them into perspective and not pay too much attention to them. However, if you overestimate the importance of these experiences, if you find them threatening and unavoidable, they become too important and start controlling your life. It is not the experiences themselves, but the interpretation of them that leads to fear, avoidance and isolation. Therefore, it is essential to think of other possible explanations for the extraordinary events. You need to stay in touch with people. Generally, acting according to your own interpretation of the extraordinary experiences is not very wise. It is much better to discuss the extraordinary experiences, and their meaning, with other people and not to act or react too quickly.

(3) Psycho-education and normalising (one session)

You already gave the patient some psycho-education and normalising information in the previous session. The patient has also read quite a lot of information. The goal of this stage in the protocol is to consolidate this information by answering any questions that the patient has, and by providing additional psycho-education where necessary. Each subject is discussed in turn.

> **TIP:** Spend enough time on this stage in the treatment protocol. Most patients are quite open to alternative explanations of their extraordinary experiences. Often, they simply have not thought of these possible alternatives. In some patients we observe a decrease in distress after receiving only this information.

Use the session forms 'start' and 'end' every session. Let the patient store the forms in the homework folder and bring them to each session.

Measurements

Hopefully, the patient will hand you the filled in DACOBS, BAI and BDI2. Explain that you will score them and discuss the results in the next session. Check whether the questionnaires are complete and whether the patient has any questions about the tests at this moment. If the patient has not filled in the questionnaires, they can do so in or after the session.

The method of this module

Discuss whether the patient understood the information from the manual about the rationale of the treatment/course. Ask them whether they have any questions about it.

> **TIP:** Let your patient summarise what they have read. Emphasise that you ask this because you find it important to ensure that the patient has understood the rationale of the treatment.

Extraordinary is normal

Repeat the psycho-education and normalising information about extraordinary experiences. Specify the information about the type of extraordinary experiences that the patient is predominantly distressed by. For example, if your patient is mainly burdened by a negative voice that he hears at low frequency, normalise perceptual abnormalities and emphasise the high prevalence of these phenomena in the general population. If he is distressed by cognitive problems, or is in doubt about whether something or someone is controlling his thoughts, then explain to the patient that intrusions and cognitive problems are quite normal phenomena with a high prevalence in the population.

> **TIP:** If the patient is ashamed of their extraordinary experiences, ask them to interview five confidants/close friends about remarkable experiences in their life, such as déjà vu, hearing things, exceptional coincidences, etc. This can have a very normalising effect, since most people experience remarkable events now and again.

Dopamine

Some patients may find the information on dopamine in the manual difficult to understand. Check whether the patient understood the information and offer to give some extra information on dopamine, 'the highlighter marker of the brain'.

EXAMPLE

> *'Prolonged stress can have the effect that the balance of substances in our brain is disturbed. In depression, serotonin is deregulated. Serotonin is a neurotransmitter, a chemical substance that conveys messages from one brain cell to the next. Depressed individuals appear to have too little of this substance in their brain.*
>
> *When the neurotransmitter dopamine is deregulated, one can experience strange things such as perceiving strange noises, getting the idea that something very important is about to happen, strange intrusive thoughts, or thoughts that appear to be alien. Also, a detail from your surroundings can suddenly grab your attention and give you the feeling that it has a special meaning to you, or that it encompasses an important message for you. The accompanying feeling of excitement and anxiety makes people fear that something terrible is about to happen. Deregulation of dopamine can also lead to an extreme drive, because it has an important function in our daily motivational systems. In the long term, this may lead to a chronic loss of interest in things that used to be important to you, such as social contacts, hobbies, sexuality and sports.*
>
> *Dopamine is usually released in the brain when a new and important phenomenon enters our perceptual field. If, for instance, you suddenly hear a very loud bang near you in the streets, your nerve endings (synapses) will release dopamine in the space (synaptic cleft) between your nerve cells. This will cause you to experience the next steps:*
>
> - *You stop what you're doing.*
> - *You fix your ears and attention on the direction from where the sounds came.*
> - *You try to comprehend what is going on.*
> - *You prepare to flee (if you conclude there is danger) or approach (if you conclude that it is safe or someone needs help).'*

Check whether your patient understands this. If they do, continue:

> *'Once you've analysed the situation and understand that there is no danger, dopamine levels will drop to normal levels. Scientists assume that in some people dopamine is sometimes released randomly. People will then react strongly, because they've learned that dopamine release means there's an important new stimulus. When dopamine is suddenly released when someone is watching the news, this person might get the feeling that what the newsreader is saying is of personal importance to him; that the presenter is actually conveying a personal message. The person will not be inclined to doubt himself, because the feeling is so real and intense.*
>
> *Random dopamine release can mislead you. Unexpected things happen and you might get the impression that something is influencing your thoughts or emotions, that strange things are happening, or that people are talking about you. Do you recognise any of these things?'*

The patient may have questions; try to answer these as fully as possible. Also give a full answer to the question of how the dopamine system can become supersensitive.

EXAMPLE

> *'A small proportion of the population probably has a genetic vulnerability in the dopamine system. Enduring daily stress doesn't lead to habituation, but to an increased sensitivity of the dopamine system. This is called 'dopamine sensitisation' or 'dopamine supersensitivity'. This means that the dopamine receptors are more easily triggered by dopamine. As a result the brain becomes supersensitive to dopamine.*
>
> *Most people that experience extraordinary phenomena have these experiences from time to time. In some people these experiences disappear, in others they linger at a fairly low level. They don't interfere with normal functioning. The extraordinary experiences worsen in a small proportion of the people. If this happens and nothing is done, a severe form of dopamine supersensitivity might develop, which we call psychosis. These people begin to suffer from perceptual abnormalities or healthy suspicion develops into paranoia.*
>
> *Cannabis influences the dopamine system and increases the chance of dopamine sensitisation. This can also happen with other drugs such as cocaine or amphetamines in XTC or speed.*
>
> *Experiencing trauma, such as childhood sexual or physical abuse, also increases the chance of dopamine deregulation. The same goes for being bullied or experiencing discrimination.*
>
> *Do you recognise any of these causes in your own situation?'*

> **TIP:** Monitor how your patient reacts to the psycho-education. Some patients will be startled by the word 'psychosis'. Most patients, however, have already linked their experiences to psychosis. Emphasise that only a minority of the people with an ARMS actually develop psychosis and that this treatment reduces this chance.

Additional idiosyncratic psycho-education

Previously, you gave the patient normalising information on the prevalence of extraordinary experiences in the general population. Here you inform the patient about specific mechanisms involved in extraordinary experiences.

EXAMPLE

'You sometimes hear your name being called while you are alone in the room. This worries you. I've explained to you that we call such experiences hallucinations and that these are highly prevalent in the general population. I would like to tell you something more about this. Our brain is extremely complex. We know quite a lot about its functioning, but there are also things that we still don't know. Several theories on hallucinations have been developed. These theories all have in common that they assume that somehow internally generated information from the memory or unconsciousness is experienced as external information. In some people we see a strong bias to do so. The 'labelling system' of the brain sometimes malfunctions, labelling internal thoughts as having an 'alien' origin. We know that almost all humans are able to hallucinate under certain conditions. Especially when they're tired or have taken certain substances. However, hallucinations also occur when we are deprived of sensory input (e.g. when we put people in a box with very soft cushioning, covered eyes, earplugs and stable temperature) or are exposed to a lot of very unclear input (e.g. staring at a television screen with snow, or listening to a radio with white noise). During lack of input, the brain appears to create its own stimulation. People who have become deaf often report hearing voices, while their hearing is not working! Also climbers who spend time in isolation in the mountains and are also deprived of oxygen tend to hallucinate.

Brain scanning techniques have shown that voices originate inside the brain. We see increased activity levels in the speech production areas of the brain during verbal hallucinating. We also see increased tension in the vocal cords when people hear voices, similar to when we 'think aloud'.

In summary, almost everybody can hallucinate, especially under certain circumstances such as during a lack of, or an excess of stimuli.

In essence, these are innocent internally produced phenomena that are experienced as external. When people don't pay too much attention to them, they are often not very distressed by them.

Do you recognise any of this in your own situation? Or do you have any questions about this information?'

> **TIP:** Feel free to adopt an expert attitude. Patients with ARMS are usually very open to new information. It helps when you are well informed, so that you can present the normalising information in a convincing manner.

Influence of beliefs and the introduction of the ABC model

Tell your patient about the importance of how extraordinary experiences are interpreted. The interpretation drives the emotional and behavioural reaction. Emphasise how safety and avoidance strategies perpetuate fear, because they take away the chance of learning that feared outcomes do not actually occur. A useful metaphor is that of a dog phobia.

EXAMPLE

'Psychologists have known for some time that it is not so much the facts in life, but the meaning we give to these facts, that determine how people react to them. When a barking dog approaches you on the streets and you think: 'He's aggressive and is going to bite me', you will probably be scared and run away. However, if you would think something completely different, such as: 'How nice, that dog is excited and wants to play with me', you will feel positive emotions and approach the animal. In both incidences the event is exactly the same. This illustrates the influence of the meaning we give to such experiences.

People who tend to give frightening meanings to situations will generally start avoiding them. As a result, fear will increase. Someone who, in fear of his life, runs away from a barking dog will probably conclude that he survived because he fled. However, actual incidences of dog bites are rare. By running away, this person deprives himself of the chance to learn that his feared outcome would not have occurred, because the dog just wanted to play. In this way avoidance perpetuates fear. Therefore, an important step in this treatment is that I'm going to motivate you to expose yourself to the extraordinary experiences that frighten you, so that you will learn that the events you fear don't actually occur. Do you have any questions about this?'

> **TIP:** Some patients will point out the importance of earlier experiences. Use this opportunity by emphasising that this is indeed highly important. Someone who was bitten as a child will be more inclined to interpret an approaching dog as dangerous than someone who was reared in a family with two nice dogs. Emphasise that life experiences will therefore be included in the case formulation.

Registration of extraordinary experiences

Give the patient an ABC form and introduce the ABC model. Explain what the function of this model is.

EXAMPLE

> 'The ABC model is a useful tool to analyse situations, the meaning we give to them and the reaction that this elicits. The model consists of several elements, the activating event, beliefs and consequences. The consequences are subdivided into emotional and behavioural reactions. The activating event is the fact as can be seen or heard without any interpretation, as you can record with a camera or microphone. This is usually the extraordinary experience (e.g. I'm lying in bed and hear a creaking noise on the stairs). The beliefs are the automatic negative thoughts that you may have (e.g. 'It is an intruder, he might hurt me'). In the emotion box you tick your emotional consequences and rate the intensity from 0 to 100 (e.g. Afraid 90). You can see that you can choose between five categories of emotional reactions, Afraid, Angry, Sad, Happy or Ashamed. Many times more than one emotion can be present at the same time. Behaviour is what you do in reaction to your interpretation of the activating event (e.g. Crawling under my bed and calling the police).
>
> When you make a correct ABC, you will see that the different elements are congruent. We make ABCs for two reasons. First, it will help us assess how much you are burdened by the extraordinary experiences. Second, it will help us understand what interpretations of the extraordinary experiences are responsible for the distress you are experiencing. Is this clear? Do you have any questions?'

> **TIP:** Ensure that the patient clearly understands the rationale and function of the ABC model. Ask him to repeat the rationale. It is of vital importance that the patient grasps the importance of the interpretations of his complaints.

Jointly make a registration of a recent extraordinary experience.

Therapist: Let's make an ABC about an extraordinary experience that you had last week. What situation would you like to start with? What was the activating event?

Patient: About what happened last Thursday. I entered the kitchen and suddenly my plate was no longer on the counter, but on the kitchen table. I totally panicked.

Therapist: Okay, so your plate was no longer where you remembered that you left it. Would you designate that as an activating event, a belief or a consequence?

Patient: That is the activating event, I guess.

Therapist: Very good. We put that down there. And panic? Is that a thought, an emotion or a behaviour?

Patient: I would say behaviour.

Therapist: It could indeed refer to acting in panic. But here it appears to refer to an emotion. What emotional category does panic belong to?

Patient: Anxiety, really bad anxiety.

Therapist: Exactly. So we tick Afraid. How afraid were you, where 0 means no anxiety and 100 means the worst fear imaginable.

Patient: Well, about 85.

Therapist: All right. We note that there ... An important question to answer next is what went on in your mind at that moment? What interpretation of the extraordinary experience frightened you so much?

Patient: I thought: 'See, there's a ghost and it's trying to make me go mad by haunting me.'

Therapist: Very well. We write that in this cell. As you can see, the thought is congruent with the emotion. What did you do?

Patient: I checked the entire apartment to see if I could find any other sign of a ghost.

Therapist: Okay, so you checked the apartment. We put that down in the cell 'behaviour'.

Patient: All right.

Therapist: In summary you see that we've made a correct ABC. You saw that your plate was no longer where you remembered you left it. You thought: 'A ghost moved the plate in order to make me go mad.' You became very anxious and checked the entire apartment for any other signs of ghosts.

Patient: That's right.

Therapist: Well, that looks like a perfect ABC, well done. Do you have any questions?

Patient: No. It's clear.

Therapist: Good. I would then like to ask you to register all your extraordinary experiences this week. Good luck!

> **TIP:** Some patients find it difficult to distinguish events from beliefs. Often they incorporate the interpretation in the event. Correct them when they do so. For example: A patient notes: 'A man in the bus was watching me because I look different'. You change this into: 'So the event was that you saw a man looking at you in the bus, and then you thought: He's watching me because I look different. Am I correct?'

> **TIP:** If people experience intrusive perceptual abnormalities, such as hearing their name being called, this is an actual event. Never say: 'Okay, so you thought you heard someone calling your name.' This is a serious misinterpretation of what the patient actually experiences. Voice hearers really hear someone speaking to them or really hear their own thoughts aloud.

> **TIP:** An ABC is a snapshot. Problematic situations often follow a kind of script. The registration can be made of different moments within this sequence of events. Ensure that the patient chooses the most important moment, so that you identify the most important negative cognitions.

Lifestyle recommendations

Give the patient four basic lifestyle recommendations. Emphasise that we give these because we know that living up to these recommendations reduces the chance that symptoms worsen and develop into severe psychiatric disorders. The lifestyle recommendations are:

1. Refrain from using cannabis and other drugs. Especially when you notice that they worsen your extraordinary experiences.
2. Stay socially active, do normal things such as seeing friends and going to work or school.
3. Discuss your extraordinary and remarkable experiences with others: for this, choose a friend or family member that you trust and know to be an understanding and stable person.
4. Do not occupy yourself too much with paranormal issues and/or complex philosophical and existential questions.

> **TIP:** Monitor and briefly discuss the level of (social) functioning at least every two sessions and, if necessary, help the patient set concrete goals for the next two weeks.

Homework

- Search the Internet for additional information on the discussed phenomena.
- Make ABCs of extraordinary experiences that occur.
- Read the following section from the manual.

Introduction on cognitive biases

We will start to collect some of your extraordinary experiences with the aid of Table 7.2. In this table you can report in the first column what happened to you. In the second column you can give a short description of your thoughts and interpretations of what happened to you. In the third column you can score your emotional response: afraid, angry, sad, ashamed or happy, with a score from 0 (not present) to 100 (extreme). In the fourth column you can describe what you did in response to your interpretation of the event.

Cognitive biases

How can you prevent extraordinary experiences from becoming the starting point of problems and complaints? You can achieve this by becoming aware of your thinking style and by correcting a risky thinking style by critically evaluating your own beliefs. The way you can accomplish this is explained in the following section about cognitive biases.

Cognitive biases are tendencies in perception, remembering and reasoning. To use a heater as a metaphor: when the room temperature is high, it does not mean the heater is broken but simply that the thermostat setting is too high. If our perception is biased, we continuously search our environment for certain cues. For example, somebody with an eating disorder is constantly aware of food around them all day and every day. Such a person is amazed by the many advertisements about food in a newspaper or magazine. Somebody with a dog phobia sees dangerous dogs everywhere. Somebody with problematic shyness sees herself continuously through the eyes of others. She thinks she is perceived as a fool and suffers from the thought that others reject her. Somebody who is paranoid continuously checks the surroundings for suspicious individuals who participate in a conspiracy against him. Every time he opens a newspaper, articles seem to indicate danger and how people will try to harm him.

If our memory is biased, some memories are easily accessible whereas others are not. We know that people suffering from depression have very easy access to memories of sorrow, failure and other unpleasant events in their lives.

Table 7.2 Registration of extraordinary experiences (ABC form)

Activating event	Beliefs	Consequences
Extraordinary experience	Automatic thoughts and interpretations	Emotion: 0–100% Behaviour [ ] Afraid [ ] Angry [ ] Sad [ ] Happy [ ] Ashamed [ ] Neutral
Extraordinary experience	Automatic thoughts and interpretations	Emotion: 0–100% Behaviour [ ] Afraid [ ] Angry [ ] Sad [ ] Happy [ ] Ashamed [ ] Neutral
Extraordinary experience	Automatic thoughts and interpretations	Emotion: 0–100% Behaviour [ ] Afraid [ ] Angry [ ] Sad [ ] Happy [ ] Ashamed [ ] Neutral
Extraordinary experience	Automatic thoughts and interpretations	Emotion: 0–100% Behaviour [ ] Afraid [ ] Angry [ ] Sad [ ] Happy [ ] Ashamed [ ] Neutral
Extraordinary experience	Automatic thoughts and interpretations	Emotion: 0–100% Behaviour [ ] Afraid [ ] Angry [ ] Sad [ ] Happy [ ] Ashamed [ ] Neutral
Extraordinary experience	Automatic thoughts and interpretations	Emotion: 0–100% Behaviour [ ] Afraid [ ] Angry [ ] Sad [ ] Happy [ ] Ashamed [ ] Neutral

Table 7.3 Cognitive biases posing a threat when judging extraordinary experiences

Perception biases

- Perceiving danger when there is none (selective attention)

Memory biases

- Attributing thoughts to others (source monitoring bias)
- Pessimism (negative expectancy bias)

Reason biases

- Jumping to conclusions
- Things are true because I know/feel they are true (dogmatism)
- There has to be a threat because I am afraid (emotional reasoning)
- Seeing too many causes; coincidence does not exist any more (covariation bias)
- 'There-you-go' reasoning (confirmation bias)

When a depressed person is asked about good and happy moments, a silence often follows and the individual finds it difficult to remember any positive moments. Such a bias of memory can also occur in anxious people.

If the reasoning is biased, we either jump to conclusions or are too slow forming a conclusion. Or we react either too optimistically or too pessimistically when judging situations and consequences.

Having described a few biases, we will now go through some specific biases that in case of extraordinary experiences can lead to dramatic interpretations of those experiences and can get you into trouble.

(4) CBT assessment and metacognitive training (six sessions)

In this phase you simultaneously gather information for the case formulation and provide a metacognitive training. The aim of this training is to help the patient identify which cognitive biases are present. Once the patient is aware of these biases, he can try to reduce their negative influence on him. During this phase, the patient is encouraged to practise coming up with alternative interpretations for extraordinary experiences.

> **TIP:** Divide each session into two halves. In the first part of the session discuss the CBT assessment; in the second part, the metacognitive training.

Discussing the results of the questionnaires

Discuss the patient's scores on the questionnaires (DACOBS, BAI and BDI2). Answer any questions, and discuss whether the patient recognises themself in these scores.

> **TIP:** It is useful to discuss the scores on the DACOBS in great detail. These scores have a clinical value and function as an impetus to discuss the metacognitive biases that the patient has read about.

Additional psycho-education

Discuss whether the patient found interesting information on the Internet about any of the phenomena that you discussed in the previous sessions. Give further psycho-education where necessary.

> **TIP:** Opportunities to give normalising and psycho-educational information will keep arising during the course of the therapy. Use these opportunities and repeat information. Remember that the patient is flooded with information in the first few sessions; repetition increases the likelihood that this information is retained.

Assessing the extraordinary experiences

Discuss the ABCs that the patient made this week. Check whether these are properly constructed. Are the different elements congruent? Are the right things noted in the right place? Does the patient make a correct differentiation between events and thoughts? Does he describe the most important interpretations?

> *Therapist:* Did you manage to make ABCs of the extraordinary experiences this week?
> *Patient:* Yes, it went pretty well. I stopped registering the sounds at night, because that was always the same.
> *Therapist:* Very well, that seems logical. Let's have a look at the ABCs that you made. Shall we start with the most distressing extraordinary experience? Which one was that?
> *Patient:* That was the incident in the city centre here (pointing to that registration on the ABC form).
> *Therapist:* Okay, and what did you note as the extraordinary event?

Patient: I passed a girl who suddenly starts filming me with her smart phone.
Therapist: All right, let's look at that situation. What we need to do is distinguish between the actual event and your interpretation of it. For the activating event we are looking for an event. Something you could have captured on camera or microphone. If you imagine that your eyes were a camera and your ears are microphones. What did you register on facts?
Patient: I see what you're getting at. What I literally saw was that she suddenly aimed the back of her smart phone in my direction as I walked by.
Therapist: Very good. That sounds like a factual event. Note that down. And how did you interpret her behaviour?
Patient: Well, I thought: 'She's filming me.'
Therapist: And how did that make you feel?
Patient: I've noted 'Afraid 75' and 'Angry 40'.
Therapist: And how did you react?
Patient: I quickly rushed into a shop and left via a different exit. Then I went home.
Therapist: Okay. You've done well. It looks like all the elements of the ABC are in the right place, and we've distinguished between the activating event and your interpretation of it. One thing remains unclear to me. What thought made you run into that shop and then go home?
Patient: How do you mean?
Therapist: Well, I'm trying to look at this situation from your perspective and do not understand your reaction. I wouldn't run away from a girl filming me. I don't think you would either. I therefore suspect that you had an additional thought. Most probably you jumped to a certain conclusion about why she filmed you. Am I right?
Patient: Now that you mention it, yes. I thought: 'She might be part of the group that may be out to get me.' But I know that this is a silly thought.
Therapist: Exactly, now that you're here. But I assume that it appeared quite realistic at that moment! Otherwise, you wouldn't have run away.
Patient: That's true. At that moment it felt dangerous. I'd rather take no risks.
Therapist: Better safe than sorry.
Patient: Exactly.
Therapist: Do you agree that we need to add this thought to the ABC to complete it?
Patient: Yes.
Therapist: Go ahead.

> **TIP:** Always perform an 'empathic check'. Put yourself in the patient's shoes and determine whether you completely understand what thoughts run through their mind and why they reacts the way they do. If you do not do this, you have probably not identified the most important cognition yet.

Attention: Just like a hallucination, an intrusive thought is regarded as an activating event. The patient interprets this intrusive experience in a problematic way. This interpretation is noted in the beliefs section. Differentiate between intrusive thoughts and thoughts in response to a stimulus. If you do not do this and regard an intrusion as a 'regular' thought, you and your patient will search for a stimulus that does not exist.

Discuss what insights the patient gained by making the ABCs during the previous week. What did he notice? And how can he use this new information?

Therapist: My compliments for how active you've been in making ABCs. In cognitive behavioural therapy most of the progression is achieved in the period between the sessions. It is good to see that you're putting in the effort. When you look at the ABCs that you've made, what did you notice?

Patient: The first thing I learned is that extraordinary experiences occur less frequently than I thought. Also I've noticed that I tend to quite easily conclude that there is danger.

Therapist: So, you appear to have a bias to jump to negative conclusions?

Patient: You could say it like that, yes.

Therapist: It is important that you notice this. Once you're aware of such a bias you can train yourself to neutralise it before it influences you in a negative way. We'll get back to this later.

Patient: Okay.

Therapist: When you look at the ABCs. What determines your emotional and behavioural reactions the most?

Patient: Clearly my thoughts. In the end my mind is the place where all the anxiety originates.

Therapist: That's correct. I explained earlier that it is the meaning we give to the facts in life that determine our reactions. It is important that you've experienced that this is also the case for your extraordinary experiences. The good thing is that thoughts can be examined and tested. Facts are unchangeable, but you can modify negative thoughts when you discover that they're false.

> **TIP:** Note the information from this session in a draft version of the case formulation in your notes. This helps you to develop an overview of the relevant events, cognitions and consequences. Moreover, it helps you to see what information is lacking to finalise the case formulation. This makes it easier to develop the case formulation in the next phase of the protocol. Also, make a short description of events, progress and clinical impression of every session. In addition, make sure that you have a copy of all the ABCs and other forms that the patient filled in. Sometimes patients lose their forms and you need the information to make the case formulation together.

Formulating alternative explanations

Introduce the extended ABC form (Table 7.4). Almost by definition, people with ARMS are not 100 per cent convinced of their frightening interpretations of extraordinary events. They usually have disease awareness. Although some amount of dogmatism does occur, most patients are quite open to examining and challenging their negative automatic interpretations of the extraordinary experiences. For many patients this is an important phase in the treatment process, because they really experience the effect of interpreting events differently.

EXAMPLE

> *'In the previous week you've made several ABCs. You've experienced how important your interpretations of events are. You've also learned that there are often many possible explanations for an event. Wise men and women have known for hundreds of years that there is rarely only one explanation for an event. Therefore, they always look at a situation from different perspectives. This ensures that they have a variety of ways (nuanced view) of seeing things, which prevents them from acting upon false conclusions.*
>
> *Starting from today, I would like to ask you to act like a wise person. This means that I ask you to think of at least one different (nuanced) alternative explanation for every extraordinary event that you encounter. You can use the new registration form (Table 7.4). As you can see, it is practically the same as you've already been using. We've only added an extra row for each extraordinary event. In this row you can note the different (nuanced) alternative interpretation. After doing this, you imagine what your reaction would have been if you (hypothetically) had directly interpreted the extraordinary event in that manner. Let's together make a registration of an extraordinary event that you experienced in the previous week on the new form.'*

> **TIP:** Do not introduce the alternative explanation as the correct interpretation. Introduce it as an exercise. 'Regardless of the question whether or not it is a realistic alternative thought, just imagine that you had directly interpreted the event in that (nuanced) way, how would you have felt then? And how would you have reacted?'

Homework

Ask the patient to register all extraordinary events. Ask him to think of at least one nuanced alternative explanation. And let him think of the (hypothetical) alternative emotional and behavioural reactions.

> **TIP:** Let the patient score the degree of credibility (0–100 per cent) of the most important negative automatic and alternative thoughts. When the alternative thoughts are perceived as more credible than the negative automatic thoughts, you can ask the patient: 'By which thoughts do you prefer to be led? By implausible thoughts that induce fear, or by credible thoughts that lead to neutral reactions?'

Again we ask you to register your extraordinary and remarkable experiences, your automatic interpretations and your emotional and behavioural responses (Table 7.4). From this week onwards, however, we also want you to think of at least one alternative explanation of the extraordinary or remarkable experience. It doesn't matter how silly or far-fetched the alternative is. What counts is that you start practising with developing alternative interpretations. There is always more than one way to perceive an event. In the second column of the second row you write down the alternative interpretation. In the third column of the third row you describe what emotion you would have felt if the alternative interpretation were true. In the fourth column of that row you note how you would have reacted behaviourally if the alternative interpretation were true. Good luck!

Table 7.4 ABC form for extraordinary experiences with alternative explanations

Activating event	Beliefs	Consequences	
Extraordinary experience	Automatic thoughts and interpretations	Emotion: 0–100% [ ] Afraid [ ] Angry [ ] Sad [ ] Happy [ ] Ashamed [ ] Neutral	Behaviour
Extraordinary experience	Alternative thoughts and interpretations	Alternative emotion: 0–100% [ ] Afraid [ ] Angry [ ] Sad [ ] Happy [ ] Ashamed [ ] Neutral	Alternative behaviour

Activating event	Beliefs	Consequences	
Extraordinary experience	Automatic thoughts and interpretations	Emotion: 0–100% [ ] Afraid [ ] Angry [ ] Sad [ ] Happy [ ] Ashamed [ ] Neutral	Behaviour
Extraordinary experience	Alternative thoughts and interpretations	Alternative emotion: 0–100% [ ] Afraid [ ] Angry [ ] Sad [ ] Happy [ ] Ashamed [ ] Neutral	Alternative behaviour

Activating event	Beliefs	Consequences	
Extraordinary experience	Automatic thoughts and interpretations	Emotion: 0–100% [ ] Afraid [ ] Angry [ ] Sad [ ] Happy [ ] Ashamed [ ] Neutral	Behaviour
Extraordinary experience	Alternative thoughts and interpretations	Alternative emotion: 0–100% [ ] Afraid [ ] Angry [ ] Sad [ ] Happy [ ] Ashamed [ ] Neutral	Alternative behaviour

Activating event	Beliefs	Consequences	
Extraordinary experience	Automatic thoughts and interpretations	Emotion: 0–100% [ ] Afraid [ ] Angry [ ] Sad [ ] Happy [ ] Ashamed [ ] Neutral	Behaviour
Extraordinary experience	Alternative thoughts and interpretations	Alternative emotion: 0–100% [ ] Afraid [ ] Angry [ ] Sad [ ] Happy [ ] Ashamed [ ] Neutral	Alternative behaviour

A therapy manual

Activating event	Beliefs	Consequences	
Extraordinary experience	Automatic thoughts and interpretations	Emotion: 0–100% [ ] Afraid [ ] Angry [ ] Sad [ ] Happy [ ] Ashamed [ ] Neutral	Behaviour
Extraordinary experience	Alternative thoughts and interpretations	Alternative emotion: 0–100% [ ] Afraid [ ] Angry [ ] Sad [ ] Happy [ ] Ashamed [ ] Neutral	Alternative behaviour

Activating event	Beliefs	Consequences	
Extraordinary experience	Automatic thoughts and interpretations	Emotion: 0–100% [ ] Afraid [ ] Angry [ ] Sad [ ] Happy [ ] Ashamed [ ] Neutral	Behaviour
Extraordinary experience	Alternative thoughts and interpretations	Alternative emotion: 0–100% [ ] Afraid [ ] Angry [ ] Sad [ ] Happy [ ] Ashamed [ ] Neutral	Alternative behaviour

Assessing intermediate assumptions

Study the completed ABCs. Explore what conditional ('If ..., then....') and instrumental ('I must ...' or 'I can't....') thoughts are most important. Often these can be found by converting automatic thoughts to a more general level or by asking the patient to verbalise what the function of his avoidance or safety behaviours is. For example, 'If I don't suppress the extraordinary experiences, I will go mad' or 'I must distrust people I don't know'. Include these conditional and instrumental thoughts in the case formulation.

Assessing basic assumptions

It is useful to identify the basic beliefs that the patient has about himself, others and the world. These are evaluative polarised statements; for example, good or bad, friend or foe, smart or stupid, competent or incompetent, loved or unloved, and so on. Patients with a negative self-esteem that are distressed by negative intrusive thoughts often believe that they are weak, weird or crazy. People who are suspicious often have negative core beliefs about others. The downward arrow technique is a useful method to identify negative basic assumptions.

> *Therapist:* When you're at work and see your colleagues talking and you have those thoughts that they want to get rid of you – what does that do to you?
> *Patient:* It makes me feel very sad and angry. It makes me wonder why these things always happen to me.
> *Therapist:* And the fact that this does happen to you. What does that say about you?
> *Patient:* That I'm someone who can't defend himself, that I'm not in control.
> *Therapist:* And if that were true – what would that say about you as a person? How would you call someone like that?
> *Patient:* Vulnerable. A weakling.
> *Therapist:* And when you say 'a weakling', I can see that those words touch you, that they activate emotion.
> *Patient:* That's correct. It's a terrible thought.
> *Therapist:* It's good that we identified this negative core belief. That's clearly something we'll have to work on!

TIP: Try to identify the 'hot cognitions'. These negative core beliefs are often of great influence. Hot cognitions are basic assumptions that activate emotional and behavioural schemas. An activated hot cognition can often be read from your patient's facial expression. Patients are usually quite capable of indicating whether cognition activates emotional and behavioural schemas.

> **TIP:** Ensure that the intermediate and basic assumptions are included in the problem formulation.

Metacognitive training

You spend the second part of each session working on the metacognitive training. Each week one or two cognitive biases are discussed. The metacognitive training comprises three elements, which are repeated for all eight included cognitive biases:

1. Reading and discussing psycho-education about the bias.
2. Performing the homework exercise in which the patient experiences the effect of that cognitive bias (not in all biases).
3. Making the new information personal. Discussing in what way the bias influences the patient.

The information and exercises on the cognitive biases are included in the manual.

> **TIP:** Ensure that you are familiar with the eight cognitive biases that are included in the manual and workbook. It is desirable that you can easily connect information and behaviour from your patient to the different cognitive biases.

> **TIP:** Include the insights you gain about the patient and his complaints during the metacognitive training in the case formulation.

Introducing the metacognitive training

Discuss the introduction on cognitive biases from the manual that the patient has read as homework. Ensure that the patient understands what metacognitions are, and that they are familiar with the goal and rationale of the training.

EXAMPLE

> *'So far we've spoken a lot about what you think when certain extraordinary events occur. I would now like to focus on how you think. You've already read some information about this. There are certain cognitive biases or 'thinking styles' that influence extraordinary experiences. In this*

training I want to examine whether certain cognitive biases are also of influence on your complaints. It is, for instance, possible that we discover that you are strongly inclined to reason on the basis of your emotions, or that you always tend to expect negative outcomes. If you discover that certain cognitive biases influence you, then you can start monitoring these biases. Once you clearly recognise the influence of these biases on your functioning, you can start neutralising this effect. In that way you prevent the biases from causing anxious or depressed feelings. In summary, this training intends to make you aware of the cognitive biases and if necessary help you neutralise them. The great advantage of changing your thinking style is that we address the problem at its roots. Moreover, it allows us to simultaneously work on various situations that are related to a certain cognitive bias.'

> **TIP:** A useful, freely translated, synonym for metacognition is 'thinking about thinking'. A useful, but not fully correct, synonym for cognitive bias is 'thinking style'.

Homework in this phase

- Make ABCs of extraordinary experiences including alternative interpretations.
- Read the information on the different cognitive biases.
- Perform the homework exercises in the manual.

Perception bias

Perceiving more danger than is probably present (selective attention)

If you see danger where there is none, or pay selective attention to anything that could be dangerous, you will perceive danger everywhere. If this is the case, then the world becomes more and more threatening. Of course, you should not stop paying attention to danger, because this might cause you to act in an irresponsible way. The key is to find a good balance.

We will perform an exercise to experience how selective attention works. In the coming week you will pay attention to something specific every workday:

1   The first day you need to score how many blue cars you have seen; you will write them down on the form. Every hour of the day you have to score blue cars, when you are outside, when you are in a tram/trolley, bus or train, when you are at school, at work or at home. Whenever you are near a window, you need to write down how many blue cars you see. The exercise continues until after supper. Then you add up the number of blue cars you have

seen that day. Also, write down what you noticed about yourself during the exercise.
2 On the second day you need to pay attention to noises or sounds that do not come from the room you are actually in. When you are inside (e.g. at work or at home or wherever you are), you need to write down which sounds you hear from outside, from neighbours, from other rooms next to the one you are in, etc. After supper you add up the number of sounds and also write down what you noticed about yourself during the exercise.
3 On day three you score the number of people you see wearing glasses. After supper you add up the number of people, and also write down what you noticed about yourself during the exercise.
4 Day four is your day off. After supper, please write down the differences you noticed when comparing today with the last few days.
5 On day five you need to focus on people who give you an unpleasant feeling. This might be because they look at you in a certain way, dressed completely differently from you, were standing in a threatening or superior way, are much taller than you, appear to be like a criminal, etc. Again, after supper you add up your scores, and write down what you noticed about yourself during the exercise as well.

Use Table 7.5 below to score, add up and describe your experiences every day.

Table 7.5 Exercise with selective attention

Time	Day 1 Blue cars	Day 2 Noises/sounds from outside the room	Day 3 People wearing glasses	Day 5 Unpleasant or scary people
08:00				
09:00				
10:00				
11:00				
12:00				
13:00				
14:00				
15:00				
16:00				
17:00				
18:00				
19:00				
Total				

Day 1 Remarks:
Day 2 Remarks:
Day 3 Remarks:
Day 4 Remarks:
Day 5 Remarks:

> **TIP:** There are videos that nicely demonstrate how strong the effect of this bias is on people. Before introducing the subject of selective attention, let your patient perform the 'Awareness Test' that can be viewed on YouTube (www.youtube.com/watch?v=Ahg6qcgoay4&list=PLACC5EB309FA7D3DB). Videos such as this can be very illustrative and also function as a useful metaphor.

Memory biases

Attributing thoughts to others (source monitoring bias)

The source monitoring bias occurs only in people who hear voices or in those who have an aptitude for hearing them. The monitoring bias has been demonstrated many times and indicates a vulnerability to hear such voices. The bias can be present during an entire lifetime and it is difficult to influence this bias. However, it is important to be aware of the bias. In short, after a certain period of time, the bias makes an individual remember their own thoughts and statements as if they are those of someone else. This also applies to thoughts, statements and writings. The brain labels all memory content, such that it indicates whether that particular memory content was produced internally or externally. The former is a thought or a memory, whereas the latter is a sensory perception. In some people, this labelling mechanism is biased, meaning that some internal memories of stimuli are wrongfully labelled as external. This mechanism of wrongful labelling is probably present during hallucinating, when internal invading thoughts are attributed to an outside source. The voice sounds different from your own, and that voice says things somebody else could say. These phenomena strengthen the idea that someone else is speaking.

Clearly there are borderline experiences as well. Some people hear their own thoughts out loud. Sometimes these spoken thoughts are repeated all the time. In this case, we are dealing with thoughts, but they differ from normal thoughts because they are clearly audible. Another experience is compulsive thoughts that suddenly become audible, such as a voice. In time, this may lead to coercive thoughts. Obsessive thoughts are intrusive thoughts that are involuntary and undesirable because of their strong aggressive or sexual nature. The person who has obsessive thoughts wants to stop them and will try anything to get rid of these thoughts, but usually fails. In this respect obsessive thoughts and voices are similar. The difference between an obsessive thought and a voice is that the first is a thought coming from oneself, whereas the latter is a voice shaped by the brain without actually being a thought. Both are predominantly intrusive and almost impossible to control. Perhaps future research will show that hearing voices is a form of obsessive thinking plus a dysfunctional labelling mechanism that is switching labels from internal to external. The content of a voice comes from a dark corner of the brain and ends up in the conscience because of a faulty filter mechanism.

> **TIP:** Customise the content of the metacognitive training to your patient. It is important to extensively discuss the source monitoring bias when the patient's most distressing problem is hearing his aggressive thoughts out loud. When the patient does not experience any perceptual abnormalities, you need only briefly discuss this bias and move on to the next.

Pessimism (negative expectation bias)

Pessimists are always afraid of a bad outcome, whereas optimists always hope for the best. Usually both are wrong. The pessimist often ends up pleasantly surprised and the optimist disappointed. Looking at it this way, it may seem that optimists experience more negative events than pessimists, but in fact it is the other way around. Pessimists undertake less and, as a result, experience less success than optimists, who will start anything. Extreme pessimism also seems to be a self-fulfilling prophecy: those who expect nothing undertake nothing and will eventually gain nothing. Pessimism can be a family trait, but it is usually acquired. Based on earlier disappointing experiences, the pessimist has decided not to expect too much in the future and therefore no longer undertakes very much. The pessimist expects to avoid disappointments this way, but is in fact preventing an active participation in life.

Pessimism is therefore an interpretation bias based on earlier disappointments. We have learned that interpretations play an important role in developing problems. Interpretations go beyond the facts. Facts are distinct events: you can film them, tape them, or measure them. Let us assume, for example, a man standing in the rain wearing a long coat. Language can state a fact as in 'That man is standing in the rain wearing a long coat'. But language can also state an interpretation as in 'That man standing alone in the rain has been dumped by his girlfriend'. Here, the interpretation goes beyond the facts and is an assumption about a fact. Usually there is no discussion about a fact, whereas interpretations can be right, a little bit right, a little bit wrong, or entirely wrong. The interpretation of being abandoned is a typical example of a pessimistic interpretation. It is also possible that the man likes the rain and has gone out for a walk simply for that reason. Another interpretation is that the man is just waiting for his girlfriend so they can go out together. This example shows that interpretation is debatable, while in fact it is not. As long as we are aware of our own interpretations, we realise that there are always other possibilities.

If you are a pessimist, it is better to acknowledge that you are one. As a pessimist you have a negative attitude towards yourself, others and life in general. Therefore, the possibility exists that you will become miserable and cynical. In this way you might well approach your moment of death unhappy and unfulfilled – while this is totally unnecessary!

Now we are going to do an exercise on pessimistic interpretations. In the coming week, before going to sleep you need to write down in Table 7.6 one or more facts you have come across, followed by a pessimistic *and* an optimistic interpretation of that fact. First, we will fill in the first column together as practice.

Table 7.6 Pessimistic and optimistic interpretations

Fact as observed	Pessimistic interpretation	Optimistic interpretation

TIP: Emphasise that this is only an exercise and challenge the patient to exaggerate his interpretations. Patients with a strongly pessimistic thinking style often find it extremely difficult to think of positive interpretations. However, do not accept a situation in which the patient leaves cells open in the column for the optimistic interpretations!

TIP: Repeatedly discuss the negative consequences of the pessimistic interpretations on affect and behaviour.

Reasoning biases

Jumping to conclusions

Jumping to conclusions is a common problem. It is partly responsible for the start of nearly all the conflicts between people and between countries. Many anxiety disorders are also based on conclusions that were drawn far too quickly and are afterwards considered to be a fact. So there are two processes at work here: drawing conclusions based on very little information, and considering the conclusion to be a factual representation of reality.

A major reason for the existence of jumping to conclusions is evolution. An organism has an evolutionary advantage if it is able to quickly form a conclusion about safety or threat. When in danger, getting away quickly, or a swift attack, is a much more useful course of action than sitting down and contemplating the situation. If the threat is imminent, harm will have overcome the contemplator before a conclusion has been formed.

A disadvantage of jumping to conclusions is that it causes many errors. A nice example of how jumping to conclusions leads to a lot of errors, but also with an evolutionary advantage, is that of the frog. The frog represents a tasty snack for storks and herons. So, imagine a frog sitting at the edge of a flowing stream, his eyes staring at the sky. Another frog (long since devoured) once tried to distinguish friend from foe. Whenever a stork or heron flew over he would jump into the water, whereas with other birds, such as a sparrow or a robin, he would just remain at the waterside. So you can understand that one day the frog was devoured because he mistakenly thought that a small stork was a fat sparrow and was then eaten up. However, the first frog does not think like this. He decides to jump into the water every time a bird flies over, to swim to the bottom and stay there for half an hour. This is a strategy that cannot fail and we also see this strategy being used by suspicious individuals. People refer to this strategy as being 'better safe than sorry'. One advantage is survival, but a disadvantage is that the frog spends a large and unnecessary part of his life alone at the murky bottom of the stream.

People still have the ability to react like frogs. When facing danger we often react quickly at the cost of accuracy. This process is rapid and without thinking. The signal travels from the eye to the recognition centre (what is it?), subsequently to the emotion centre (beware, danger!) and, finally, to the movement centre (get out!). The time elapsing between perception and response is a split second. When, for example, someone throws a giant bug on to your lap, it only takes milliseconds to jump up, scream and jump backwards. In the meantime your heart rate has risen, you are sweating and panting, and your muscles are tense and ready for action.

Then a second process starts, which is a slow and conscious assessment of the situation. In our example, you now see that the bug is motionless. On closer inspection you realise that the bug is a plastic toy, and this comforts you. Your conscious perception centre now sends a message to the emotion centre, indicating a false alarm. The emotion centre returns to normal, your heart rate drops, your sweat glands are no longer stimulated and, after a deep sigh, your respiration returns to normal. For those interested, Figure 7.1 shows a more technical explanation of the processes described above.

In the brain the hippocampus is the recognition centre and the amygdala the emotion centre. The prefrontal cortex (PFC) is the conscious judgement centre.

In a suspicious individual, with a strong selective attention to danger, over-activity in the emotion centre (amygdala) and an under-activation of the conscious judgement centre (PFC) is present. In a manner of speaking, the system is locked. The individual keeps reacting with strong

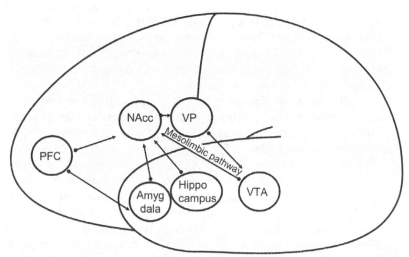

PFC = prefrontal cortex; NAcc = nucleus accumbens; VP = ventral pallidus; VTA = ventral tegmental area

Figure 7.1 The mechanism of switching between a fast and emotional, and a conscious and well-thought, response.

emotions, even though this is unnecessary under the given circumstances. The hippocampus is locked too: there is no evaluation of reactions and new learning is not possible. This state of anxious increased attention can be shut down by rhythmic signals from dopamine cells in the ventral tegmental area (VTA). If the nucleus accumbens (NAcc) is subsequently activated, activity in the ventral pallidus (VP) decreases and activity in the PFC increases. Then a conscious re-evaluation can occur and the PFC, in cooperation with the NAcc, can unlock the amygdala and hippocampus. Tranquillity of mind returns and new learning can take place.

In short, elevated anxiety associated with suspicion and selective attention causes people to react quickly and in a stereotypical way, which prevents new learning. To get out of this cycle, the anxious person needs to be induced to come to second or third thoughts about the events, by means of questions and stimulation of thinking. Aid comes from realising again that interpretation is not yet a fact, and that different interpretations can exist for the same events.

Therefore, jumping to conclusions is not a disorder, but can simply serve survival. Things go wrong when conscious re-evaluation stops. To prevent problems it is important to:

1 distinguish facts from interpretations;
2 come up with two or more interpretations about a fact;
3 not act on an interpretation before it has been discussed with others.

A therapy manual 103

> **TIP:** The material of the metacognitive training developed by Moritz and Woodward (2007b) about jumping to conclusions can be very instructive. This can be downloaded for free (www.uke.de/kliniken/psychiatrie/index_17380.php). When you use elements from the training by Moritz and Woodward with patients with ARMS, be aware of the fact that this training was developed for people with schizophrenia.

We are going to do an exercise. Think of an extraordinary experience you had recently. Describe it in a factual way. Then describe your interpretation of it. Come up with two other interpretations and discuss these with a close friend, acquaintance or relative. Make sure that you ask someone that you know to be a stable and rational person, someone who can help you think of non-frightening alternative interpretations. Use Table 7.7 below.

Table 7.7 Preventing mistakes by use of conscious re-evaluation

Recent extraordinary experience. Describe factually

Your interpretation of the experience when it happened

Alternative interpretation 1

Alternative interpretation 2

Results of discussion with someone else. What are your feelings now towards the extraordinary experience?

> **TIP:** Ensure that the patient chooses a friend or relative who is a stable and reasonably rational person. The purpose of discussing the extraordinary event with someone else is that the other person can help the patient think of nuanced and relativistic alternative interpretations that reduce the credibility of the original negative interpretation.

> **TIP:** This exercise is similar to making ABCs with an alternative interpretation. Here you try to increase metacognitive awareness. Does the patient recognise this bias in his situation? If so, what is he going to do about it? It can be very helpful to start using 'stop and think' procedures at moments when the patient notices that he has jumped to a conclusion.

Things are true, because I know/feel they are true (dogmatism/belief inflexibility)

Convictions can become so powerful that they are assumed to be true. In this case, an interpretation becomes a fact. If something happens that does not coincide with your idea of how things work, you disregard it and you do not change your idea. In history, the carrier of an unwanted message was often murdered.

The advantage of this attitude is that you do not go along with the 'madness of the day'. In this way political ideologies and religions can continue to exist for a long time, despite the continuous changes in the world. A disadvantage of this resoluteness is that it can become dogmatic: we can no longer listen, let alone learn from other people with different opinions. A dreadful example of dogmatism is the banning of so-called heretics from the Church by a religious community. A strong dogmatic individual is no longer interested in what other people think. He assumes he has the wisdom and whoever does not think the same is a fool. The way dogmatic people deal with other ideas is to cast them aside and feel pity; in the worst case they feel contempt for those other stupid people.

Fortunately, very few people are completely inflexible. It is much more common for people to tend to stick to their own opinion. This is achieved by mainly focusing on information and events that support their own opinion and paying less attention to information that contradicts their ideas. This latter bias is much more common. In this case, the advantage is also a certain stability of opinions, but the disadvantage is that people can maintain catastrophic opinions. Below we will discuss this so-called confirmation bias.

> **TIP:** Do not start a discussion with patients who are strongly dogmatic in their reasoning. Most patients with a strong bias to dogmatism are well aware of their trait: 'experiencing is believing'. This rule of thumb applies especially to patients scoring high on dogmatism. Do not spend too much time working on cognitive interventions with these patients, and start exposure and behavioural experiments as soon as possible. Ensure that the outcomes of these exercises are beyond dispute.

There-you-go reasoning (confirmation bias)

People tend to focus more on evidence supporting their ideas than on evidence contradicting it. If uncertainty or fear increases, this bias becomes stronger. An example of this is Robin's colleague at work. Robin asked him to open his email and handle the urgent mail while he is on holiday. On his return 14 days later, all his mail is there – untouched. When Robin asks about this, his colleague looks down on him and says he did not have enough time to do it. Robin thinks, 'He probably dislikes me.' One week later, during a meeting at work, the same colleague opposes a proposition made by Robin but does not give any valid reason for this; he just does not think it is a good idea. Robin thinks, 'Now he's being mean to me again. He hates me.' The day after that, the colleague passes Robin on the stairs. The colleague looks down and does not greet him. Robin thinks, 'There you go. I'm certain. He hates me.' It is possible the colleague hates Robin, but there can be another explanation. For example, he really did not have enough time to handle the email because other colleagues were on holiday as well; it might indeed have been a bad idea proposed by Robin; and he may have been lost in thought when walking down the stairs and simply did not notice Robin. Since Robin has more or less decided the colleague is an unfriendly person who hates him, he will focus more on the confirmation of this idea and less on the disconfirmation. In the worst case, a friendly act from the colleague, such as congratulating Robin on his birthday or getting him a cup of coffee, will be met with distrust. 'Why is he suddenly friendly? Does he want something from me?'

When you have opinions that tend to lead to negative feelings or cause you to avoid people or places, it is wise to take a more critical viewpoint. You need to try to find other interpretations for the events. Also, it will help if you can find (similar) events and occurrences that contradict your own opinion.

For the next exercise you need to think of a person somewhere around you, who you think dislikes you. You must have reached that conclusion based on a number of incidents with that particular person. It might be a relative, neighbour, colleague or somebody else. It should not be someone you are having an argument or fight with, just someone you think dislikes you.

Use Table 7.8 in this exercise. After you have written down the name, use the second line to explain what happened that made you start thinking that the person might dislike you. On the third line you note the incident in which you thought, 'There you go, I'm certain now'. Use the fourth and fifth lines to describe other possible explanations for the behaviour of the other person. Think of what needs to happen to change your opinion about the other person to a friendlier one, and use the sixth line to describe it.

> **TIP:** As you can see, the last question of this exercise builds up to a behavioural experiment (e.g. monitoring factual behaviour of the other person or asking the person if he is indeed angry, agitated, etc. with the patient). Let the patient perform this experiment if possible and useful.

Table 7.8 From confirmation bias to looking for counter-evidence

What is the name of the person who you think dislikes you?

Briefly describe the incident when you first concluded that the person dislikes you

Briefly describe the incident where you thought: 'There-you-go, it is true'

Describe a different interpretation of the initial incident

Describe a different interpretation of the there-you-go incident

What needs to happen for you to change your opinion?

There has to be a threat, because I am scared (emotional reasoning bias)

If somebody tells you he will 'get you' some time, this information is very frightening. If there is a threatening situation, we are scared. But the reverse is not always true. If you feel depressed, it is not simply a fact that you are having a miserable life. When you feel uncomfortable in a new environment this does not mean a threat is present. Nevertheless, people often reason like that. They notice a certain mood in themselves and start looking for the reason. If the reason is searched for in an external circumstance or in an individual, we call it emotional reasoning.

In case of emotional reasoning you think your feelings are caused by facts. But feelings are not caused by facts, but by interpretations. Our own interpretations, not the facts, make us anxious. Thus, we should not ask ourselves initially what is scaring us in the environment, but ask ourselves what thoughts we have at the moment we get scared. People are afraid of the dark, not because ghosts are really present, but because they *think* ghosts are present. Small noises in the house are not just noises from the heating or the cat on the stairs, but become sounds produced by ghosts in the house. This thought increases anxiety and might even turn into panic. In Table 7.9 we see perfectly innocent facts, which do not have to lead to feeling anxious. It is the interpretations that cause a panic attack.

Extraordinary events can also become frightening because of how they are interpreted. In the next exercise we will use Table 7.10. In the first column, describe extraordinary events you have encountered in the past few months. It can be events, voices, visions, strange sensations in your body, and events with an exceptional mysterious, meaningful ambiance, etc.

Table 7.9 It is not the facts, but our interpretation that scares us

Fact	Interpretation	Emotional response
It is dark in the house	There must be ghosts	Fear
Ticking from a central heating pipe cooling down	I can hear them knocking; they are poltergeists	Extreme fear
Cat walking down the stairs	They are coming down from the attic; they are after me	Panic

Write down your interpretation of the extraordinary events in column two and your emotional response in column three.

Table 7.10 Interpreting extraordinary events and accompanying emotions

Extraordinary experience	Interpretation	Emotional response

TIP: There are always two possible explanations for sudden fear:

1. Fear is the result of negative automatic thoughts. These thoughts can be intrusive thoughts that suddenly come into awareness, or are interpretations of a certain event. The credibility of these thoughts can be challenged later in therapy.
2. Fear is caused by a sudden release of dopamine, which we call 'delusional mood'. Patients who have this describe that they suddenly experience a great anxiety, tension or vividness without having any thoughts. If this is the case, discuss how dangerous this really is and how the patient can react next time it happens.

Seeing too many causes; coincidence does not exist any more (covariation bias)

Coincidence sometimes does not appear to be a coincidence. Your girlfriend says you smoke too much 'weed' and she is going to monitor your cannabis consumption. Your boss is dissatisfied with your work and tells you he will observe you closely and judge you. After a rough game an opponent says to you in the dressing room he will 'get you' some time. Cameras are hanging in the shopping mall and when you pass by they rotate and follow you. You read in the newspaper that all email from @gmail.com is stored in the files of the American secret service. A vagrant jumps up from the street and starts yelling, 'I know who you are, I know everything about you, filthy bastard!' You think, 'Are they watching me or what?'

In recent years, all exceptional weather was attributed to the 'greenhouse effect'. That is what is thought to be causing storms, droughts and hurricanes. Ten years earlier, in 1997–1998, all exceptional weather patterns were attributed to El Niño. This is a warm Gulf Stream, which appears every 10 to 15 years near the coast of Peru. In the 1960s we did not expect a greenhouse effect but a small ice age was thought to be approaching! It is true. Whenever it rained, or there was a storm or the wind blew, the weatherman on television said a new ice age was coming. Everyone tends to connect circumstances as being more-or-less coincidental, and then assume a causal effect.

Someone running away from his pursuers hears a fragment of the national anthem on the radio; is that a signal that he is safe after all? In the distance he hears a siren; they are tracking him. He runs inside and calls a friend for a safe house. While he is on the phone, he hears strange crackling sounds; he thinks they are bugging him. He hangs up and runs outside before they can trace him. A jet passes over; is it taking pictures of him? Now they have seen him. Things go wrong! He throws his jacket into the water; a tracking device may be hidden inside!

You concentrate on the dice and say softly to yourself 'A six, a six, a six'. You throw the dice and indeed a six turns up. You can do it!

In the Middle Ages people were certain that dangerous gases caused the plague. In Great Britain during the plague large groups of people moved out of town into the mountains. Nobody became ill in the mountains; the air was healthy, the connection obvious. Afterwards it turned out that the quality of the air had nothing to do with this; the disease proved to be caused by bacteria transferred to humans by fleas from rats.

In the nineteenth century throat cancer was very common among smokers. There had to be a causal effect. Tobacco smoke was at its hottest and most concentrated with dangerous substances at the moment it passed over the larynx. Afterwards, the smoke spread through the lungs. Because the lungs have a surface area of about half the size of a soccer field, the smoke is diluted and rapidly cools down. Laryngeal cancer reduced naturally during the course of the twentieth century. Nowadays the relation between smoking and lung cancer is much clearer, but nobody understands why this shift took place.

A coincidence sometimes does not appear to be a coincidence. Nevertheless, if you throw the dice six times, the series 6–6–6–6–6–6 is just as probable as the series 3–4–1–3–2–5. The first series does not appear to be a coincidence, but in fact it is. After each throw, the chance to get a six or a five or a two or a four is still one out of six.

Similarly, on the roulette table the chance after six times red again is 48.6 per cent red, 48.6 per cent black and 2.8 per cent zero (green), irrespective of the previous outcome.

People do not understand the phenomenon of chance very well. A lot of personal misery arises from overestimating chances (e.g. the plane crashing on your holidays) and underestimating the chances (e.g. cardiovascular diseases and lung cancer from smoking). Many people confuse synchronicity with cause, as illustrated by the examples described above.

The motto is: if events occur simultaneously they can be causally related, but usually it is a coincidence.

Summary

People are exceptional creatures because they can think about themselves and their surroundings. People have been able to solve problems because of thought, technical development, and the attitude that they are able to do anything. Nevertheless, our mind can get us into trouble. On several points our mind falls short in our everyday life because our emotions are also present all of the time. We are simply not good when it comes to judging very large and very small numbers, that is, we estimate chances poorly. Because of that we overestimate danger one time and underestimate the adverse consequences of our actions another time.

If we get scared, selective attention makes us see the things we are scared of – all the time. By avoiding the alleged source of danger, we are unable to experience that our interpretations were incorrect. We tend to see our interpretations and conclusions as facts. We tend to avoid people who try to make us think otherwise, by contradicting us.

Based on far too little information we jump to conclusions and try to find evidence only for our own opinions. We see causality in coincidences and sometimes perceive bad intentions in others, when in fact there are none.

Extraordinary events are extraordinary because not everyone is familiar with them. Therefore, it is difficult to talk about these experiences with others. Someone else may contradict you and tell you it is your imagination. But it is not. The experiences are real experiences, and they are caused by slight imbalances in our brain. Over time, in most people they will fade away, whereas in others they will remain but not in a dominant way. The danger is in thinking that other people or 'intelligent beings' are involved. You perceive some sort of system in it, which makes one suspect premeditation. It happens to you involuntarily and you have little control over it. That would suggest involvement of others. Despite the fact that these explanations seem obvious, they are incorrect. We know the brain regularly lacks the ability to understand reality and we know how these kinds of extraordinary events come into existence. An appropriate understanding, and keeping calm and not becoming afraid or angry because of the events, is very important. The deregulation of dopamine is responsible for these extraordinary events. It is not necessary or desirable for you to use medication. It is more helpful for you to learn to evaluate your way of thinking. Only then will you be able to correct yourself and to put the interpretations into a reasonable perspective by coming up with a number of alternative interpretations.

Eventually, reality is something we all agree upon. Whoever does not embrace the shared reality becomes alienated. For that reason, it is a good thing to share your interpretations of extraordinary events with others, and to evaluate them together. If that does not work out with friends and family, then turn to a professional. In the middle of the stream of opinions of people in your environment, you are safe.

Homework

- Read the last chapters of the manual.

If extraordinary experiences become intrusive and dominant

We have explained how extraordinary experiences are the result of the release of dopamine or dopamine supersensitivity in our brain at unexpected moments, and how selective attention biases, memory biases and reasoning biases could play a role. Now we focus on what to do when extraordinary experiences reoccur too often, evoke too much fear and become too dominant in our life.

If alienating experiences occur more often and become frightening

Depersonalisation is the feeling that you lose contact with yourself. Depersonalisation often goes hand in hand with derealisation, that is, the feeling that the world does not seem real, that you lose touch with reality. It is like being in a dream and looking at the world from behind glass. These kinds of experiences are quite common in the general population. Various estimates report that from 34 per cent to 70 per cent of the population sometimes undergoes these kinds of experiences. Every year about 23 per cent of the population suffers from depersonalisation and derealisation. So, basically, this phenomenon is relatively harmless. It tends to occur more often in people who were traumatised during childhood and in people with an anxiety disorder or depression. Prolonged stress with fatigue, and intoxication with alcohol or drugs, can also evoke sensations of depersonalisation and derealisation.

As long as people attribute these experiences to circumstances and succeed in tolerating the experiences, the problem remains limited. Things can go wrong when the sensations of depersonalisation and derealisation are interpreted in a catastrophic way. For example, as a sign of impending madness, or an omen of impending loss of control, or the idea of dissolving, disintegrating or becoming invisible, or of the symptom of a serious brain disease. In those cases fear increases.

Strangely enough, it has been shown that there is no increase in the activity of the autonomic nervous system during depersonalisation. The autonomic nervous system regulates heart rate, blood flow to muscles, respiration and excretion of sweat, etc. By contrast, there is a decrease in autonomic activity during depersonalisation and this coincides with the feeling of loss of involvement of one's self with the world around us.

This increase in fear often goes hand in hand with mechanisms that make the fear permanent. In the long term, the fear grows stronger and stronger, and the feelings of depersonalisation occur more often. By avoiding certain situations in which feelings of depersonalisation have occurred, one's work, school, friends and relations become jeopardised. In addition, avoiding people and places prevents the possibility for new learning. The individual cannot experience, for example, that depersonalisation does not occur again in the same situation as before. Furthermore, selective attention occurs during the experience of mild signs of depersonalisation. Paying attention to these signs all day long causes many moments of slight panic, which can trigger a new episode of depersonalisation. The individual often looks for different ways to protect themself. For example, when shopping, they will always keep an eye on the emergency exit, will avoid elevators and escalators, and will only enter shops that are not crowded.

Therefore, in case of feelings of depersonalisation and derealisation, it is important to remain calm until it passes. These are relatively harmless experiences and only a catastrophic interpretation, namely, that the experiences are serious, will lead to more fear and more feelings of depersonalisation and derealisation. Figure 7.2 depicts the cognitive model of depersonalisation and derealisation.

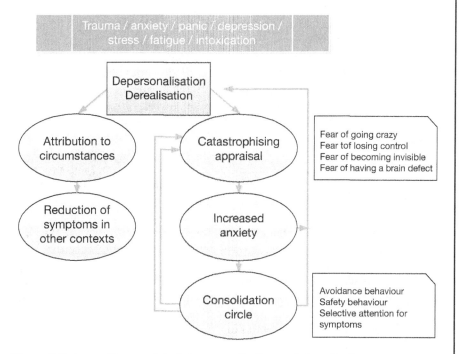

Figure 7.2 A cognitive model of depersonalisation and derealisation.
Source: Hunter et al. (2003)

If thoughts and behaviour seem to be influenced more frequently

Sometimes it seems as though your hand is doing something all by itself, without you controlling it. But it is not true that you have lost control over your hand. If you repair a bicycle tyre, your hand will not suddenly play the piano. It just *feels* as though an outside force is controlling your hands. The control has not been lost, only the experience of control is missing. This can happen to thoughts as well. We all know the appearance of an unpleasant thought of an aggressive or sexual nature. That thought interrupts any other thoughts we have at that moment and seems to invade consciousness. We do not want to think that thought, and we do not identify with the content of which we disapprove. It can also happen that we get thoughts that seem to come from outside, as though someone else has put them into our mind. Here too, the experience of control is disturbed. Sometimes thoughts can become blocked, and you can have the sensation that someone else is doing it. You can think that someone else is intervening with your thoughts, preventing you from thinking what you want to think about. Physical sensations, such as tingling arms, can also give the impression that someone else is sending electricity through your skin, or that emotions (such as happiness, grief or gloom) are being forced upon you. In all of these cases we feel, think or do something, but we do not experience having initiated it ourselves. The notion of control is missing. How is this possible?

If we do something, there is a double guiding system. A feed-forward system calculates how to perform a movement; for example, picking up a cup of tea and bringing it to our mouth. This system estimates the distance to the cup, notes where the handle is, calculates the position of your lips, etc. It designs the complex movement of the arm very rapidly, so that movement can be performed. A feed-backward system also exists. This system compares the calculated position of the hand to the actual position of the hand during the movement: it is a monitor. A correction takes place after only the smallest deviation from the calculated position by the actual position. This indeed allows us to pick up the teacup, lift it and bring it up to our mouth. In a diagram form, it looks something like Figure 7.3.

A goal is made into a plan. The plan is sent through and converted into a programme of actions and estimates: a willed intention. This programme is being performed by our locomotor system. At the same time a message is sent to the monitor and the programme is about to be carried out. The monitor controls the movement and thus the goal is achieved. If the movement deviates from the planned one, the monitor detects it and passes this through to the planning centre and the centre of intention will adjust the programme accordingly.

In the extraordinary experience of being controlled, something goes wrong, probably at the stage of informing the monitor. The movement is being performed but you did not know that this was about to happen. It feels as though you did not do it yourself and so you experience it as though you are not doing it yourself, but someone else is controlling you. This can happen with actions, but also with thoughts and emotions.

We more or less know the mechanism related to this in the brain, as shown in Figure 7.4.

A therapy manual 113

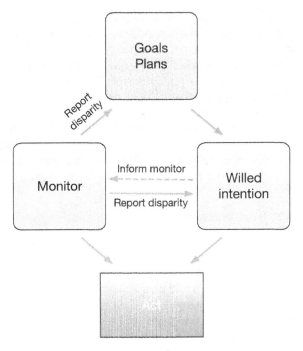

Figure 7.3 Diagram showing the feed-forward and feed-backward systems illustrating the feeling of being controlled.

Feed-forward and feed-backward systems in behaviour

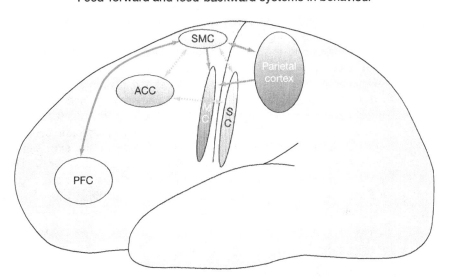

PFC = prefrontal cortex; SMC = supplementary motor cortex; MC = motor cortex; SC = sensory cortex; ACC = anterior cingulate cortex

Figure 7.4 Planning and controlling of movement by feed-forward and feed-backward systems in the brain.

The plans and goals are shaped in the frontal part of the brain (prefrontal cortex: PFC). The supplemental motor areas (SMA) convert the plan into a series of movements, which are fine-tuned in collaboration with the parietal cortex. This latter area enables us to imagine things spatially. The motor cortex (MC) controls the muscles and the movement starts. The sensory cortex (SC) in cooperation with the anterior cingulated cortex (ACC) performs the monitoring function. In the sensory cortex we feel our body and movement. The ACC compares the plan and the performance. Deviations are detected and passed through to the supplementary motor cortex and the plan of execution is adjusted. (Please do not bother memorising or understanding all these names!)

If being threatened becomes paranoia

The mechanism that causes enhanced suspicion is avoidance. Anyone who has had a car accident will feel tense during the next drive. Those who persist with driving will conquer their fear. Those who decide to abandon the car at the height of their fear learn to avoid cars and will probably have a raised heart rate when they are still in the car park the next time they plan to drive. Avoidance makes people more scared, and avoidance of driving a car increases fear. It is similar to the fear of dogs after having been bitten by one. Renewed contact with dogs, and experiencing that not all dogs bite, allows one to conquer fear. Those who decide to remain at a distance will always be taking (ever-increasing) safety measures. In the end, this may result in someone only going outdoors when wearing a thick coat, gloves and steel-tipped shoes! Such an individual will run away at the slightest sign of a dog, run into a building, or jump on a bus. In a short period of time the world has become engulfed with dogs that are after the person who has a dog phobia.

This description can also apply to suspicion. Paranoia increases through avoidance. The group of people opposing you seems to expand with other suspicious people, thus creating a world full of danger in which practically nobody can be trusted any more. Similar to the above-mentioned types of fear, going into the source of the fear is the best cure if it seems that the fear was not justified in the first place. However, in the case of extreme suspicion, people are usually not able to do that any more. The assumption of the extremely suspicious individual is that seeking out your pursuer could lead to death. Trying to see what the pursuer will really do is out of the question. Fear and avoidance form a sort of continuous whirlpool, and anyone caught in it will inevitably drown emotionally.

If voices make you angry or scare you

Many voices feed on the anger and fear of the person hearing them and that is why they try to make that person feel emotional. How does that work? Voices are language productions coming from a dark corner of our brain and are not thought up by us. Because the voices use vocal characteristics from someone else and because there are often recurring themes, the impression is created that others are involved. Sometimes the voices claim to have knowledge that the person hearing the voices does not; however, this is never the case once it has been tested. For example, ask the voice for today's (or tomorrow's) headline in the newspaper before you have read or heard it on the news. They do not know. Voices know what you know, never anything more. When we make a scan of the brain of someone at the precise moment voices are heard, we see that the same areas are active as those areas used during thinking and speaking. There is one exception to this (see Figure 7.5).

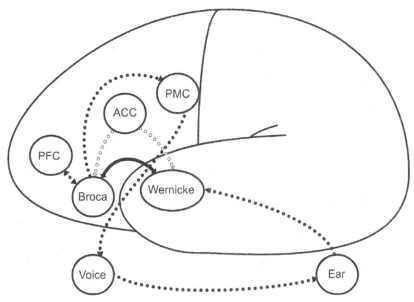

PFC = prefrontal cortex; ACC = anterior cingulate cortex; PMC = premotor cortex

Figure 7.5 The routes involved in thinking, speaking and listening.

Speech in the environment travels from our ear (Ear in Figure 7.5) to the area of listening, Wernicke's area. This is located just behind the ear. If we perceive our own thoughts as inner speech, this enters from the prefrontal cortex (PFC) and the area of speech (Broca's area) and subsequently travels into Wernicke's area too. How can Wernicke's area tell whether the speech has an internal source, initiated by us, or an external one? This is indicated by the anterior cingulate cortex (ACC). Thoughts travel directly from Broca's to Wernicke's area, but also indirectly through a monitoring centre in the ACC, which labels our thoughts as our thoughts. Speech travelling through the ear lacks such a label and Broca's area considers this to be external speech. The ACC is less active during hallucinations and so it can occur that thoughts coming from within are perceived as speech coming from outside.

Sometimes people hear their thoughts out loud and this experience is explained by the ACC letting something pass without labelling it as 'internal'. In other cases, people hear statements that they feel cannot come from themselves. One example is a man who hears that his mother cannot be trusted, yet he loves her very much and knows she is very sincere. How is that possible? It can happen with a surplus of dopamine in the mid brain. Dopamine deregulation leads to abnormal 'gating'. This means that all sorts of strange thoughts and peculiar ideas, but also coincidental observations, feelings on the skin, etc., are not being filtered but reach our consciousness. All sorts of unnecessary events are noticed and the worst part is that we pay attention to these events. We are used to the fact that events that enter the consciousness are important. It has been shown scientifically that only a fragment of all information in our brain at a certain moment is processed by our consciousness. For example, we are not aware of our digestion, whether our heart rate needs to go up or down, in which order we need to tighten which muscles, and which force to apply during cycling. A lot of information is filtered out and is dealt with at a subconscious level.

Whoever hears voices is therefore not responsible as a person for whatever the voices are saying. We are dealing with a temporary mutiny in the brain, causing strange things to enter our consciousness. Thus, voices originate from your own brain and nothing or nobody has anything to do with that. This fact detaches the voices from your own personality. On one hand that is a comfort; you have nothing to do with them. On the other hand, this can be threatening. Your personality is no longer in charge of the contents of your consciousness. So we need to restrain the voices and not give them too much power and freedom. How do you accomplish that? The most important advice is to remain calm. Voices get worse if you become emotional. The ability of the director in the ACC to guide your thoughts improves when your emotion centre (in the amygdala) remains calm. When dealing with an increased emotional state, the controlling parts of the brain in the frontal area and the ACC have a harder time to do their work.

A person who hears a voice talking to them without someone being present and who considers this to be a strange phenomenon of a psychological nature and who does not pay attention to it, is generally doing well. This often applies to people who consider the voice to be friendly and helpful, without this voice getting a grip on their own life.

It is different for people who conclude that the voices originate from beings that have a considerable influence over them and will harm them if they are not obeyed. The group of people who hear voices and are occupied all day long with their voices experience fear, lose friends, and avoid work and school. These people will often get into such trouble that professional treatment and the repression of the voices by medication is required.

Once the voices have gained a foothold, they often pursue a continuous existence. They can best achieve that goal when they are successful in scaring or upsetting the person hearing them. Voices evoking emotions, weakening the controlling and regulating influence of the ACC have an even greater chance of getting through to the consciousness. This might explain why people hearing voices do not experience them as particularly unpleasant at the beginning. People often relate that the voices turned increasingly against them over the course of many years. During that time, the voices usually discover the weak spots: remarks that can hurt and make the person feel emotional. Through the process of selection, as in evolution, neutral and friendly voices will not increase, while unfriendly, threatening and hurting voices will be present much longer. Just as rain is able to erode rocks in the long term, neural pathways in the brain become increasingly worn out and these pathways are travelled more often. Therefore, it is important to prevent paying any attention to the voices, or becoming emotional because of their content, and/or acting upon what the voices tell you to do.

When withdrawal is making your world smaller and smaller

Some people tend to withdraw from social contacts when troubles arise. This also occurs when extraordinary experiences demand increasing attention from the individual and when (at the same time) the environment becomes negative towards the explanations the individual presents for these extraordinary experiences. In this way, time spent in the outside world shifts towards time spent in the world of strange and extraordinary experiences. Those experiences can have such an impact that attention for school, work, friends and relatives decreases. Some people become completely fascinated by their experiences and become isolated from their social environment.

Earlier we read about the vulnerability of our brain when it comes to understanding reality. In fact, we constantly tend to make faulty assumptions, jump to conclusions, search to confirm our opinions, find connections that do not exist, etc. We really do need others to correct us and put our opinions into perspective. In this respect, an objective reality actually does not exist. Reality is a social construction. We agree upon what we assume to be a reality and what is not. With the passage of time, and cultural and scientific changes, each new period creates its own view on reality. The immutability of the universe has been replaced by the idea of a constantly changing and expanding one. Bacteria and viruses have replaced the idea of dangerous vapours as the cause of diseases. Physicians have abolished bloodletting.

The current scientific view on reality will keep on evolving. To be part of it, it is necessary for you to participate in the current ideas about reality. If you remain alone and isolated from others, sticking to your opinions will increasingly alienate you from others. For a better life it is therefore essential to keep in touch with other people. It is wise, before undertaking any action, to discuss your conclusions and proposed actions with someone else. One individual tends to wander off track, but a group of people is able to put things into proper perspective, which enables a sensible conclusion to be formed.

Convictions and habits to help you

We end this manual by listing the most important changes you need to achieve in your way of thinking:

1. Always come up with more than one explanation for every extraordinary experience. Putting things into perspective is the key to controlling negative feelings such as fear, anger, panic and despair.

2   Discuss your opinions with others and keep in mind that usually the majority are right. Talk about and negotiate possible explanations for whatever is happening to you with the people around you.
3   Be careful when you act upon your interpretation. We have seen that many interpretations have a weak foundation. Acting based on faulty assumptions can lead to trouble, and can also lead to ostracism/expulsion by others.
4   In the end, even extraordinary experiences are also just experiences. Generally, these experiences are caused by a disruption of the neuro-transmitters in the brain. In many cases the disruption eventually disappears in a natural way.

Good luck with keeping your negative emotions and extraordinary experiences under control!

Evaluate the metacognitive training. What did the patient learn? Ensure that you incorporate the most important information in the case formulation that you will develop in the next phase of the protocol.

(5) Case formulation and goal setting (one session)

Case formulation

Discuss the outcome of the CBT assessment phase with your patient and fill in the case formulation form (Appendix D) together (with the same text on both your and the patient's form). The outcomes are included in the case formulation on a general level (see Figure 7.6 for an example). In that way they do not cover one, but several situations within the same theme (A–D). You also include relevant life experiences and possible predispositions that influence symptoms (E). Basic (F) and intermediate assumptions (G) that are important are added in the appropriate boxes. Lastly, you describe the life experiences (E) that have led to the development of relevant basic and intermediate assumptions (see the next paragraph 'Why life experiences are included in the case formulation'). The case formulation has a collaborative character. It is very important that the patient recognises themself to a large extent in the case formulation. It is very positive if the patient suggests the text and the therapist agrees. The case formulation is very important because it forms the basis of the treatment plan and the interventions.

> **TIP:** Often there are many different extraordinary experiences that distress the patient. It can help to make a problem list with your patient on which you build a hierarchy of the symptoms. Just include the most important extraordinary experiences in the case formulation.

> **TIP:** Include the cognitive biases that have a strong influence on the patient's symptoms in the case formulation. Usually this is done best by verbalising them as automatic or intermediate assumptions, for example:
> - 'I quickly jump to the conclusion that people are of malicious intent' (jumping to conclusions bias).
> - 'If I don't regularly check my room, something might sneak up on me' (selective attention bias).
> - 'If I feel anxious, there must be danger' (emotional reasoning bias).
> - 'Coincidence does not exist' (covariation bias).

> **TIP:** Contextual factors, such as a parent with a severe mental disorder, or having a lot of socio-economic problems, can strongly influence symptoms. Someone who has debts and no money will benefit little from CBT when nothing is done about the financial problems. It is therefore important to include these contextual factors in the case formulation.

Why life experiences are included in the case formulation

The core of the CBT protocol is made up out of:

- challenging the negative automatic thoughts;
- becoming aware of the influence of cognitive biases;
- changing the reinforcing avoidance and safety behaviours that the patient performs.

In some patients, knowing what life experiences and underlying beliefs are of influence can be important, even at the start of therapy. Many ARMS individuals have suffered adversity in childhood or have been traumatised later in life. Sometimes clear and direct connections can be made between these previous experiences and extraordinary events in the present (e.g. a patient that sometimes hears a voice threatening him in a way similar to the way his mother used to when he was a child). Sometimes these interactions are indirect (e.g. a patient developed delusional-like ideas as a consequence of many previous violations of his trust). Besides this, many patients report certain (non-traumatic) experiences that they see as evidence for their negative expectations. In summary, connections between life experiences and extraordinary experiences can often be made. These interactions can be direct or indirect.

Direct influence of life experiences

Sometimes the connections are very clear. Someone, for instance, develops mild paranoid ideas after being assaulted or starts experiencing mild hallucinations after being sexually abused. But also less invasive experiences can be part of the 'evidence' that a patient has for their negative expectations. Direct questioning is often enough to determine what experiences are of influence:

> *T:* 'What happened that started you thinking that your colleagues wanted to get rid of you?'
> *T:* 'So you're afraid that at night a ghost might grab you. Where does that thought come from?'
> *T:* 'Do you see any relation between your current fears and earlier life experiences?'

Including these experiences in the case formulation is important. Often the evidence that patients have is quite thin. The realisation of this fact can have a therapeutic effect:

> *T:* 'So if I understand you correctly, this fear of ghosts started after you saw a frightening movie? And you never saw or experienced any proof of the existence of ghosts?'

Understanding the direct impact of adverse life experiences can function as an alternative explanation of extraordinary experiences in the present:

> *T:* 'Are you actually in that much danger when you go out? Or might it be that you have learned to expect danger because you were mugged in such an aggressive way?'

Indirect influence of life experiences

Life experiences also indirectly influence fear of extraordinary experiences. We know that adverse life events, such as childhood abuse or neglect, influence the development of basic assumptions about self, others and the world. These beliefs in turn influence intermediate assumptions and strategies that people develop. These factors influence how patients interpret and react to extraordinary experiences. Often patients with mild paranoia have 'learned' to mistrust others. And people who are burdened by hearing their own negative thoughts out loud frequently have 'damaged' self-esteem. In determining the indirect influence of adverse life experiences it is usually a good strategy to start with establishing what basic and intermediate beliefs are of influence. Sometimes these cognitions can be derived from what the patient verbalises during sessions:

> *P:* 'I just freeze when I lie in bed and see a fleeting shadow. Then I feel so vulnerable. I feel that I must stay in control. Or else ... or else I'll go mad.'

Sometimes interviewing techniques such as the 'downward arrow technique' are necessary to determine what core beliefs are in play:

> T: 'When you hear a strange sound in the house at night, what does that do to you?'
> P: 'It feels like I can't do anything.'
> T: 'The fact that you can't do anything, what does that mean to you?'
> P: 'It means that they can just kill me any minute.'
> T: 'What does that say about you?'
> P: 'That I'm totally defenceless.'

Setting treatment goals

Fill in the treatment goals form together (Appendix E). The treatment goals form differentiates between the reduction of symptoms and the improvement of the level of social functioning.

Formulate the goals in SMART terms (Specific, Measurable, Attainable, Relevant and Time bound). Operationalising the treatment goals in this manner helps you and your patient to stay focused on what the therapy is about.

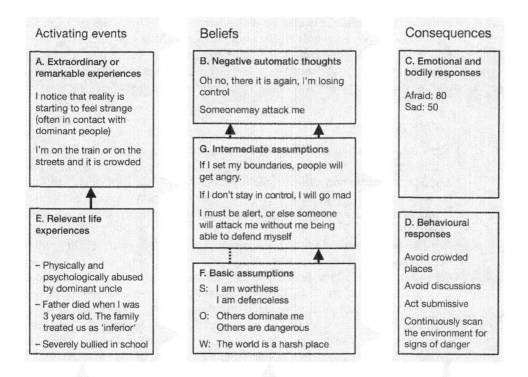

Figure 7.6 Completed case formulation form (S = self, O = others, W = world).

> **TIP:** Evaluate the therapy every five sessions using the formulated treatment goals.

(6) Cognitive behavioural intervention (6 to 12 sessions)

In some patients hardly any CBT interventions have to be used. Their distress caused by the extraordinary experiences decreases strongly after the normalising psycho-educational information and the insights that they have gained in the metacognitive training. In others, extensive CBT has to be given in order to make changes occur. You tailor the treatment to the individual patient.

The most important intervention within the CBT protocol is without a doubt the performance of behavioural experiments and exposure. 'Experiencing is believing'. Patients with ARMS are less inflexible in their thinking than patients with frank psychosis. Moreover, you and your patient have already worked together on a few things. In this phase of the therapy the patient usually already doubts his negative expectations to a certain extent. If this is the case, design a behavioural experiment and let the patient carry it out. Within this protocol you are always working towards a behavioural experiment or exposure assignment. Continuously ask yourself: 'Is the patient prepared to perform a behavioural experiment?' If this is not the case, investigate what causes the patient's reluctance and use cognitive techniques to challenge those assumptions.

Treatment plan

The case formulation should incorporate all the relevant information about the extraordinary experiences. Important questions to ask are: 'What central assumptions cause and maintain the distress?' and 'What behaviours reinforce those assumptions?' A central question is: 'What assumptions have to be modified in order for this patient to give up his avoidance strategies and continue his normal functioning?'

The next question is: 'What assumptions are most easily challenged by performing behavioural experiments?' The following interventions are used, depending on the motivation of the patient and the content of the case formulation.

Generally you start challenging automatic negative interpretations with cognitive techniques such as Socratic questioning. Asking questions in such a way that patients start to think about their dysfunctional beliefs can induce change. Socratic questioning usually has more effect than trying to convince patients. The aim is to induce doubt about the veracity of the interpretations or reinforce the doubt that is already present. This will motivate the patient to perform behavioural experiments or exposure assignments in the session, or as homework. Extensively discuss the results of the behavioural experiments or exposure assignments. The patient has to integrate this new information into his changing cognitive explanatory model of the extraordinary experiences. This cycle sometimes has to be repeated for each relevant dysfunctional assumption.

> **TIP:** Choose wisely at what level you intervene. In some patients with a fear of ghosts, therapy will, for instance, focus on the question: 'Do ghosts really exist and haunt your house?' In others this question will be ignored, for instance, because the patient is so convinced that ghosts exist that this question would only lead to fruitless discussions. The question to then ask is: 'Are ghosts actually out to hurt you?' Once the patient starts to doubt this, the question may be posed whether it would not be wiser to start ignoring the ghosts.

Intervening with psycho-education

Psycho-education plays an important role in the entire treatment protocol. Also in this phase psycho-education can be selectively used to challenge negative interpretations of extraordinary events (see earlier examples and descriptions on how to apply psycho-education).

Cognitive challenging

In this phase you use all the CBT techniques that you have at your disposal to challenge negative automatic thoughts and to stimulate the patient to consider alternative interpretations. By this time in therapy, the patient has already been practising with developing alternative interpretations for several weeks. If the patient finds it difficult to think of alternative explanations, for instance, as a result of a strong dogmatic reasoning bias, you can use the 'pie chart technique' (see Appendix F). This technique can be used and repeated for several situations, until the patient is able to do it himself. Classify each explanation as 'somewhat coincidental' or as a reason that has nothing to do with the patient.

> *Therapist:* Sometimes you think that your neighbour doesn't like you and wants to bully you until you move. You just told me that you base this presumption on her behaviour. As an example you mentioned an incident last week. You met her in the hallway and instead of stopping she said hello and rushed on. You indicate that you can't think of an alternative interpretation for her behaviour other than that it proves that she wants you to move. You find this thought 80 per cent credible.
> *Patient:* That's correct.
> *Therapist:* Let's look into this. If we would take a different situation in mind, a situation that isn't about you. What can be the reasons that people say hello and then rush on when they encounter someone they know?

Patient: Well. It can be that the person is late for an appointment or for his work.
Therapist: Very well. We'll put that in the left column on the form. The person's running late for an appointment or is in a hurry. What are other possible reasons?
Patient: Maybe the person has a bad mood or is cranky and therefore avoids talking to others.
Therapist: Okay. And what else?
Patient: hum, difficult . . .
Therapist: Can it be that someone is shy and finds it scary to talk to others?
Patient: Yes, that's possible. It's also possible that the person thinks that the other person doesn't like them.
Therapist: Exactly. So there are two additional possibilities; let's note them. Any other possibilities?
Patient: It could be that the person is deep in thought. I have that myself sometimes.
Therapist: Very good. We include that as a possible reason. Let's see, we've thought of five possible reasons why someone would say hello and then rush on when they encounter someone they know. We also add a sixth category 'other' because for sure we have missed some reasons. Let's look at these alternative reasons and see to what extent these could apply to your situation. What do you consider the chance that your neighbour was late for an appointment or work?
Patient: Well, she's a nurse and works quite hard, so I would say 50 per cent.
Therapist: Okay, we note that behind it and include it in the pie chart.

The therapist and patient do this for all the possible explanations and, finally, when the pie chart is already (partly) filled, for the original assumption. After doing this the therapist and patient discuss the credibility of the original interpretation.

TIP: Don't linger too long in cognitive techniques when the patient strongly doubts his negative assumptions. Despite great doubt about the credibility of negative assumptions, most patients would rather avoid than perform a behavioural experiment.

Other useful techniques that go well with the pie chart technique are the historical test or discussing the evidence in favour and against certain assumptions.

Therapist: So you find the idea 75 per cent credible. What matters are in favour of the presumption that when derealisation occurs, you will totally lose control and be stuck in derealisation forever?

Patient: Well. It worsened lately. And I've noticed several times that only cutting myself takes away the derealisation. Plus, my mother sometimes says that I'm a crazy child.

Therapist: All right. Let's write that down in the left column. And what matters indicate that this negative thought is not true?

Patient: ... (thinks) Well, I haven't gone mad yet, while I've been having derealisation for more than six months now.

Therapist: That's a very good point. What else?

Patient: I don't know.

Therapist: How often do you think that you had those derealisation feelings in the last six months?

Patient: Pfff, more than 50 times.

Therapist: Okay, and did you cut yourself every time?

Patient: No, I think that happened about eight times. Often I'm with other people. I can't start cutting myself with other people around. They'd freak out.

Therapist: So do I understand correctly that in the 42 remaining times the derealisation stopped without you hurting yourself?

Patient: It does take longer, usually about half an hour. But yes, up till now it did stop every time.

Therapist: Okay, we note that in the right column. What else pleads against the idea that you'll be stuck in derealisation forever?

Patient: I've also read in the manual that it is actually quite a normal phenomenon. You told me that there's no disorder in which people are constantly in a state of total derealisation. You also explained that it most probably increased because it worries me so much.

Therapist: That's correct. You remembered that very well. Let's note those things. What else?

Patient: My mother tells me that I will be all right now that I've started this therapy. She also told me that she has these kinds of experiences every now and then.

Therapist: Good. We also note that. In summary, there appear to be quite a few indicators that contradict your negative expectations. We are inclined to look at things that confirm our frightening ideas. This makes us miss other things; that's the selective attention bias about which we spoke during the metacognitive training. Because you were so afraid, it was difficult for you to take a moment and view it from a more objective standpoint. If you now look at it, how convincing do you find the thought that you will lose control and be stuck in derealisation forever?

Patient: A lot less convincing, about 30 per cent.

The negative scenarios that patients expect to occur are often not impossible, but usually highly unlikely. Therefore, calculating cumulative probability can be very useful (Appendix G). It is comforting to the patient when the odds of an event actually occurring are very low. Anxious patients initially always overestimate the chance that a certain catastrophic event will occur.

(The therapist and patient look at the cumulative probability calculation form)

Therapist: You are afraid that a paedophile will abduct and abuse your son who is 7 years old if you don't constantly keep an eye on him on the playground. How do you estimate the odds that this will actually happen?

Patient: . . . about 85 per cent.

Therapist: All right. Before your child is actually abducted and abused several events have to occur. Just like in a movie scenario. It doesn't just happen. Several conditions have to be met. Do you understand what I mean?

Patient: Yes.

Therapist: Let's have a look at those different steps in the process. What's the first step?

Patient: Well, there will have to be a paedophile looking for a victim at the playground when we go there.

Therapist: That's correct. Actually these are two steps. There must be a paedophile while you are there and he must be looking for a victim to abuse. We note those two steps. What are the next steps?

Patient: He'll have to lure my son with candy or some sort of excuse.

Therapist: That's correct, we write that down. But before that there's another step, because he then apparently chose your son as his potential victim.

Patient: Yes, that's correct.

Therapist: So we note that as well. What's next?

Patient: He will have to take my son without anyone noticing it.

Therapist: All right. Is that the last step?

Patient: I think so, yes.

Therapist: Now please determine how probable you find each step.

Patient: That a paedophile is at the playground while we are there I find 50 per cent probable. That he will choose my son as his victim I give 20 per cent – there are always many children. That he is able to lure my son I find 20 per cent probable. My son knows how I think about talking to strangers. That the paedophile will be able to abduct my son without anyone noticing I give 25 per cent. There are always a lot of parents from our neighbourhood around.

Therapist: Do you agree that all these steps will have to occur for your worst nightmare to actually happen?

Patient: Yes.

Therapist: That means that we must multiply all these steps. When we do so, we see that the total chance that a paedophile will abduct and abuse your child is only 0.45 per cent.

Patient: Yes . . . that's quite a bit lower than I imagined . . ., I hadn't really thought about the fact that several conditions have to be met for it to actually happen.

Therapist: It is very important that you realise that. How credible do you now find the thought that a paedophile will abduct and abuse your son if you don't constantly keep an eye on him on the playground?

Patient: A lot less, say 40 per cent.

Therapist: Okay, that's quite a bit less. Would you now also dare to let go of your safety behaviour? For instance, by not paying attention to your son for ten minutes while he plays and instead read a magazine with your back turned towards him?

In addition to cumulative probability calculation, gathering information from the Internet can also be useful.

Therapist: You believe that there is a great chance that someone will break into your house and hurt you. How often do you think burglaries occur in the Netherlands?

Patient: I have no idea.

Therapist: Me neither, let's find out. Look, here on the site of the Dutch Central Bureau of Statistics. It reports yearly on all kinds of societal phenomena such as crime figures. Here it says that in 2011 about 1 per cent of the Dutch population was confronted with some form of burglary. That appears to include attempts at burglary. What do you think about that figure?

Patient: Wow, that is quite low. I thought it would be more. Apparently it happens less than I thought. You do read and hear a lot about burglary.

Therapist: Yes, the media report about these things, because sensation sells. And people like to talk about these matters. That makes it seem as though it occurs very frequently, while in reality it does not. Here we see the effect of selective attention once more.

Sometimes it is necessary to enhance the motivation to change. Discussing the pros and cons of a certain avoidance or safety strategy is a useful technique. This can be done by making two columns, or by Socratic interviewing.

Therapist: So you are afraid that ghosts will kill you in your sleep. In the daytime, you doubt this thought. But you perform a lot of safety strategies, such as leaving the door and the curtains open, and sleeping with your head underneath the blankets.

Patient: That's right. I know that it sounds silly. I realise that it is highly unlikely, but at night I'm just terrified.

Therapist: Very clear. I wonder, have you ever really been attacked?

Patient: No. Not yet. But I always sleep with the door and curtains opened and always fully underneath the blankets.

Therapist: Always?

Patient: Well, I don't do those things when my girlfriend sleeps over. I don't want her to know of my fear of ghosts.

Therapist: Okay. And have you ever been attacked when your girlfriend slept over?

Patient: No, otherwise I wouldn't be sitting here . . .
Therapist: I see. And how do you explain that? I mean, since you closed the door and curtains? How does the presence of your girlfriend protect you?
Patient: I don't know actually. I think I'm more afraid that they'll grab me when I'm alone. I don't really know why . . .
Therapist: Okay. . . . There's something else that I'm hoping you can explain to me. Can you tell me something more about those ghosts? What are they made of? Do they consist of matter? Can you touch them?
Patient: No. I don't think that ghosts have matter like you and me. They can go through everything. That's what makes them so scary. You don't see them, but any second they could come through a wall and grab you.
Therapist: So you believe that they can go through walls without any problem.
Patient: I think so, yes.
Therapist: And floors and doors . . .?
Patient: Also I guess. . . .
Therapist: (thinks). . . . There's something that I find difficult to grasp. Maybe you can help me understand it. If ghosts can go through walls, doors and floors, why would pulling the duvet over your head protect you? Can't the ghosts easily go through your duvet as well?
Patient: Ha-ha . . . that's a good question. I really never thought about that. . . . Well, it does sound very contradictory. Maybe they can, maybe they cannot. . . .

Discuss how the patient can obtain additional information to determine whether the automatic negative thought or the alternative thought is more realistic. In most cases this is done in the form of a behavioural experiment.

Behavioural experiments and exposure assignments

The behavioural experiments and exposure assignments usually target intermediate assumptions. You try to test the credibility of the negative assumptions and the utility of the avoidance and safety behaviours. Use all your creativity to devise valuable experiments. An important question in doing this is: 'What experiment does the patient need to perform, or what situation does he need to expose himself to, to become fully convinced that his original negative expectation is actually false?'

TIP: Actively involve the patient in designing the behavioural experiments and exposure assignments. Most patients are quite capable of doing this after an explanation of the rationale.

Vignette

A patient was afraid that thinking about something would also make it happen (thought–event fusion) or would make her do it (thought–action fusion). She constantly monitored her thoughts and was afraid to lose control, because losing control would result in catastrophe. Once she understood what the most important maintaining cognitions were, the patient devised several behavioural experiments as homework. She finalised them with her therapist. Each experiment lasted a week. In the first experiment the therapist bought a lottery ticket. The patient programmed her smart phone to help her remember to think about her therapist winning a big prize (more than 1,000 euros) at least ten times a day. He did not win. In the next experiment she thought about herself getting the flu. In the following experiment she thought about the therapist dying in a traffic accident. She then thought about slashing her plant with a big kitchen knife. Lastly she thought about running over her sister (who approved of the thought experiment) with her parent's car. Her preoccupation decreased considerably after performing these experiments, because she experienced that thinking about an event did not result in an actual event or behaviour. She was able to let go of her avoidance behaviours after these experiments.

> **TIP:** Make sure that the possible outcomes of the behavioural experiment are well defined. In the first few experiments you can use the 'behavioural experiment form' (Appendix H). Ensure that the possible outcomes are mutually exclusive and that there are no other possible outcomes.

> **TIP:** Let the patient use the 'behavioural experiments and exposure assignments homework form' (Appendix I). Let him fill these in before and after performing the exercises.

Therapist: You are convinced that you will become totally depersonalised and stay like that for hours if you don't suppress the mild feeling of depersonalisation.
Patient: Yes.
Therapist: Let's see how we could investigate whether this is actually true. Do you have any idea how we could test this assumption?
Patient: I could try not to suppress the depersonalisation feelings. A problem is that I don't have them every day.
Therapist: Looking in the mirror for a longer period evokes feelings of depersonalisation in most people. Could we use that?

Patient: Yes. We could do that and test whether I will stay depersonalised for several hours.

Therapist: Very well. That seems like an appropriate experiment to me. What we need to do now is neatly work out the experiment, just like scientists do. I would like to use this form [therapist gives the behavioural experiment form to the patient]. The belief that you want to test is: 'If I don't suppress the depersonalisation, then I will stay depersonalised for hours.' Is that correct?

Patient: Yes, that's correct.

Therapist: We note that in A. And how convinced are you now that this will actually happen?

Patient: About 60 per cent.

Therapist: Noted. And what's the alternative thought that we want to test? Make sure to formulate it as an 'if . . . then . . .' expectation as well.

Patient: If I don't suppress the depersonalisation, then it will automatically disappear within an hour.

Therapist: That looks like a fine alternative thought to me. How credible do you find this thought?

Patient: That would be the remaining 40 per cent.

Therapist: Okay. Next is designing the experiment that we are going to perform. Like I explained earlier, repetition is important. Five experiments are more convincing than one. Could you practise with evoking derealisation feelings by looking in the mirror every night this week?

Patient: Yes, I will.

Therapist: So we write down that in the coming week you're going to stare into the mirror until depersonalisation feelings start at least once a day. You don't suppress these feelings and just let them be. You wait and observe how long the feelings persist. After the depersonalisation feelings are gone, you note on the homework form 'behavioural experiments and exposure assignments' – how it went. All right?

Patient: Yes.

Therapist: What outcome would confirm your original thought or conviction?

Patient: If the depersonalisation feelings would indeed persist.

Therapist: How long exactly?

Patient: On average, at least one hour.

Therapist: All right. We note that: 'If the depersonalisation feelings persist longer than an hour on average', and if the depersonalisation feelings last less than an hour on average – would that confirm your alternative thought?

Patient: Yes it would.

Therapist: Do you feel that this experiment is convincing enough?

Patient: Definitely. I find it a bit scary, but I know that I have to confront my fears sooner or later.

> *Therapist:* Very well. Do you want to practise it here or are you going to manage to do it at home?
> *Patient:* I'll manage.
> *Therapist:* Okay, good luck then. Don't forget to use the homework form. Call or email me if you have any questions concerning the experiment.

During the week the patient performed the experiment.

> *Therapist:* How did the experiment go?
> *Patient:* Actually quite well. Looking in the mirror indeed evoked feelings of depersonalisation.
> *Therapist:* Good. And did you succeed not to suppress those feelings?
> *Patient:* Yes. It went pretty well. I just sat down on the couch and waited.
> *Therapist:* And what happened when you did that?
> *Patient:* Not too much actually. The mild depersonalisation persisted for a while, but also subsided quite quickly. On average it didn't persist for more than 15 minutes.
> *Therapist:* My complements for the work you've done this week. What did you learn from the experiments?
> *Patient:* Mainly that my biggest fear didn't become reality. I mean, it is still a very unpleasant feeling. But I've learned that it disappears after a while and doesn't last for hours.
> *Therapist:* Okay. And what conclusion do you draw from this?
> *Patient:* Apparently I don't have to go through that much trouble to suppress the depersonalisation feelings. They aren't harmful and maybe it would be better to just ignore them.
> *Therapist:* Very good. Let's see how you can assure that you will actually start doing that.
> *Patient:* Okay.

TIP: A hierarchy can be used in the exposure assignments, because by organising the exposure assignments from easier to more difficult, the step to start with the assignments becomes reduced. Alternatively, using a hierarchy you may unconsciously convey the message that the patient is not able to perform more difficult assignments. This may have the opposite effect of what you are trying to achieve, that is, letting the patient realise that his fearful expectations are unrealistic.

TIP: Repeat experiments in different contexts. The result of one experiment can be coincidental. That is less likely for five experiments with the same outcome. Ask the patient what is necessary for him to really believe that the results are not based on coincidence or luck.

In association with your patient, design all kinds of appropriate behavioural experiments and exposure exercises to test conditional and instrumental thoughts. Focus on replacing avoidance and safety strategies by alternative behaviours that match the formulated treatment goals.

> **TIP:** Table 7.11 shows several examples of behavioural experiments.

Homework in this phase

Perform homework assignments (cognitive or behavioural challenging techniques).

> **TIP:** Extensively discuss the homework assignments every session. For example, How did it go? Did you manage to register what we agreed upon? What was the effect of omitting your safety strategies? What new experiments could be useful?

Distancing

Distancing oneself from the extraordinary experiences is an automatic reaction in most patients when the credibility of the dysfunctional beliefs decreases. They increasingly ignore extraordinary experiences and focus their attention more and more on normal, everyday activities. They often notice that this results in a decrease in frequency and intensity of extraordinary events. In other patients, distancing is an important and explicit step in the treatment process. This occurs especially in patients who suffer from negative aggressive or sexual intrusive thoughts or low frequent negative voices that they try to suppress.

Evaluate your patient's symptoms and discuss whether distancing from the extraordinary experiences is something that requires explicit attention. If this is the case, discuss distancing with your patient.

EXAMPLE

'Distancing from intrusive extraordinary experiences is an important step in achieving your treatment goals. You've learned a lot and made quite considerable progress. However, some extraordinary experiences keep attracting your attention. I would like to investigate whether it would be possible for you to distance yourself more from these experiences that bother you. Distancing means a decreased involvement and decreased reacting to a once-disrupting activating event. It is interesting to see what

you could do with this knowledge. Many people that are distressed by negative intrusive thoughts feel addressed by these thoughts or draw negative conclusions about themselves, because they have them: 'I must be a bad person, otherwise I wouldn't have these nasty thoughts.' And someone who is distressed by hearing a negative voice that calls him a 'loser' will only feel involved when deep down inside he believes or fears that he is indeed a loser. Extraordinary experiences, such as negative intrusive thoughts or negative voices, resemble bullying children. They can only hurt you with their verbal abuse if you let them; remember 'sticks and stones may break my bones . . .'

Also, you don't recognise yourself in the content of your intrusive experiences. Could you imagine feeling less involved with the intrusive experiences? What would be necessary to achieve this?'

Discuss how the patient could reduce his involvement with the intrusive experiences.

> **TIP:** Start working on self-esteem (see next paragraph) if the patient involves strongly with the content because he/she believes or fears that the content of the intrusive thoughts is true, or when he draws very negative conclusions about himself. Motivate the patient to start trying to ignore the extraordinary experiences parallel to this.

EXAMPLE

'Once you've decided to stop feeling addressed by the content of the intrusive extraordinary experiences, the next step is to stop reacting to these experiences. The metaphor of bullying children is again useful. What bullying children want is to elicit a reaction. That's what they're after. Just like bullying by children your intrusive experiences will reduce in frequency and intensity if you ignore them. A bullying child will quickly be bored and look for something else to do when it notices that the potential victim doesn't even notice his actions. Suppression appears to be an effective strategy in the short term. In the long term, however, it results in you constantly being occupied with these negative experiences. It is as though you're standing in the ocean and try to push a ball under water. Paradoxically, the harder you push it, the more counterforce it will produce and the more you get caught in a never-ending struggle. This law of physics also applies to extraordinary experiences. They appear to thrive on the negative energy that is released by your irritation or anxiety. But what would happen if you just let go of the ball? It will be right in your face for a moment. But eventually it will drift away on the waves or current. Ignoring the ball will have the effect that it disappears out of

Table 7.11 Examples of behavioural experiments

Dysfunctional assumption	Alternative assumption	Behavioural experiment
Having extraordinary experiences means I'm crazy	Extraordinary experiences are also normal experiences	Ask ten friends/acquaintances whether they have ever experienced anything extraordinary
If I have a negative feeling, something very bad is going to happen	If I have a negative feeling, this doesn't necessarily mean something bad will happen	Monitor negative feelings on a form, and bad events on another form during several weeks. Then compare the two lists
If I experience feelings of derealisation, I will totally lose control	If I experience feelings of derealisation, nothing terrible will happen	Evoke derealisation and test whether control is lost and disaster occurs
If I don't suppress depersonalisation feelings, they'll never subside	If I don't suppress depersonalisation feelings, they'll subside automatically	Evoke depersonalisation and test whether the feeling subsides
If I don't protect myself, I will be attacked by a ghost	If I don't protect myself, nothing will happen	Stop using safety strategies
I must suppress negative thoughts, or else I will perform them (in thought action fusion)	Thinking something doesn't mean that I will actually do it	Consciously evoke negative thoughts/not suppressing negative thoughts/explicitly worsening negative thoughts
If someone walks behind me in the street, then he is probably following me	If someone walks behind me in the street, that doesn't mean that he's following me	Choose unusual routes and see if the person follows you; or stop and let the person pass. Then look and see whether the person turns to check on you
Everybody looks at me while I'm riding the subway	Some people look at me in the subway. However, most have something better to do than to look at me	Count how many times someone looks at you in the subway. Also count how often people don't look at you

Table 7.11 continued

Dysfunctional assumption	Alternative assumption	Behavioural experiment
People know what I think	My thoughts can't be heard or read by others	Think things 'out loud' that should lead to certain consequences if the person hears it. For instance: thinking something that should evoke a reaction, e.g. that his shoelaces are untied, that there is a large sum of money lying behind him, insults, etc
People often talk about me	People don't talk about me	If you see two people talking and think that they are talking about you, then go over there and listen to what they're talking about or find out whether the conversation suddenly stops
My colleagues laugh at me behind my back	My colleagues laugh about all kinds of things, they're not laughing at me	When you hear your colleagues laugh, then go over there and try to participate in making jokes
Something or someone moves things in my house, because things are not always where I left them [excessive trust in own memory]	My memory isn't perfect. If things are misplaced, it could be that I did that myself but forgot about it	The patient leaves the therapy room. The therapist moves one item. The patient has to determine what was moved (can also be done at the patient's home)
If I look at someone in the street too long, he will harm me	Most people in the street don't harm me	Look at people longer than usual and note their reactions

sight. Not involving and not reacting that's what it's all about. Ignoring these experiences is something that you will have to learn. With ignoring I mean literally acting as if you don't even notice the extraordinary experience. That is something that you are not used to and requires some practice. Can you imagine that not feeling involved and not reacting could have the effect that you will be less distressed by these extraordinary experiences? Can you imagine yourself ignoring these experiences?'

> **TIP:** Make sure that the patient understands how you ignore something. Some patients will keep suppressing the negative experiences covertly. It can help to practise ignoring with your patient. For instance, let him read a magazine for five minutes while you try to distract him by talking to him. Let the patient experience how it feels to act as if he really does not hear you and focuses on the task, reading the magazine.

It may be helpful to perform an imaginary 'theatrical exercise' in distancing from the extraordinary experiences.

EXAMPLE

'Close your eyes and imagine you're in an empty theatre standing on the podium . . . you're all alone. . . . Take your time. . . . Look around you. . . . Please describe how the theatre looks on the inside. . . . What else do you see? What do the chairs look like? . . . Now imagine that the intrusive experiences start. . . . What does that look like? [let the patient visualise his experiences]. . . . Okay, now leave the podium . . ., walk down the aisle towards the last row. . . . Have a seat in the last row. . . . You now become a spectator of what is happening in your own mind, namely the intrusive extraordinary experiences. . . . Relax . . ., just relax . . . you have no part in this play, you just observe it . . . . Observe the intrusive extraordinary experiences . . ., don't feel involved . . ., don't react . . ., just let them be . . ., distance yourself from them . . ., become indifferent to them. . . . You know that you can be strong and indifferent. . . . You don't feel involved . . ., you don't fight the intrusive extraordinary experiences . . ., you don't need to suppress them . . ., you just relax. . . . The intrusive experiences will disappear eventually. . . . They will become weaker . . ., and weaker. . . .'

> **TIP:** In performing this exercise you have to make a little theatre yourself. You're directive and induce detachment and relaxation. Help the patient to 'get into the exercise'. Ask for sensory details. Make him the director of it all.

Negative basic assumptions

Many patients have negative basic assumptions that influence their interpretations of events. That is why they are included in the case formulation. Working on basic assumptions can have the effect that patients start interpreting extraordinary events in a less negative way. Moreover, it is probable that this will decrease the chance of reinstatement of the distress caused by the extraordinary experiences. Working on negative basic assumptions is done in two ways:

1. challenging basic assumptions (focused on the present);
2. doing trauma work with the experiences that have led the patient to develop those negative basic assumptions (focused on the past).

Together with your patient, determine whether there are important negative basic assumptions that influence the distress caused by the extraordinary experiences.

Cognitive challenging

Negative basic assumptions about the self and negative expectations of others are often polarised thoughts, such as: 'I'm a loser', 'I'm a bad person', 'I'm defenceless', 'Others are untrustworthy', or 'Others are evil'. These cognitions are susceptible to challenging by cognitive techniques such as the historical test or behavioural experiments.

Vignette

Farid is a 22-year-old student. His father was an abusive man who used to emphasise that Farid was a useless boy. His mother was a weak woman who did not stand up for her son. Farid was bullied at school and developed very negative ideas about himself, such as 'I am a loser' and 'I can't do anything right'. Recently, Farid became depressed and started to hear an 'inner voice' at low frequency that negatively comments on his behaviour. This occurs especially when he has to perform in his studies; for example, when he has to give a presentation. He is distressed by the voice. He fears that the voice is correct when it criticises him. Farid and his therapist decided to start working on his negative self-esteem. They reviewed the evidence that Farid has for and against his negative thoughts. They used multidimensional evaluation to target the dichotomous nature of Farid's negative self-esteem and performed several behavioural experiments in which Farid carried out complex tasks and experienced that he did most things 'right'. Challenging his negative self-esteem with cognitive techniques made Farid judge himself more realistically. He learned how damaging his youth had been. He also realised that the negative basic assumptions were totally incongruent with his actual functioning. The idea that he was a loser and an incompetent person lost credibility. This made it a lot easier for him to ignore the negative inner voice, since it was clearly wrong. Ignoring the voice had the effect that the frequency decreased, further empowering Farid's self-esteem.

Multidimensional evaluating is a useful technique in challenging negative basic assumptions. You can use the form 'multidimensional evaluating' (Appendix J). First, you have the patient judge themself on the dimension that you want to challenge (e.g. 'I'm a weakling, 80 per cent credible'). Then the patient selects two people who have extreme scores on the selected dimension (e.g. weak versus strong), one person who scores very high (e.g. 'Jasper, a very strong person') and one person who scores very low (e.g. 'Bernard, a weakling'). You then ask the patient to determine what five characteristics made them decide to select those two people. You put these characteristics on the form with their counterparts on the other end of the line (e.g. physical strength–physical weakness). In the end the patient has selected ten different characteristics that they apparently find important in determining someone's score on that dimension. The next step is to let the patient rate the two other people and lastly self-rating on all ten characteristics (0–10) by putting a mark on the line on the form. After doing this, discuss the patient's mean total score, which usually is less negative than the patient's original judgement.

> *Therapist:* When we view the judgements of 'weak' Bernard, strong 'Jasper', and yourself, we see that you rate yourself very low on having support from others. On many other characteristics, such as perseverance, toughness, physical strength and optimism you rate yourself well above Bernard. Your mean score is also above average. Apparently you're not that much of a weakling. What do you think of this outcome?
>
> *Patient:* I've never really thought about it that much. I've just always believed that I was a weakling. When I look at these scores, that doesn't appear to be correct.
>
> *Therapist:* That's right. You are now looking at this question in an objective way. It is important to realise that you yourself choose what characteristics determine whether someone is a weak or a strong person. It is also important to notice that you give yourself pretty high rates on those factors.
>
> *Patient:* That's correct. Somehow I just never paid attention to those things.
>
> *Therapist:* When people have assumed something, they usually don't tend to critically think about it that much any more. We usually seek for confirmation of our beliefs.
>
> *Patient:* I recognise that.
>
> *Therapist:* How credible do you now find the thought 'I'm a weakling' after we did this exercise?
>
> *Patient:* A lot less . . ., about 40 per cent.
>
> *Therapist:* Very well. That is a much more realistic judgement of yourself. Your strong characteristics also deserve some place in the sun! Let's strengthen them.

TIP: Again, if possible let the patient perform behavioural experiments or exposure assignments. Are there situations that the patient avoids because of negative expectations based on their negative self-esteem? If so, motivate the patient to expose themself to these stimuli and test whether their negative expectancies actually occur.

Reinforcing self-esteem

There are several useful CBT techniques to improve self-esteem. For instance, the 'reinforcing self-esteem exercise', which was found to be effective in a randomised clinical treatment trial (Hall and Tarrier, 2003) (see Appendix K). Possibly, competitive memory training (van der Gaag, van Oosterhout, Daalman, Sommer and Korrelboom, 2012) can be used as a technique to let the patient feel what they already rationally know, such as feeling strong or valuable. In case of excessive worry, metacognitions about the worrying can be challenged. Depending on the case formulation, other interventions can be used here.

Trauma-focused interventions

In some patients the negative self-esteem or negative expectations of others do not respond well to cognitive challenging. Certain life experiences have been so damaging for the patient, as it were, that they still prove that no one can be trusted or that he is a loser or guilty. It can be very useful to treat these damaging experiences with trauma-focused interventions such as *in vivo* exposure with rescripting or eye movement desensitisation and reprocessing. This can take away the negative basic assumptions by reducing credibility in the present. Treating the effects of damaging life experiences can reduce the distress caused by the extraordinary experiences.

In other patients direct relations between traumatic events and extraordinary experiences in the present are clearer. For instance, people develop mild paranoia after being aggressively victimised, start to fear ghosts after a relative has died, or become burdened by negative intrusive thoughts that are directly related to psychological abuse in their childhood. Trauma-focused techniques can be a valuable addition to cognitive challenging in these patients.

Vignette

A year ago two men sexually confronted Jessica. She just escaped from being raped. In that same period her brother was severely beaten up in a bar fight. She started to feel unsafe on the streets after these two experiences. She started to think that there might be people out in the streets who are trying to hurt her. She knows these thoughts are probably not true, but she is afraid and avoids going out as much as possible. She stopped going out at night and avoided eye contact with other people. In the end Jessica stopped going to work because of her fears. Her employer advised her to seek help.

Jessica was not easily motivated for exposure assignments. Considering this fact and also the obvious relationship between the start of the anxiety and her negative life experiences, Jessica and her therapist decided to use prolonged exposure on the memories of the sexual assault and seeing her brother on the intensive care. After three sessions of exposure Jessica notices that she was less occupied with the negative memories. She also became more receptive to cognitive challenging of her negative expectations. As a response to this, the credibility of her belief that people may be trying to hurt her decreased. Jessica started *in vivo* exposure assignments, such as walks and bicycle rides in her neighbourhood. Eventually she visited the crowded city centre on her own.

Homework in this stage

- Perform behavioural experiments and exposure assignments.
- Practise with cognitive techniques, such as multidimensional evaluation of negative self-esteem.

(7) Post-assessment (one session)

Administer the CAARMS (or SIPS), DACOBS, BDI2 and BAI in the same manner as in the pre-assessment.

The most important instrument to discuss is the CAARMS (or SIPS) interview. There are three possible outcomes:

1. Symptoms have decreased significantly; the patient no longer meets ARMS criteria.
2. Symptoms have not changed significantly; the patient still meets ARMS criteria.
3. Symptoms have worsened or the patient transitioned to psychosis.

Discuss the CAARMS (or SIPS) score extensively. In most cases the patient will no longer meet ARMS criteria. Discuss the differences between the baseline and post-assessment scores on the other measurements. Link these changes to the work done in therapy. What was the effect of challenging negative thoughts and stopping avoidance behaviours? What did the patient consider the most useful things that were learned?

If symptoms did not change significantly, then consult one of your colleagues for advice. If you and your colleagues do not see any options for further intervention, then discuss with the patient what to do next. First, discuss how the patient feels about the therapy not delivering what they probably hoped for. Second, discuss alternative treatment options, such as omega-3 fatty acid or antidepressants. The patient's motivation will be dependent on the level of distress that they experience.

If the patient has indeed made a transition to psychosis (what you probably have already identified), it is important to follow treatment guidelines (NICE, 2009). Of course, the patient has an important say in this decision. We recommend to continue the CBT treatment when the patient starts using antipsychotics for instance. There are also CBT protocols available for patients with a first episode of psychosis (e.g. Jackson and Iqbal, 2000)).

TIP: If possible, let a colleague administer the CAARMS (or SIPS) interview. This ensures that the assessment is objective and therefore more reliable.

Homework

- Reread all session forms.
- Browse the workbook.
- Reread the last page of the workbook.
- Describe in one A-4 page maximum:
    a) What were the most important things that the patient learned during therapy?
    b) What would the patient advise, if they were ever to start feeling distressed again by extraordinary experiences?

(8) Consolidation (one session)

Evaluation and relapse prevention

Look back at the original level and intensity of the symptoms and discuss whether things have improved. Evaluate which steps the patient has made towards their improved levels of functioning and what challenges they still face in this area.

Discuss the homework that the patient has done. Reinforce the insights that the patient has gained and the steps made to overcome the complaints. Therapy is hard work and the patient has done most of it.

Give compliments and adjust the document that the patient has made where necessary. If possible, summarise conclusions in mottos or metaphors that are easy to remember; let the patient write them down in their workbook. Emphasise that the patient can use this written evaluation to refresh their knowledge of what they learned in therapy or when they notice that anxiety might be coming back.

Discuss the treatment goals: decreasing distress caused by the extraordinary experiences and reducing the chance of more severe problems in the future. Tell the patient that they can always contact you with questions or should their complaints unexpectedly increase. Booster sessions can be planned when you think that there is an indication to do so, or when the patient indicates that they would appreciate it.

(9) Booster sessions (for instance, four sessions)

These sessions can be planned in whatever way you and the patient prefer. Usually we plan three to four sessions with a one-month interval. In these sessions you briefly discuss how the patient is functioning and whether they have experienced any distress caused by extraordinary experiences in the previous period. You can repeat certain important concepts from the therapy or perform interventions if necessary.

TIP: Avoid continuing the booster sessions for too long. If you do so, you may implicitly convey the message that you feel that the patient is not yet ready to function without these contacts. Some patients also need a little push to let go of the safe idea of being in therapy.

8

Typical vignettes of treatment cases

This chapter demonstrates the clinical application of the cognitive behavioural therapy protocol on extraordinary experiences by briefly describing several typical vignettes.

When suspicion starts to impede functioning

Suspiciousness is a selective attention for potential threat in everyday life. There is no distinct transfer from a protective coping style to a disabling coping style to, finally, a psychiatric symptom. Suspiciousness is on a continuum ranging from a beneficial to a disabling trait. ARMS subjects are somewhere in between the healthy normal end and paranoid delusion. The case of Mike will illustrate the therapeutic approach as described in the manual.

Introduction and assessment

Mike is 17 years old. He is doing the eleventh grade for the second time. He is quite intelligent, used to getting A grades. He has been missing classes and his grades have dropped since he started playing the internet game World of Warcraft last year. Mike does not go out at weekends and avoids going outside alone. Mike's mother found him shaking in the kitchen a couple of months ago. He said he was afraid he was going crazy and told his mother that he felt like everybody was watching him at school. Mother convinced him to seek help. Mike has a 16-year-old sister. From the third to the sixth grade at primary school he was severely bullied. In the sixth grade he did a training in assertiveness on the recommendation of his school; after this, the bullying subsided. In high school Mike has been bullied, but not very often.

Mike often feels anxious outside and in school. He sometimes thinks that someone wants to harm him. He avoids walking the streets alone. When he does he scans the environment for people who might pose a threat. When he rides his bike to school he cycles very fast to avoid possible attacks. Mike considers almost everyone his age or older to be suspect. He is afraid that his classmates are secretly talking or laughing about him. Therefore, he sits at the back of the classroom and tries to keep everything in sight. Mike's schoolwork is suffering from this. His bedroom is the only place where he still feels really safe. Mike says that he knows that what he is thinking is not realistic, so he can to some extent distance himself from the negative thoughts. Nevertheless, it produces some anxiety and impedes his functioning.

The last few months Mike has sometimes heard his name spoken around school or at home. This often happens when he wears his headphones. When he checks whether someone called him, usually there is no one there. Mike does not know what to make of this. A few times a week Mike sees something out of the corner of his eye. He interprets this as a door opening or someone who is watching him.

Mike has a few friends from his former class. However, he never shares his most intimate thoughts because he distrusts everyone. He says that everything he tells others can be used against him. Mike has never had a girlfriend. He goes to bed around 1 or 2 am and has difficulty getting out of bed in the morning. At the weekends he stays in bed until late in the afternoon. Mike has never used drugs and only sporadically drinks alcohol.

Normalising information and alternative explanations

Mike is glad to hear that the therapist is familiar with fears like his and he does not think that he is crazy. He quickly picks up the fact that his attribution determines his reactions to extraordinary experiences. He is motivated to start treatment. He would like to be less burdened by his suspicious thoughts, get his diploma next year and go to college. As homework he reads information about extraordinary experiences and the influence of dopamine on the genesis of these experiences. Mike is very interested in all the information. He understands that dopamine can trick his mind into highlighting experiences that are actually harmless, such as people laughing or whispering. Mike expresses that he is afraid of going mad. He knows this is not necessarily true, but he cannot get it out of his head.

Mike's therapist explains why it is very important to keep going to school and meeting friends. In this session the ABC model is introduced (activating event, beliefs, consequences). They make two ABCs together.

- Activating event (extraordinary experience):
  - I am walking through the crowded hallway at school.
- Beliefs (automatic negative thoughts or interpretations):
  - They are watching me and talking about me.
- Consequences (emotion and behaviour):
  - Afraid
  - I fled the situation.
- Activating event (extraordinary experience):
  - I am sitting in the classroom, it is noisy and I hear someone saying my name.

- Beliefs (automatic negative thoughts or interpretations):
  - My classmates are looking at me and talking about me.
- Consequences (emotion and behaviour):
  - Afraid
  - Tried to convince myself that it wasn't true.

As homework Mike will try to make ABCs about extraordinary experiences himself. He is encouraged to produce alternative explanations for the extraordinary events.

Metacognitive training

Mike and his therapist discuss the information on selective attention. Selective attention has an evolutionary function, but can malfunction. For example, if you are afraid of dogs you continuously notice dogs and therefore feel frightened all day long. As homework for the next session, Mike will read the information in the manual about selective attention and he will try to do the exercise. The first day he has to pay attention to blue cars all day long, noting the number of blue cars every hour, and describing his experiences. The next day he has to pay attention to noises in the adjacent rooms, the third day to people wearing glasses, the fourth day is a rest day (comparing not paying attention to certain details to the previous day), and the last day Mike has to pay attention to suspicious-looking people.

The next session Mike describes that he had difficulty carrying out the exercise. He was so distracted by it that he almost got run over by a yellow car! In addition, because he does not walk alone on the streets very often, he was unable to do the outdoor exercise. He did perform the exercise with the noises in the adjacent rooms. He heard all sorts of sounds he usually does not notice. Mike and his therapist discuss how selective attention may play a role in causing his fears. Mike recognises that he is preoccupied with monitoring his surroundings, making him perceive all kinds of threats.

For the next session Mike reads the information about jumping to conclusions and carries out the exercise, that is, formulating alternative explanations:

- extraordinary experience: a passer-by looks at me with an unfriendly expression on his face;
- automatic negative interpretation: he may want to harm me. I am in danger;
- emotion: scared;
- behaviour: cling on to mother;
- alternative interpretation: 1) The passer-by was unhappy because be had an argument with his wife or boss; or 2) I colour the intentions of others with my negative experiences with my peers in primary school.

Mike notices that formulating alternative explanations decreases anxiety. His therapist asks Mike to keep monitoring his automatic thoughts and encourages him to think of alternative interpretations of extraordinary events.

Case formulation

Mike has good grades on his recent school report and he is happy about that. Mike and his therapist make a case formulation. Mike thinks that the basis for his suspiciousness lies in primary school where he was bullied. He acknowledges that his extreme vigilance and selective attention are no longer adaptive. He also knows that he often jumps to conclusions that are not supported by facts. On the other hand, he emphasises that the reason he has not been attacked yet is the fact that he avoids walking outside alone.

Cognitive behavioural therapy

Mike still avoids many situations, but he has started to question whether his negative expectations are realistic. Mike is willing to start testing the thought that other people will attack him when he is alone and outside. A fear hierarchy of situations (0 = no fear, 100 = extreme fear) that are avoided by Mike is made.

Fear hierarchy:

- Sitting alone on a bench in the park when it is quiet: 10
- Travelling with public transport: 20

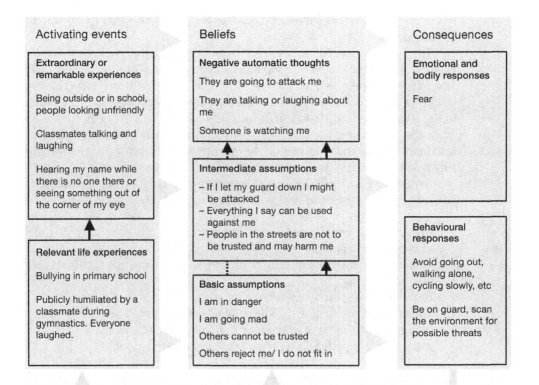

Figure 8.1 Case formulation: Mike.

- Walking around in the classroom: 30
- Walking on the street with other people I know: 40
- Speaking to a group of people (e.g. giving a presentation): 50
- Walking alone past groups of people at school: 60
- Confiding in someone: 70
- Walking alone on the streets: 80

We agree on starting with the least feared situation of the fear hierarchy to test out what happens if the feared situations are sought out. Mike is prepared to go to a bench in the park on Sunday morning when not many people are outside and sit there for ten minutes before the next session. He will try to pay attention to children and the surroundings instead of suspicious-looking people. If people leave him alone, Mike will accept this as evidence that his thought is untrue in that situation. If other people bother him, Mike will give more credibility to his negative thought.

The next session Mike explains that he performed the experiment twice. He first went in the morning; there was hardly anybody in the park. After experiencing that nobody bothered him, he was confident enough to go back in the afternoon when the park was more crowded. Mike was happy to experience that nobody spoke to him, let alone attack him. Consciously aiming his attention to non-threatening stimuli such as children and the surroundings helped him to feel less frightened. Mike is willing to try some other situations such as travelling with public transport and walking around in the classroom.

Owing to the behavioural experiments, Mike learns that nothing happens when he walks outside alone. Maybe he is in less danger than he thought he was. He also notices that manipulating his attention decreases fear. Slowly Mike feels more comfortable about going outside alone. Mike recognises himself in the information in the manual about paranoia and withdrawal from social contacts. He would like to be more sociable and is willing to do a behavioural experiment about entrusting someone with personal information. He will tell someone he likes in his classroom something personal about himself. If he finds out that this person has passed on the personal information to others in the following two weeks, or when this person uses the information against Mike, his idea that others cannot be trusted will be confirmed. If not, he will consider it as evidence for the contrary hypothesis.

After several behavioural experiments without leakage or other abuse of personal information, Mike feels more comfortable speaking freely to classmates that he likes and friendships begin to develop.

Relapse prevention and end of therapy

After 12 sessions Mike is less frightened in several situations. He can walk outside alone and some social relations are starting to develop. An appointment for a booster session after three months is made. Three months later, Mike has passed to the next year of his school. He is still less socially active than many of his peers, but he now has some social contacts at school. He is no longer convinced that other people are out to get him. Sometimes he still hears his name in the classroom but it does not bother him very much. He has more hopes for the future and is no longer worried about going crazy.

When coincidence does not exist

From time to time we all have experiences in which coincidence no longer seems to be a mere coincidence. Everyone has the tendency to assume causal relations when events coincide in a specific time. In general, people do not have a good understanding of 'chance'. Chances are often overestimated or underestimated. Interpreting coincidence in a delusional way and focusing too much attention on it can result in the development of psychosis.

Introduction and assessment

In the first session Charles and his therapist meet and talk about his complaints. Charles is referred to the Early Detection and Intervention Team (EDIT). He is 19 years old and has always been an anxious boy. In primary school he was severely bullied and could not stand up for himself. He has a difficult relationship with his father who is a strict and rigid man. Charles is rather dependent on his mother. He lives with his parents and is doing a vocational business study. In the past there were periods in which he used cannabis on a daily basis, but he has not been using cannabis in the last few months.

Charles sometimes has the fleeting idea that someone is putting thoughts in his head. About once a week when walking on the street, he suddenly feels he is being chased and occasionally sees strange things, such as shadows, which frighten him. Charles expects that most people will think he is weird. However, his main complaint is the fact that he can sense when negative things are going to happen to himself or to people close to him. Sometimes he has predictive dreams, or thoughts that come true. Most of the time he just has a very ominous feeling. When this occurs he knows something is about to happen and he avoids 'dangerous' activities, such as cycling. He has many examples in which he predicted catastrophe. Every time he has the ominous feeling something negative happens. For instance, he felt that his grandmother, who was sick, was going to die; she passed away two days later. About a month ago he sensed that something was going to happen and he was right, because that afternoon he had a bicycle accident and sprained his wrist. Although he keeps finding corroborative evidence that his tension precedes catastrophe, he indicates that he is not absolutely sure that he really has a gift of foresight. On the other hand, he is certain that there is more going on than mere coincidence. Charles' preoccupation with these events is putting a lot of strain on him since he feels rather responsible. He wonders whether he should do more to prevent future disasters. His behaviour related to being 'safe' is starting to interfere with his functioning and he has missed some classes in school.

Charles is diagnosed with a panic disorder. His complaints meet the criteria for an ARMS. The therapist explains the rationale and design of the therapy. When asked, Charles explains that he is scared that he is losing control of his mind; he feels he is not normal. Charles is highly motivated to undertake therapy and agrees to see his therapist on a weekly basis.

Normalising information and alternative explanations

Charles is relieved to hear the information about extraordinary experiences. His therapist explains the working of dopamine on the brain and hypothesises that Charles' anxious or ominous feelings might in fact be caused by a sudden release of dopamine in his brain. It is as though the alarm system of Charles' brain 'cries wolf' a lot. On request, Charles' therapist explains how intrusive thoughts can arise in the brain, and how voices and intrusive thoughts are similar experiences. His therapist advises him not to use cannabis because this increases the dopamine levels in the brain. The rationale behind the ABC model is introduced and together the therapist and Charles complete several ABCs about extraordinary experiences. Charles is asked to make ABCs for every extraordinary event he encounters during the coming week.

Metacognitive training

A total of eight cognitive biases are discussed. Charles is enthusiastic about the insight he gets from reading about cognitive biases and performing exercises that demonstrate the effect of these biases. He concludes that he is a rather pessimistic person who generally expects failure, although this is not always realistic. Moreover, he understands that his brain is programmed for classification of input and therefore continuously makes connections that are not actually there. As a result of the training Charles becomes more aware that he is rather rigid in his opinions – in fact, just like his father. In the 'jumping to conclusions' exercise he discusses a recent extraordinary experience with his brother. They were on holiday a few weeks earlier when Charles suddenly saw a strange shadow on the wall of his hotel room. His immediate assumption was that there was a ghost. He woke his brother up and asked him whether he saw the same thing. However, his brother did not react and Charles had almost no sleep on that holiday.

The exercise entails Charles asking his brother to help him think of alternative explanations for this extraordinary event. Together they produce some alternative interpretations of the shadows; for example, that they are shadows from passing cars, humidity stains or grease marks. At the end of the training Charles concludes that most events can be interpreted in several ways and that less terrifying thoughts lead to more pleasant consequences. Charles states that from now on he will ask himself the following question when he notices fear: 'Is there an actual threat or is this just my bias to jump to frightening conclusions?'

Case formulation

Based on the ABCs and the information from the previous sessions, a shared case formulation is made. The influence of previous life experiences are integrated in the formulation. While making the case formulation it becomes clear that some of Charles' complaints have already subsided. He is less worried about the

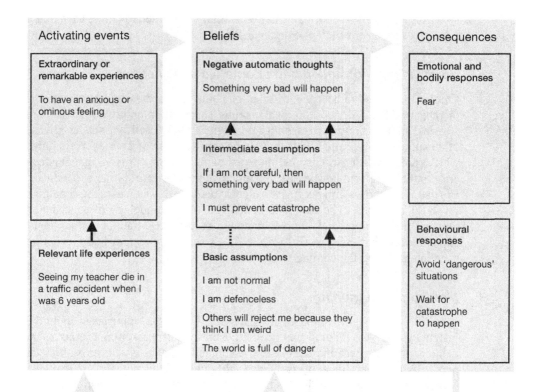

Figure 8.2 Case formulation: Charles.

extraordinary experiences and understands what causes them. This makes it easier for him to ignore his negative thoughts and feelings. What remains are the anxious and ominous feelings. When they occur Charles still fears something negative will happen. Although the credibility of the idea that he is not normal has decreased, it still feels slightly realistic.

Cognitive behavioural therapy

Charles' therapist teaches him progressive muscle relaxation, which helps him to relax. At this point Charles thinks of different explanations for every extraordinary event he encounters. Moreover, he has learned that it sometimes takes a few minutes, and sometimes even three days, before something negative happens after he has had an ominous feeling. Charles and his therapist decide to perform a behavioural experiment. During the next two weeks Charles will monitor and register all the incidences in which he feels ominous or anxious. On another list he will register all the negative events that happen to him or his family members. The next session the lists are put together and examined. The first thing Charles notices is that there were only a few moments of anxiety during the last two weeks. This concurs with Charles reporting that he had two relatively good weeks. However, the most important thing that Charles learns from the experiment is that there appears to be no relationship at all between anxious feelings and negative events. And, if there is a relationship, it is more likely to be the reverse. To be sure, Charles repeats the experiment for two more weeks. This produces the same result as the first experiment. Charles concludes that he was wrong. He does not sense approaching catastrophe; the alarm system of his brain is tuned to sensitively creating biases that lead to fear.

The idea that he is not normal is challenged with several cognitive techniques, such as multidimensional evaluation, in which Charles is asked to come up with five characteristics of the most normal person he knows, and five characteristics of the most 'weird' person he knows. These are divided into dimensions; for example, 'has many friends' versus 'is a total loner'. Charles is then asked to rate himself on these dimensions. He experiences that he rates himself as normal. After this exercise Charles concludes that he is different from others, but that he is normal. As a behavioural experiment he discusses his idea with a friend, who confirms that Charles is a perfectly normal guy. This friend also denies that others think Charles is weird. In the next session evidence for and against the idea that others think he is weird is discussed. Charles concludes that he has no proof that others think so negatively of him and that this would be strange considering the fact that his friends encourage him to go out with them. Charles is doing well. He no longer misses classes, goes out more frequently, and has taken a part-time job in a restaurant. Charles no longer thinks he is going crazy.

Relapse prevention and end of therapy

As homework Charles is asked to make an abstract of his session forms. Based on this an emergency card is drawn up. This is a card with rationalising self-speech on it, which Charles can use in future extraordinary experiences. Charles and his therapist plan a few two-monthly booster sessions. At the second booster session Charles reports that he did not experience any extraordinary experiences worth mentioning. The therapy is terminated with the message that Charles can always contact his therapist again for any questions or a booster session.

When experiences and thoughts become intrusive

Intrusions are related to several disorders, such as PTSD, OCD and psychosis. The diagnosis that a person receives depends on several factors; for example, whether the person experiences the intrusive thoughts as 'own' or 'alien'; whether or not the intrusions are related to trauma; whether or not the theme is bizarre; and whether the theme matches the cultural setting of the client and the diagnostician. A significant proportion of people with PTSD or OCD indicate that their intrusions have perceptual qualities. Psychosis can develop when intrusions are interpreted in a delusional way, that is, as alien, powerful and of malicious intent.

Introduction and assessment

Aisha is a 27-year-old North African woman who has been living in Europe for over ten years. Between the age of 12 and 15 years a family member had sexually abused her. She lives alone. Most of her family members still live in her country of origin. Aisha is diagnosed with PTSD for which she receives treatment. Besides the PTSD symptoms she has certain extraordinary experiences. Every day she hears her own thoughts out loud; she is a 100 per cent certain that these are her own thoughts. About twice a week she hears a negative voice that often commands her to harm herself; for instance, to jump into water even though she cannot swim. Aisha has no intention of performing these commands, but the voices do worry her. When Aisha is in bed she sometimes has the feeling that someone is there. At these moments she thinks a man is in her room. Aisha ruminates daily and for hours on end. At a certain point she often feels she loses touch with reality and then 'awakes' half an hour later. This scares her a lot. Aisha is afraid of losing control and often thinks that she is not normal. When she has a bad week, Aisha can have suicidal thoughts. She has called in sick at her work as a chemist and has withdrawn from her social life.

Aisha's trauma therapist and her Early Detection and Intervention Team (EDIT) therapist agree on a collaborative treatment. The trauma therapist focuses on the prolonged experiences in Aisha's past, while the EDIT therapist aims at reducing the distress caused by the extraordinary experiences in the present.

Normalising information and alternative explanations

A first step is to give Aisha normalising information about PTSD symptoms and extraordinary experiences. Her therapist explains that many of the extraordinary experiences can in fact be conceptualised as post-traumatic stress symptoms. Her therapist explains what happens in the human brain when someone hears voices, and presents data that show that voices originate in the brain and not in the outside world. Aisha is encouraged to perform several brief experiments when she hears the voice, like plugging her ears or walking towards the voice. Hearing voices is normalised and the importance of attribution is emphasised. Her therapist explains that many voice hearers report that the voices started after a traumatic or very emotional event. Aisha is encouraged to resume social contacts, meaningful activities and sports. Aisha is an intelligent woman and all resources are still available – she just has to start using them again.

Metacognitive training

In the metacognitive training, emphasis is placed on the section about source monitoring. Aisha takes in all the information and indicates that she is convinced that the perceptual experiences originate in her own brain. Several coping strategies are discussed; for example, humming when she hears the voice and, most importantly, ignoring instead of analysing the experiences.

Aisha recognises herself in the negative expectation bias. She used to be an optimist. She feels that her positive ideas about the world were shattered by the abuse she suffered. In the accompanying exercise, she notices that optimistic

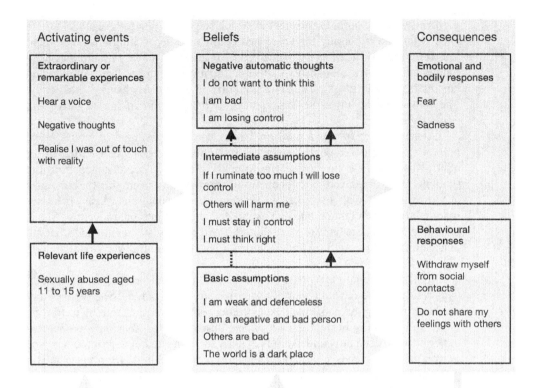

Figure 8.3 Case formulation: Aisha.

interpretations of ambiguous events are at least as realistic as her pessimistic thoughts and lead to more pleasant feelings.

Case formulation

Aisha still hears the voice every now and then, which causes moderate concern. She is now fully convinced that the voice originates from her own brain. However, she still ruminates a lot and is afraid of losing control. She feels she is a bad person. This makes her feel anxious and sad. She often starts intensive discussions with herself, which she calls internal dialogues. She tries hard to 'think right' and does not share her thoughts with others.

Cognitive behavioural therapy

The power, origin and intent of the voice are clarified and discussed. The Voice Power Differential Scale and the Social Comparison Rating Scale are administered and discussed. The conclusion is that Aisha experiences that the voice has a lot of negative influence, but that she feels she is in control. To test this, Aisha performs a behavioural experiment in which she walks along the canals in town even when she is hearing the voice that commands her to jump into the water. The frequency of hearing the voice drops to less than once a month and it no longer causes distress. Aisha explains that the most important factor in reducing her distress is the fact that her interpretation of the voice changed drastically. She now sees the intrusive experiences as a reflection of her negative life experiences.

Aisha and her therapist perform a behavioural experiment in which Aisha practises letting go of control over her thoughts. She learns that letting go of control has a paradoxical effect and quickly leads to more distance from the thoughts and to a relaxed state. They discuss how Aisha can employ the strategies she uses to deal with the voice in reducing her ruminations. Aisha practises manipulating her attention and distancing herself from internal processes. She is encouraged to ignore her intrusive thoughts and manipulate her attention. Doing everything in slow motion, and therefore in a very mindful way, is a strategy that works well for Aisha.

Additional cognitive work is done to challenge Aisha's negative self-esteem. This results in the development of more realistic basic beliefs. She realises that she is actually a good person and an extremely strong woman, coming to Europe alone and finishing her university studies despite all the abusive acts she had experienced. Aisha now understands that her thoughts do not determine who she is as a person. Friends who she has linked up with again confirm that she is a good and very strong woman.

Aisha is doing well. She no longer hears the voice, the rumination has decreased significantly, and the accompanying symptoms have subsided. She has started swimming lessons, exercises a few times a week, and is reintegrating at her work.

Relapse prevention and end of therapy

Aisha makes an abstract of her session forms and her therapist encourages her to think in a rational way, to consider alternative explanations, and always seek additional information – preferably from others. The therapy is terminated after several booster sessions.

When ghosts are haunting

In any group, about 50 per cent believe in supernatural beings such as ghosts or devils. Fear of ghosts is common and can be seen in different disorders. Sometimes the fear is based on hallucinations that are attributed to a ghost. These people hear, see, smell, taste or feel strange things; or they have awkward experiences, such as things being misplaced. They conclude that a ghost must be responsible for these sensations or experiences. In a second group the fear resembles a specific phobia. These people do not have any distinct experiences that they attribute to ghosts; they often indicate they have had this fear since childhood and used the same safety behaviours for many years. In a third group the fear of ghosts can be conceptualised as a form of OCD; these people often suffer from 'thought–event fusion'. They feel that performing (or not performing) certain activities may result in a ghost attacking them or their loved ones, or in terrifying experiences such as a ghost taking over their body. They therefore conduct avoidance behaviours.

All these different routes to a fear of ghosts can be seen in ARMS subjects. Because an idiosyncratic case formulation has been developed, the CBT protocol in this book can be used for every type of fear.

Introduction and assessment

June's general practitioner has referred her because she is very anxious. During the past year she has been sleeping with her mother in her parents' bed. Her father moved into the guestroom without any protest. June told her mother that the reason for sleeping in her parents' bedroom was that she found it cosy. Recently, she told her mother the truth: she does not dare to sleep alone. June is afraid that ghosts might attack and kill her while she is asleep. June explains that she is aware that her fear is childish and that she feels like her 7-year-old nephew who is afraid to sleep alone. At the moment of referral June has started sleeping in her own bed again. She can barely cope with this, is extremely tense and only gets a few hours of sleep every night. June has developed an arsenal of safety behaviours. Instead of walking, she runs up and down the stairs, jumping the first few steps. She sleeps with the covers pulled over her head, leaves the door open, the radio playing and the lights on. June is at the end of her first year in university and failed most of her courses. She complains about fatigue, and for the first time in her life has difficulty concentrating. When asked, June explains that she does not need any proof that ghosts actually do exist or reside in her house. One day she realised there might be a ghost and started to avoid sleeping alone. She started paying close attention and observed some strange events that confirmed her presumption. When she lies in her bed, she sometimes hears strange noises or sees odd flashes or shadows. Moreover, lately she noticed that objects are sometimes suddenly misplaced. At this moment she is certain that there is a ghost that is teasing her in the daytime and waiting for an opportunity to kill her at night. She tells her therapist that he will not be able to change her mind and that she will not give up her safety behaviours. In a rational way she understands that she is wrong, but explains she will not take the risk. The expected negative consequences are too horrifying to her and somehow she just knows that she is right.

Normalising information and alternative explanations

The design and rationale of the therapy are discussed, and normalising information about extraordinary experiences is presented. This evokes considerable resistance in June. She explains that she is not crazy. Her therapist emphasises that no one thinks that she is crazy, but that she is distressed by her current situation. He explains that the treatment goal is to reduce her distress and prevent an increase of her anxiety in the future, which otherwise could develop into a severe disorder.

June is glad to hear this and indicates that she is afraid that her anxiety will increase. June explains that part of her reluctance also comes from the fact that she needs some time to start trusting others again. She had some experiences with girlfriends who told personal things about her to other people, and this damaged her trust. June accepts all the information about extraordinary experiences, and the influence of attribution and dopamine as possible explanations of what she is experiencing, but is reluctant to let go of her current convictions. The ABC model is introduced and an ABC is filled in for a situation that she experienced the previous week. In this situation her hairdryer was suddenly set on a different blowing mode. June concluded that a ghost must have done this to freak her out. June is encouraged to make ABCs for every extraordinary experience and to think of at least one alternative explanation when she does this.

Metacognitive training

June recognises herself in the information about emotional reasoning and dogmatism. She says that she is extremely stubborn and is not able to doubt her own ideas. If she starts doubting her ideas she feels she will be lost. She is afraid that she will then lose control over her life. June has no idea why she has become so afraid of losing control.

Following the information from the manual, June and her therapist discuss the poor reliability of human perception and memory. June has an exceptionally large amount of trust in her memory; for example, with respect to misplaced objects. To test this, June and her therapist perform a short behavioural experiment in which she leaves the room and he misplaces one object. She then has to determine what object was misplaced. In eight trials she only notices one misplacement, thus challenging her trust in her memory.

Her therapist also gives examples that show how poor our perception and memory actually is. He shows video clips in which June's attention is manipulated, making her miss vital information. June is particularly surprised by a video in which she missed a man that walked straight through the image wearing a 'bear suit' because her attention was focused on some other people playing with a ball.

They discuss the negative consequences of her safety behaviours. June's insight is increasing rapidly and she now fully accepts a theory of biased cognition as possible alternative for what she is experiencing. She understands that she has no firm evidence; that she selectively aims her attention at signs of threat; that she is inclined to quickly jump to negative conclusions; that she is dogmatic in her reasoning and therefore does not view all the evidence; and that her safety behaviours are preventing her from learning that she might actually be wrong.

Case formulation

Although insight into her complaints is increasing, June's safety behaviour remains unchanged and she indicates that she is not ready to start giving this up. June and her therapist make a case formulation based on the information they have gathered so far. June's main goals are to be able to live and sleep in her own house without fear, and to resume her studies and social life.

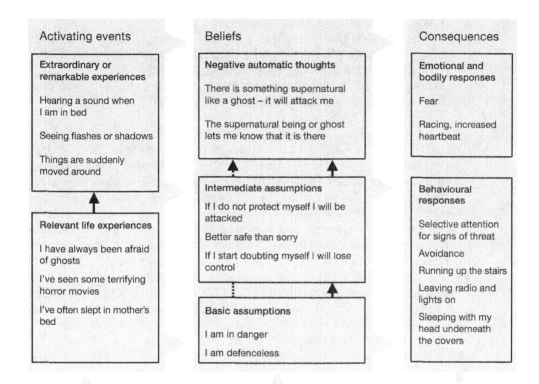

Figure 8.4 Case formulation: June.

Cognitive behavioural therapy

The evidence that June has for the existence of ghosts is collected. One by one these pieces of evidence are critically examined and alternative interpretations are discussed; for instance, for the hairdryer incident. A role change via the 'pie-chart technique' makes it easier for June to come up with alternative explanations; for example, her sister might have used it and might be afraid to admit this, or the control button might have accidentally been moved when putting it away. Alternatives are also produced for the sounds and shadows at night. June is working hard and her earlier conviction is starting to crumble.

In the next phase they review June's safety behaviours. June's thoughts and strategies are challenged, for example:

> *Therapist:* . . . 'If ghosts can go through walls, how can sleeping under your duvet defend you against them?'
> *June:* 'That's a good one, I never thought about that. That doesn't make any sense. . . .'
> *Therapist:* . . .'What makes it safer to sleep with your mother? Does she have protective powers? Do ghosts never attack when you're not alone?'

June: 'I haven't thought about all these things.'
Therapist: 'You haven't really thought it all through, yet you are allowing it to greatly influence your life. What do you think about that?'
June: 'It sounds quite silly when you put it like that. . . .'
Therapist: . . .'You say that these ghosts have been haunting you for a while now; why don't they just finish the job?'
June: 'I don't know. . . .'

After this cognitive work, June is prepared to start the exposure. Because June is not motivated to directly perform a behavioural experiment in which she lets go of all her safety behaviours, she and her therapist decide to make a hierarchy of the situations she is avoiding. Every week June performs a step on the hierarchy. Every day she monitors whether her negative expectations actually become reality and what she has learned about her fears that day. June emails about her progress and any questions or problems that she has in performing the exposure assignments. She starts by walking up and down the stairs slowly. In a later stage she gradually lets go of her safety behaviours related to sleeping. Relaxation exercises and attention manipulation help her to persevere in changing her behaviour when she is in bed. 'Experiencing is believing' for June. After two months of exposure she is sleeping alone in her room, with the door closed, the radio and lights switched off, and with her head above the duvet.

Relapse prevention and end of therapy

A few booster sessions are planned. After the summer June restarts her first year in university and is doing very well. She has picked up most of her social network and is planning to move to a student dormitory in the near future. She makes an abstract of her session forms and indicates that therapy can be terminated.

Losing touch with reality

Derealisation (the subjective experience of losing touch with reality) and depersonalisation (losing touch with yourself) are harmless by nature and very common among the general population. When these experiences are interpreted in a non-frightening way and ignored, they usually just disappear. Derealisation or depersonalisation can become a problem when interpreted in a catastrophic way, resulting in avoidance behaviours. Again, when these phenomena are interpreted in a delusional way, they may result in psychosis.

Introduction and assessment

Beatrice is a 26-year-old administrative worker who called in sick a few months ago. She was feeling depressed and started to become increasingly anxious. Beatrice did not feel at ease at her work any more. She felt that her colleagues, and also people on the streets, were talking about her behind her back. She has no idea what they were saying and why they were doing this. Beatrice often feels that she is losing touch with the world. At those moments she feels detached, as though she is looking at the world rather than taking part in it. She then fears that she does not exist and in her panic calls a friend or family member for help. Beatrice does not dare to look in the mirror for more than a second at a time and avoids crowded places.

Sometimes she experiences blackouts; she comes back to awareness and realises that it is half an hour later. This worries her, because all kinds of things might happen to her when she is in such a state. She also fears that it might worsen, making her lose control. She thought she might have a tumour in her brain and underwent a MRI scan. No somatic reason for the blackouts was found and no additional treatment was offered.

Every now and then Beatrice feels she receives signs, for instance from the television. For example, one evening she felt depressed and that very night a programme was shown about recovering from depression. These kinds of experiences never used to cause her any distress. Lately, however, it is happening more often. Beatrice is starting to wonder whether she should do something with it to prevent negative events. She has no idea who or what could be behind this.

Beatrice has a good relationship with her parents and sister. However, her uncle used to terrorise her and her sister, which greatly damaged her self-esteem. In primary school she was bullied, which confirmed her negative ideas about herself and others. Two years ago she ended an abusive relationship. Her ex-boyfriend repressed her and financially ruined her. She is still paying for the debts he left her with.

Normalising information and alternative explanations

The treatment manual is introduced and Beatrice is informed about extraordinary experiences, dopamine, lifestyle and the importance of attribution. The ABC model is introduced and practised. Beatrice's therapist explains that she appears to be suffering from derealisation and dissociation. Beatrice receives additional information from the manual about these types of experiences. She is relieved to hear that these experiences are quite common and harmless. Her therapist explains that these experiences are more common in people who feel anxious or depressed or who were maltreated during their childhood. Moreover, dissociation is regarded as a coping strategy in extremely stressful situations. Beatrice recognises this; she frequently used to 'black out' as a child when her uncle rampaged against her. Lastly, her therapist explains that it is the interpretation and not the experience itself that causes the distress.

Beatrice is asked to monitor her complaints with ABCs and formulate alternative explanations.

Metacognitive training

Beatrice learns from the metacognitive training that she is preoccupied with bodily signs of losing touch with reality. She constantly monitors whether she is light-headed or tensed. The panic model is introduced to show how selective attention for bodily signs and catastrophic misinterpretations of these experiences can trigger negative vicious cycles that eventually result in a panic attack. Beatrice is instructed by her therapist to stop paying attention to bodily symptoms of derealisation. Beatrice also learns that she tends to jump to negative conclusions. She has a pessimistic view of herself and others, and often expects the worst to happen. Knowing this, she can critically judge her interpretations to ensure they are realistic.

Case formulation

Receiving normalising information, thinking of alternative explanations and the metacognitive training lead to a decrease of distress caused by the extraordinary experiences. Beatrice is no longer worried about coincidences or people talking about her. The derealisation and dissociation appear less frequently. Beatrice no longer interprets them as an indication that she is not alive, but they are still present and still evoke some amount of distress. By monitoring her complaints, Beatrice learns that the dissociation and derealisation are difficult to unravel. She and her therapist decide to consider them as experiences that lie on the same continuum. Four types of events appear to trigger derealisation and dissociation: 1) Ruminating; 2) being confronted with dominant people; 3) looking in a mirror; and 4) being in a crowded place.

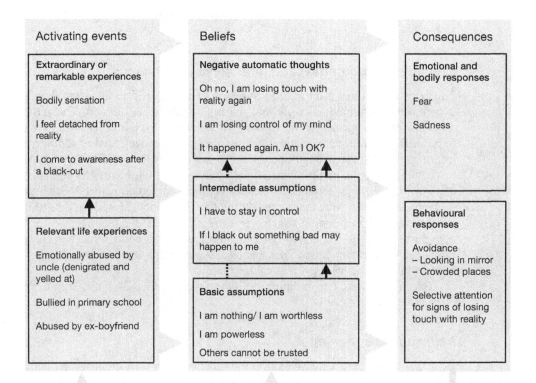

Figure 8.5 Case formulation: Beatrice.

Cognitive behavioural therapy

The worst case scenarios of Beatrice are critically examined. She is afraid of losing control of her mind and that something bad will happen while she is in the dissociated state. So far these things have not happened, so why does she expect them in the future? Beatrice is invited to try to evoke the derealisation in the therapy and to experiment with letting go of control, and looking at it as if she was a neutral bystander. This experiment fails because Beatrice cannot induce the derealisation. Some interoceptive exposure (such as hyperventilation and high muscle tension) is done and Beatrice is instructed to remain calm and just wait until the derealisation passes the next time it occurs. Beatrice learns from this that her bodily sensations are normal and that she does not lose control due to the derealisation.

Beatrice is feeling less depressed and does not ruminate as much as before. She is advised to avoid situations in which she knows she often ruminates extensively. Imagery exposure with rescripting is used to work on several experiences associated with her uncle, the bullying, and her ex-boyfriend. Beatrice learns from this that she is stronger now; that she is an adult; and that she can now stand up for herself.

Behavioural experiments are performed revolving around looking in the mirror for longer periods, something that evokes depersonalisation in most people. Beatrice is encouraged to visit crowded places. All experiments produce some distress at first, but are performed without anxiety after several attempts.

Some cognitive work is done on Beatrice's negative core beliefs, and elements from an assertiveness training (e.g. role playing) are used to increase her defence capacity.

Relapse prevention and end of therapy

During therapy Beatrice met a new boyfriend who is treating her 'like a princess'. His compliments and love for her boost her self-esteem much more than any cognitive intervention by her therapist. Beatrice hardly ever experiences derealisation or dissociation now. She has not panicked in the last two months and she no longer feels depressed. She and her therapist make an emergency card on which Beatrice notes the most important lessons she has learned during the last five months. The therapy is ended after two monthly booster sessions.

Magical thinking

The border between OCS and psychosis can easily be crossed. If convictions about germs in food are so strong that a person starves themself to death, one may say that this conviction has become a delusion. The *Diagnostic and Statistical Manual of Mental Disorders* (DSM)-IV (APA, 2001) treats OCD and Psychotic disorders as separate classification categories. However, OCS and mild psychotic symptoms often co-occur and are difficult to disentangle. OCS can be viewed as a form of magical thinking that also often occur in subjects with a psychotic disorder. Because of similarities between OCS and (mild) psychotic symptoms, treating the mild psychotic symptoms sometimes reduces anxiety, leading to a positive effect on OCS. Otherwise, CBT for OCS also often shows a positive effect on mild positive symptoms. The treatment of co-occurring OCS and mild psychotic symptoms is illustrated by the case of Jennifer.

Introduction and assessment

Jennifer is 17 years old. She has had OCS since she was 12 years old. She has to walk up and down the stairs several times at one moment, because if she walks down the stairs with the wrong thought (e.g. cancer), she is afraid that one of her relatives will become ill. Walking down the stairs is causing her problems every day. She also washes her hands 20 times a day and she has to check locks 15–20 times. Fortunately, she does not spend a lot of time doing these activities (less than an hour). Although she finds the thoughts frustrating, she can usually control herself and is able to get to school on time. In the last six months she also (infrequently) hears voices, especially when she closes her eyes. The voices tell her in a scary tone that she needs to go to sleep. She often wonders if they are real or imaginary. Furthermore, Jennifer is afraid of ghosts since she had a boyfriend who claimed that he could communicate with the ghosts of dead people. In addition, she sometimes has the thought that cameras are recording her in her room. In answer to the therapist's question whether she ever looks for these cameras in her room, she replies: 'In that case, I would declare myself crazy.'

Her uncle was diagnosed with schizophrenia when he was 18 years old and committed suicide when he was 30. Jennifer's symptoms are starting to interfere with her functioning and she is afraid that she will get the same diagnosis as her uncle. Fortunately, she is still going to school, although her grades have dropped and she has become more socially isolated. She has not yet received any treatment.

Normalising information and alternative explanations

Jennifer is relieved that her therapist does not think that she has schizophrenia like her uncle. She is really motivated to start therapy because she has become increasingly frightened by her unusual experiences. The information about hearing voices in the manual is comforting because she realises that people without schizophrenia also sometimes hear voices. Her goals in therapy are to become less scared, to get her school diploma next year, and to improve and expand her social contacts. Early in the therapy the ABC model is introduced (activating event, beliefs, consequences). Jennifer and her therapist make two ABCs together.

- Activating event: I am walking down the stairs and a wrong thought about illness comes into my mind.
- Beliefs: If I do not walk up and down the stairs again with the right thought, someone in my family may die of an illness.
- Consequences: I become very scared and frustrated and walk up and down the stairs until I succeed in walking down the stairs with the right thought.
- Activating event: I am lying in bed and a voice talks to me in a scary tone.
- Beliefs: I may be going crazy like my uncle.
- Consequence: Terror and not being able to sleep.

Jennifer grasps the concept of the ABCs easily and she makes several ABCs as homework assignment:

- Activating event: I touch the door knob of the toilet door.
- Beliefs: I may become sick because of germs.
- Consequence: Fear and washing hands twice for five minutes.
- Activating event: I lock the door before going to bed.
- Beliefs: I am not 100 per cent certain that the door is locked.
- Consequence: Fear of burglars and checking the lock over and over again.

Metacognitive training

Jennifer recognises the covariation bias in herself. For her, touching door knobs is associated with the expectation of fear. Furthermore, she remembers in her childhood she once thought about illness while walking down the stairs, and a few days later her father suffered a mild heart attack and had to be admitted to hospital. Reading the information makes her doubt that the co-occurrence of the thought, and this event a few days later does not necessarily imply that the thought and the event are causally related.

Case formulation

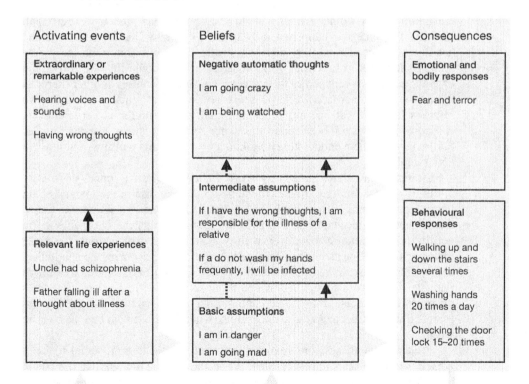

Figure 8.6 Case formulation: Jennifer.

Cognitive behavioural therapy

Jennifer is willing to test the thought that if she walks down the stairs with the wrong thought, a relative may become ill. However, she is afraid that, if she tries it out, a family member will actually get cancer. The damage will be done and she will be to blame, and she thinks she could not live with the feelings of guilt following such events. After some discussion, Jennifer and her therapist devise a behavioural experiment with a thought about her cat. She is willing to take the chance with her cat. They fill in the behavioural experiment form (also available on the website). The thought that Jennifer wants to test is: If I accidentally think about my cat falling ill when I walk down the stairs, the cat will become terminally ill within three weeks. Conviction is 50 per cent. The alternative thought she wants to test: if I walk down the stairs with a wrong thought about the cat, the cat will remain healthy during the coming three weeks. Conviction is 50 per cent. They list as evidence for her first hypothesis: the cat becoming terminally ill within three weeks. As disconfirmatory evidence we list: the cat remaining healthy the coming three weeks, or experiencing a non-terminal illness. Jennifer promises to do the experiment the coming week and they will discuss the outcome during the next session.

The next session, Jennifer says proudly that she has performed the experiment. She was scared but she read the information about the covariation bias again and was able to calm her nerves thinking about the information. Jennifer felt a knot in her stomach when the cat sneezed the day after the experiment. Luckily, the sneezing happened only once. Until now the cat had remained healthy. Jennifer learned that, when she walks down the stairs with the wrong thought about her cat, her cat will not necessarily become ill. The conviction of the thought was reduced to 40 per cent. However, Jennifer and her therapist have to wait another two weeks to see whether the cat remains healthy. Two sessions later the cat has not fallen terminally ill. Jennifer is very relieved. Her conviction has not been reduced to 0 per cent but it is a lot less than it was. She is now confident enough to try walking down the stairs with a wrong thought about a relative.

At night, when Jennifer is lying awake in bed and hears a sound, she is very afraid of ghosts. Jennifer and her therapist do the exercise in the manual about the interpretation of events (Table 7.6). When Jennifer hears a sound, she thinks that a ghost of a deceased person is in the room and that the ghost may harm her. In therapy, Jennifer comes up with two alternative explanations: the pipes of her central heating are ticking because they are cooling down, or the neighbours are making a noise. When she talks to her mother about it, her mother confirms that the pipes are also ticking in her room, and that she is also sometimes disturbed by the noise from the neighbours. Jennifer is relieved and already less scared. She promises to do the same exercise when she is lying in bed the coming week.

At the seventh session, Jennifer reports that she is better able to calm herself when she hears noises at night. When she gets the thought that there may be a ghost in the room, she convinces herself that other explanations are more likely. Generally, she is able to go back to sleep. Moreover, the walking up and down the stairs has been reduced to once or twice week. However, Jennifer has experienced an increase in her lock-checking activity. It takes her about half an hour to get to bed. Although she has checked that the door is locked, she walks back to check again because she is not 100 per cent certain that the door is locked. She is afraid that a burglar will come into the house. Jennifer and her therapist make a list of reasons for (pros) and against (cons) checking the lock 15–20 times.

Pros	Cons
Reducing fear	I never found the lock to be open when I checked it again
	A lock is not alive, it cannot open itself
	Nobody can open the lock from outside
	Even if the lock is open, the chance that a burglar would notice is minimal
	I am frustrated that I am busy for half an hour with the lock before I can go to bed

Seeing the pros and cons she had listed during the session, Jennifer realises that the reduction in fear is only temporary and that the cons outnumber the pros 5 to 1. She is motivated to try to reduce the lock checking. As homework she will try to keep in mind or read the pros and cons again, and try to reduce the checking.

The next session, Jennifer tells that she has been able to reduce the checking to ten times every night. She is better able to calm herself and generally feels less afraid.

Relapse prevention and end of therapy

After 15 sessions Jennifer's functioning has improved as she is less tired than before. The OCS take less time and energy and she is better able to sleep. As a result she has more energy to see her friends and to do her homework. She still hears the voices occasionally, but she is less 'spooked' by them. Jennifer is also more optimistic about the future because she is not so afraid that she will get schizophrenia like her uncle. An appointment is made for a booster session after three months.

Three months later, Jennifer spends about three minutes a day checking, walking up and down the stairs and washing her hands, which is acceptable to her. She is still prone to anxiety but has learned to reduce anxiety by making lists of pros and cons, and doing experiments to test her anxiety-provoking thoughts. Her therapy notebook is of help doing these exercises. Her therapist explains that Jennifer can make an appointment whenever she experiences an increase in symptoms in the future.

Concluding remarks

Our research and clinical experience has shown that identifying ARMS subjects in secondary mental health services is possible and that these subjects benefit from CBT. Screening with a 16-item version of the Prodromal Questionnaire (Loewy *et al.*, 2005) in secondary mental health services is a feasible method to filter out subjects with possible ARMS and/or psychotic symptoms (Ising *et al.*, 2012). These individuals can then be interviewed using the CAARMS to verify their ARMS/psychotic status. Based on the ever-increasing scientific evidence, and the fact that ARMS/psychosis is often not recognised even in mental health services (Boonstra, Wunderink, Sytema and Wiersma, 2008; Nieman *et al.*, 2009), it seems that the time has come to start extensive implementation of the screening for and treatment of ARMS.

Although many ARMS subjects do not make the transition to psychosis, the chance of developing another severe mental illness is higher than in typically developing adolescents and young adults (Rössler *et al.*, 2011). McGorry and colleagues have developed a model of clinical staging for mental disorders. In this model, mental disorders are divided into stages ranging from mild symptoms with a better prognosis, to a severe mental disorder with a worse prognosis (McGorry, 2010; McGorry, Hickie, Yung, Pantelis and Jackson, 2006). In current clinical practice, mental disorders are categorised using the DSM-IV (APA, 2001). However, psychiatric comorbidity and the biological invalidity of categorising DSM-IV diagnoses is leading to a major shift in contemporary psychiatry. It may be clinically and biologically more valid to diagnose subjects based on symptom dimensions (e.g. psychosis, depression) ranging from mild to severe (Miller and Holden, 2010). The psychotic symptoms in ARMS subjects are rated with the CAARMS in a dimensional way and treatment can be offered for ARMS symptoms irrespective of the present or future DSM-IV diagnosis (McGorry, 2011). Even for the false-positive cases (i.e. subjects who would not make a transition to psychosis without this intervention) this therapy can be beneficial without adverse side effects. Offering help to subjects who are at increased risk of developing a severe mental disorder is promising because it entails intervention in the early stages (McGorry *et al.*, 2006). However, more research is needed to further explore the effect of CBT on ARMS subjects regarding the incidence of severe mental disorders, and to replicate our findings in an independent sample.

Some critics are of the opinion that treating subjects early in the course of mental illness may lead to stigmatisation. We do not agree with this standpoint from either a clinical or research perspective. In our institutes we treat help-seeking subjects; these individuals and their families are already very concerned about the symptoms, otherwise they would not have sought help. In our experience, they are very relieved when they receive normalising information about their symptoms and are offered individually tailored help. These patients and their families do not report that they feel stigmatised.

Another possible criticism in the treatment of ARMS subjects is that the symptoms might remit without therapy. Until we have better tools to predict which subject is heading in which direction, it may be wise to offer help-seeking ARMS patients a benign and usually short intervention that has no known side effects. If schizophrenia or another severe mental illness is prevented in even a small minority of the ARMS patients, offering the therapy will probably prove to be cost-effective in financial terms and certainly with respect to a reduction in human suffering.

Appendix A

Session form 1 (start)

Name: .... Date: ....

What did we discuss in the previous session?
....
....
....
....
....

Do you have any questions or remarks about the previous session?
Was there anything that you found unpleasant or confusing or unclear? If so, what?
....
....
....
....
....

How was your week? And do we need to put any of the events of last week on the agenda?
....
....
....
....
....

Agenda for the session:
1 ....
2 ....
3 ....
4 ....

Session form 2 (end)

Name: .... Date: ....

What has been discussed? What has to be put on the agenda for the next session?
....
....
....
....
....

Session notes (write down anything that you feel is important).
....
....
....
....
....
....
....
....
....
....

What is your opinion on/how would you rate this session? Do you have any feedback or suggestions for the therapist?
....
....

What is the homework for the next session?
....
....
....
....
....

Appendix B

Additional ABC forms

Activating event	Beliefs	Consequences	
Extraordinary experience	Automatic thoughts and interpretations	Emotion: 0–100% [ ] Afraid [ ] Angry [ ] Sad [ ] Happy [ ] Ashamed [ ] Neutral	Behaviour
Extraordinary experience	Automatic thoughts and interpretations	Emotion: 0–100% [ ] Afraid [ ] Angry [ ] Sad [ ] Happy [ ] Ashamed [ ] Neutral	Behaviour
Extraordinary experience	Automatic thoughts and interpretations	Emotion: 0–100% [ ] Afraid [ ] Angry [ ] Sad [ ] Happy [ ] Ashamed [ ] Neutral	Behaviour

Activating event	Beliefs	Consequences	
Extraordinary experience	Automatic thoughts and interpretations	Emotion: 0–100% [ ] Afraid [ ] Angry [ ] Sad [ ] Happy [ ] Ashamed [ ] Neutral	Behaviour
Extraordinary experience	Automatic thoughts and interpretations	Emotion: 0–100% [ ] Afraid [ ] Angry [ ] Sad [ ] Happy [ ] Ashamed [ ] Neutral	Behaviour
Extraordinary experience	Automatic thoughts and interpretations	Emotion: 0–100% [ ] Afraid [ ] Angry [ ] Sad [ ] Happy [ ] Ashamed [ ] Neutral	Behaviour
Extraordinary experience	Automatic thoughts and interpretations	Emotion: 0–100% [ ] Afraid [ ] Angry [ ] Sad [ ] Happy [ ] Ashamed [ ] Neutral	Behaviour

Appendix C

ABC form for extraordinary experiences with alternative explanations

Activating event	Beliefs	Consequences	
Extraordinary experience	Automatic thoughts and interpretations	Emotion: 0–100% [ ] Afraid [ ] Angry [ ] Sad [ ] Happy [ ] Ashamed [ ] Neutral	Behaviour
Extraordinary experience	Alternative thoughts and interpretations	Alternative emotion: 0–100% [ ] Afraid [ ] Angry [ ] Sad [ ] Happy [ ] Ashamed [ ] Neutral	Alternative behaviour

Activating event	Beliefs	Consequences	
Extraordinary experience	Automatic thoughts and interpretations	Emotion: 0–100% [ ] Afraid [ ] Angry [ ] Sad [ ] Happy [ ] Ashamed [ ] Neutral	Behaviour
Extraordinary experience	Alternative thoughts and interpretations	Alternative emotion: 0–100% [ ] Afraid [ ] Angry [ ] Sad [ ] Happy [ ] Ashamed [ ] Neutral	Alternative behaviour

Activating event	Beliefs	Consequences	
Extraordinary experience	Automatic thoughts and interpretations	Emotion: 0–100% [ ] Afraid [ ] Angry [ ] Sad [ ] Happy [ ] Ashamed [ ] Neutral	Behaviour
Extraordinary experience	Alternative thoughts and interpretations	Alternative emotion: 0–100% [ ] Afraid [ ] Angry [ ] Sad [ ] Happy [ ] Ashamed [ ] Neutral	Alternative behaviour

Appendix D
Case formulation form

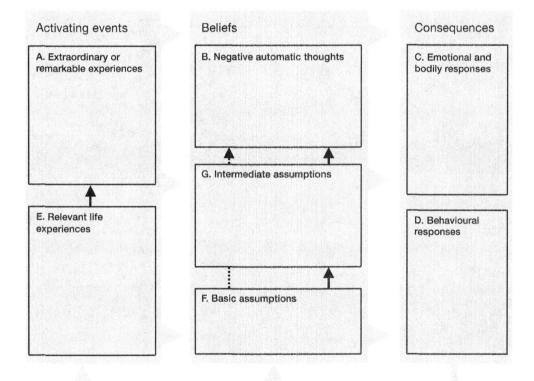

Appendix E

Treatment goals form

Name: .... Date: ....

Summary of the case formulation in words
....
....
....
....
....
....
....
....
....
....
....

Reduction of symptoms
....
....
....
....
....
....

Improvement of (social) functioning (in SMART formulation: specific, measurable, attainable, relevant and time bound)
....
....
....
....
....
....

Appendix F
Pie chart form

Name: .... Date: ....

Event:...
....
....
....

Credibility before the event?............................. %

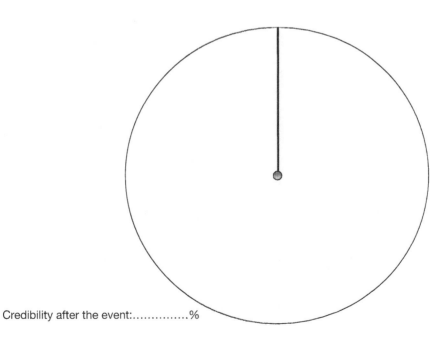

Credibility after the event:...............%

180 *Appendices*

Possible explanations for the event	*Chance %*

Other/unknown explanations

Appendix G
Cumulative probability form

Name: .... Date: ....

Description of the expected event: ....
....
....
....
....

What is your estimation of the chance that this event will occur? ....%

Necessary conditions to let the event actually occur

Step	Chance	Cumulative chance

From this probability calculation I can conclude that: ....
....
....
....

Estimated odds after the event: .... %

Appendix H
Behavioural experiment form

Name: .... Date: ....

What thought or conviction do you want to test? How credible do you consider this?
A: ....
....
....
....%

What alternative thought or conviction do you want to test? How credible do you consider this?
B: ....
....
....
....%

What experiment are you going to perform to test these thoughts or convictions?
....
....
....
....
....

What results would confirm your original thought or conviction?
A is true if: ....
....
....
....
....
....

What results would confirm your alternative thought or conviction?
B is true if: ....
....
....
....
....
....

Perform the experiment.
In your opinion how successful (or unsuccessful) was the experiment?
....
....
....

What did you learn?
....
....
....
....

Appendix I

Behavioural experiments and exposure assignments homework form

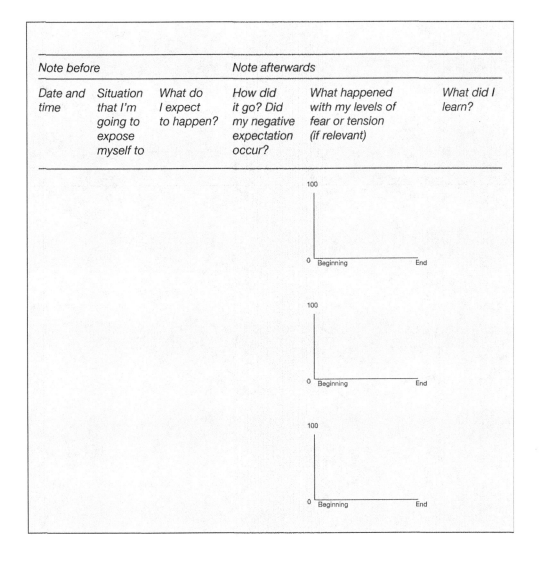

Note before			Note afterwards		
Date and time	Situation that I'm going to expose myself to	What do I expect to happen?	How did it go? Did my negative expectation occur?	What happened with my levels of fear or tension (if relevant)	What did I learn?

Appendix J
Multidimensional evaluation form

Name: .... Date: ....

Conviction: ....
....
....
....

Credibility before multidimensional evaluation: ....%

●──●

DIMENSIONS

●──●

....
....

●──●

....
....

●──●

....
....

●──●

Credibility after multidimensional evaluation: ....%

Conviction after multidimensional evaluation: ....

Appendix K

Reinforcing self-esteem exercise

1. Have the patient name their ten most positive characteristics or qualities.
2. Let the patient judge to what extent they really possess these qualities. Let the patient note specific events from the previous week that show that they really possess these qualities. Let the patient rate these on a scale from 0 to 100.
3. Ask the patient to repeat the list to themselves and imagine the events. Then ask the patient to rate the qualities again (0–100). Emphasise that the credibility level is dependent on the amount of proof.
4. For the following week, ask the patient to selectively focus their attention on positive things they do and to register these behaviours on a list.
5. The following session give feedback on any items on the list. Let the patient report on several of the events.
6. Ask the patient about the effect of focussing their attention on their positive behaviours. Let them rate their positive qualities again and discuss the effect of the positive focus on their self-esteem.
7. Repeat this procedure and emphasise that our self-esteem can change over time and is strongly influenced by what we focus our attention on.
8. Let the patient continue with the positive logbook for a while.

(Hall and Tarrier, 2003)

References

Abercrombie, H., Larson, C., Ward, R., Holden, J., Turski, P., Perlman, S. *et al.* (1996). Medial prefrontal and amygdala glucose metabolism in depressed and control subjects. An FDG–PET study. *Psychophysiology, 33*(suppl.), S17.

Addington, J., Epstein, I., Liu, L., French, P., Boydell, K. M. and Zipursky, R. B. (2011). A randomized controlled trial of cognitive behavioral therapy for individuals at clinical high risk of psychosis. *Schizophrenia Research, 125*, 54–61.

Aghotor, J., Pfueller, U., Moritz, S., Weisbrod, M. and Roesch-Ely, D. (2010). Metacognitive training for patients with schizophrenia (MCT): Feasibility and preliminary evidence for its efficacy. *Journal of Behaviour Therapy and Experimental Psychiatry, 41*, 207–11.

Alden, L. E. and Bieling, P. (1998). Interpersonal consequences of the pursuit of safety. *Behaviour Research and Therapy, 36*(1), 53–64.

Allen, P. P., Johns, L. C., Fu, C. H. Y., Broome, M. R., Vythelingum, G. N. and McGuire, P. K. (2004). Misattribution of external speech in patients with hallucinations and delusions. *Schizophrenia Research, 69*(2–3), 277–87.

Alloy, L. B. and Tabachnik, N. (1984). Assessment of covariation by humans and animals: The joint influence of prior expectations and current situational information. *Psychological Review, 91*(1), 112–49.

Alloy, L. B., Abrahamson, L. Y. and Whistehouse, W. G. (1999). Depressogenic cognitive styles: Predictive validity, information processing and personality characteristics and developmental origins. *Behaviour Research and Therapy, 37*, 503–31.

Alvarez-Jiménez, M., Gleeson, J. F., Henry, L. P., Harrigan, S. M., Harris, M. G., Killackey, E. *et al.* (2011). Road to full recovery: Longitudinal relationship between symptomatic remission and psychosocial recovery in first-episode psychosis over 7.5 years. *Psychological Medicine, 42*, 595–606.

Amaral, D., Price, J., Ptikanen, A. and Carmichael, S. (1992). Anatomical organization of the primate amygdaloid complex. In J. Aggleton (ed.), *The amygdala: Neurobiological aspects of emotion, memory and mental dysfunction.* (pp. 1–66). New York: John Wiley & Sons.

Amminger, G. P., Schäfer, M. R., Papageorgiou, K., Klier, C. M., Cotton, S. M., Harrigan, S. M. *et al.* (2010). Long-Chain Ω-3 fatty acids for indicated prevention of psychotic disorders: A randomized, placebo-controlled trial. *Archives of General Psychiatry, 67*(2), 146–54.

Anderson, K. K., Fuhrer, R. and Malla, A. K. (2010). The pathways to mental health care of first-episode psychosis patients: A systematic review. *Psychological Medicine, 40*(10), 1585–97.

APA (American Psychiatric Association) (2001). *Diagnostic and statistical manual of mental disorders. 4.* Washington, DC: American Psychiatric Association.

Armony, J. and Ledoux, J. (1999). Towards a systems, cellular, and computational understanding of cognitive–emotional interactions in fear circuits. In M. Gazzaniga (ed.), *The cognitive neurosciences.* (pp. 1067–80). Cambridge: MIT Press.

Arntz, A., Rauner, M. and van den Hout, M. (1995). I feel anxious, there must be danger: Ex-consequentia reasoning in inferring danger in anxiety disorders. *Behaviour Research and Therapy, 33,* 917–25.

Averbeck, B. B., Evans, S., Chouhan, V., Bristow, E. and Shergill, S. S. (2011). Probabilistic learning and inference in schizophrenia. *Schizophrenia Research, 127,* 115–22.

Avery, R., Startup, M. and Calabria, K. (2009). The role of effort, cognitive expectancy appraisals and coping style in the maintenance of the negative symptoms of schizophrenia. *Psychiatry Research, 167*(1–2), 36–46.

Bak, M., Delespaul, P., Hanssen, M., de Graaf, R., Vollebergh, W. and van Os, J. (2003). How false are 'false' positive psychotic symptoms? *Schizophrenia Research, 62*(1–2), 187–9.

Bar-Haim, Y., Lamy, D., Pergamin, L., Bakermans-Kranenburg, M. J. and van IJzendoorn, M. H. (2007). Threat-related attentional bias in anxious and nonanxious individuals: A meta-analytic study. *Psychological Bulletin, 133*(1), 1–24.

Beard, C. (2011). Cognitive bias modification for anxiety: Current evidence and future directions. *Expert Review of Neurotherapeutics, 11*(2), 299–311.

Beauregard, M., Lévesque, J. and Bourgouin, P. (2001). Neural correlates of conscious self-regulation of emotion. *The Journal of Neuroscience, 21,* 1–6.

Bechdolf, A., Wagner, M., Ruhrmann, S., Harrigan, S., Putzfeld, V., Pukrop, R. *et al.* (2012). Preventing progression to first-episode psychosis in early initial prodromal states. *The British Journal of Psychiatry: The Journal of Mental Science, 200,* 22–9.

Beck, A. T. (1976). *Cognitive therapy and the emotional disorders.* New York: International Universities Press.

Beck, A. T. and Steer, R. A. (1993). *Manual for Beck anxiety inventory.* San Antonio, TX: Psychological Corporation.

Beck, A. T., Emery, G. D. and Greenberg, R. L. (1985). *Anxiety disorders and phobias: A cognitive perspective.* New York: Basic Books.

Beck, A. T., Grant, P. M. and Perivoliotis, D. (2009). Cognitive therapy for negative symptoms and functioning. Unpublished paper. Philadelphia, PA: University of Pennsylvania.

Beck, A. T., Rector, N. A., Stolar, N. and Grant, P. (2009). *Schizophrenia: Cognitive theory, research, and therapy.* New York: The Guilford Press.

Beck, A. T., Steer, R. A. and Brown, G. K. (1996). *Manual for Beck depression inventory-ii.* San Antonio, TX: Psychological Corporation.

Bell, V., Halligan, P. W. and Ellis, H. D. (2006). Explaining delusions: A cognitive perspective. *Trends in Cognitive Sciences, 10*(5), 219–26.

Bennett, K. and Corcoran, R. (2010). Biases in everyday reasoning: Associations with subclinical anxiety, depression and paranoia. *Psychosis, 2*(3), 227–37.

Bentall, R. P. and Fernyhough, C. (2008). Social predictors of psychotic experiences: Specificity and psychological mechanisms. *Schizophrenia Bulletin, 34*(6), 1012–20.

Bentall, R. P. and Kaney, S. (1996). Abnormalities of self-representation and persecutory delusions: A test of a cognitive model of paranoia. *Psychological Medicine, 26*(6), 1231–37.

Bentall, R. P., Baker, G. A. and Havers, S. (1991). Reality monitoring and psychotic hallucinations. *The British Journal of Clinical Psychology/The British Psychological Society, 30*(3), 213–22.

Bentall, R. P., Corcoran, R., Howard, R., Blackwood, N. and Kinderman, P. (2001). Persecutory delusions: A review and theoretical integration. *Clinical Psychology Review, 21*(8), 1143–92.

Bentall, R. P., Kaney, S. and Dewey, M. E. (1991). Persecutory delusions: An attribution theory analysis. *The British Journal of Clinical Psychology/The British Psychological Society, 30,* 13–23.

Bentall, R. P., Rowse, G., Shryane, N., Kinderman, P., Howard, R., Blackwood, N. et al. (2009). The cognitive and affective structure of paranoid delusions: A transdiagnostic investigation of patients with schizophrenia spectrum disorders and depression. *Archives of General Psychiatry*, 66(3), 236–47.

Birchwood, M., Mason, R., MacMillan, F. and Healy, J. (1993). Depression, demoralization and control over psychotic illness: A comparison of depressed and non-depressed patients with a chronic psychosis. *Psychological Medicine*, 23(2), 387–95.

Bishop, S. J. (2008). Neural mechanisms underlying selective attention to threat. *Annals of the New York Academy of Sciences*, 1129, 141–52.

Bishop, S. J., Jenkins, R. and Lawrence, A. D. (2007). Neural processing of fearful faces: Effects of anxiety are gated by perceptual capacity limitations. *Cerebral Cortex (New York, N.Y.: 1991)*, 17(7), 1595–603.

Blackmore, S. J. (1984). A postal survey of OBEs and other experiences. *Journal of the Society for Psychical Research*, 52(796), 225–44.

Blackmore, S. J. and Troscianko, A. (1985). Belief in the paranormal: Probability judgements, illusory control and the 'chance baseline shift'. *British Journal of Psychology*, 76, 459–68.

Blackwood, N., Howard, R., Bentall, R. and Murray, R. (2001). Cognitive neuropsychiatric models of persecutory delusions. *The American Journal of Psychiatry*, 158, 527–39.

Bleuler, E. (1911). Dementia preacox oder der gruppe der schizophrenien. In G. Aschaffenburg (ed.), *Handbuch der geisteskrankheiten*. Leipzig: Deuticke.

Boonstra, N., Sterk, B., Wunderink, L., Sytema, S., De Haan, L. and Wiersma, D. (2011). Association of treatment delay, migration and urbanicity in psychosis. *European Psychiatry: The Journal of the Association of European Psychiatrists*, 27(5), 500–5.

Boonstra, N., Wunderink, L., Sytema, S., and Wiersma, D. (2008). Detection of psychosis by mental health care services: A naturalistic cohort study. *Clinical Practice and Epidemiology in Mental Health: CP and EMH*, 4, 29.

Brakoulias, V., Langdon, R., Sloss, G., Coltheart, M., Meares, R. and Harris, A. (2008). Delusions and reasoning: A study involving cognitive behavioural therapy. *Cognitive Neuropsychiatry*, 13(2), 148–65.

Brébion, G., Gorman, J. M., Amador, X., Malaspina, D. and Sharif, Z. (2002). Source monitoring impairments in schizophrenia: Characterisation and associations with positive and negative symptomatology. *Psychiatry Research*, 112(1), 27–39.

Brennan, J. H. and Hemsley, D. R. (1984). Illusory correlations in paranoid and non-paranoid schizophrenia. *The British Journal of Clinical Psychology/The British Psychological Society*, 23(3), 225–6.

Brockner, J. and Rubin, J. Z. (1985). *Entrapment in escalating conflicts: A social psychological analysis*. New York: Springer.

Broome, M. R., Johns, L. C., Valli, I., Woolley, J. B., Tabraham, P., Brett, C. et al. (2007). Delusion formation and reasoning biases in those at clinical high risk for psychosis. *The British Journal of Psychiatry. Supplement*, 51, s38–42.

Broome, M. R., Woolley, J. B., Johns, L. C., Valmaggia, L. R., Tabraham, P., Gafoor, R. et al. (2005a). Outreach and support in south London (OASIS): Implementation of a clinical service for prodromal psychosis and the at risk mental state. *European Psychiatry: The Journal of the Association of European Psychiatrists*, 20(5–6), 372–8.

Broome, M. R., Woolley, J. B., Tabraham, P., Johns, L. C., Bramon, E., Murray, G. K. et al. (2005b). What causes the onset of psychosis? *Schizophrenia Research*, 79(1), 23–34.

Brüne, M. (2005). 'Theory of mind' in schizophrenia: A review of the literature. *Schizophrenia Bulletin*, 31(1), 21–42.

Brunelin, J., d'Amato, T., Brun, P., Bediou, B., Kallel, L., Senn, M. et al. (2007). Impaired verbal source monitoring in schizophrenia: An intermediate trait vulnerability marker? *Schizophrenia Research*, 89(1–3), 287–92.

Brunet, K., Birchwood, M., Lester, H. and Thornhill, K. (2007). Delays in mental health services and duration of untreated psychosis. *Psychiatric Bulletin*, *31*(11), 408–10.

Buchy, L., Woodward, T. S. and Liotti, M. (2007). A cognitive bias against disconfirmatory evidence (BADE) is associated with schizotypy. *Schizophrenia Research*, *90*(1–3), 334–7.

Candido, C. L. and Romney, D. M. (1990). Attributional style in paranoid vs. Depressed patients. *The British Journal of Medical Psychology*, *63 (Pt 4)*, 355–63.

Cannistraro, P. A. and Rauch, S. L. (2003). Neural circuitry of anxiety: Evidence from structural and functional neuroimaging studies. *Psychopharmacology Bulletin*, *37*(4), 8–25.

Cannon, T. D., Cadenhead, K., Cornblatt, B., Woods, S. W., Addington, J., Walker, E. *et al*. (2008). Prediction of psychosis in youth at high clinical risk: A multisite longitudinal study in North America. *Archives of General Psychiatry*, *65*(1), 28–37.

Carpenter, W. T. and Strauss, J. S. (1991). The prediction of outcome in schizophrenia. IV: Eleven-year follow-up of the Washington IPSS cohort. *The Journal of Nervous and Mental Disease*, *179*(9), 517–25.

Chapman, L. J. and Chapman, J. P. (1967). Genesis of popular but erroneous psychodiagnostic observations. *Journal of Abnormal Psychology*, *72*(3), 193–204.

Christensen-Szalanski, J. J. J. and Willham, C. F. (1991). The hindsight bias: A meta-analysis. *Organizational Behaviour and Human Decision Processes*, *48*(1), 147–68.

Chudleigh, C., Naismith, S. L., Blaszczynski, A., Hermens, D. F., Hodge, M. A. and Hickie, I. B. (2011). How does social functioning in the early stages of psychosis relate to depression and social anxiety? *Early Intervention in Psychiatry*, *5*(3), 224–32.

Colbert, S. M. and Peters, E. R. (2002). Need for closure and jumping-to-conclusions in delusion-prone individuals. *The Journal of Nervous and Mental Disease*, *190*(1), 27–31.

Connolly, K. M., Lohr, J. M., Olatunji, B. O., Hahn, K. S. and Williams, N. L. (2009). Information processing in contamination fear: A covariation bias examination of fear and disgust. *Journal of Anxiety Disorders*, *23*(1), 60–8.

Conway, C. R., Bollini, A. M., Graham, B. G., Keefe, R. S., Schiffman, S. S. and McEvoy, J. P. (2002). Sensory acuity and reasoning in delusional disorder. *Comprehensive Psychiatry*, *43*(3), 175–8.

Corcoran, R., Rowse, G., Moore, R., Blackwood, N., Kinderman, P., Howard, R. *et al*. (2008). A transdiagnostic investigation of 'theory of mind' and 'jumping to conclusions' in patients with persecutory delusions. *Psychological Medicine*, *38*(11), 1577–83.

Costafreda, S. G., Brébion, G., Allen, P., McGuire, P. K. and Fu, C. H. (2008). Affective modulation of external misattribution bias in source monitoring in schizophrenia. *Psychological Medicine*, *38*(6), 821–4.

Davidson, R. J. (2002). Anxiety and affective style: Role of prefrontal cortex and amygdala. *Biological Psychiatry*, *51*(1), 68–80.

Davies, M., Coltheart, M., Langdon, R. and Breen, N. (2001). Monothematic delusions: Towards a two-factor account. *Philosophy Psychiatry and Psychology*, *8*(2/3), 133–58.

Davies, M. F. (1993). Dogmatism and the persistence of discredited beliefs. *Journal of Personal and Social Psychology*, *19*(6), 692–9.

Davies, M. F. (1998). Dogmatism and belief formation: Output inference in the processing of supporting and contradictory cognitions. *Journal of Personal and Social Psychology*, *75*(2), 456–66.

De Jong, P. J., van den Hout, M. and Merckelbach, H. (1995). Covariation bias and the return of fear. *Behaviour Research and Therapy*, *33*(2), 211–13.

De Jong, P. J., Merckelbach, H., and Arntz, A. (1995). Covariation bias in phobic women: The relationship between a priori expectancy, on-line expectancy, autonomic responding, and a posteriori contingency judgment. *Journal of Abnormal Psychology*, *104*(1), 55.

de Koning, M. B., Bloemen, O. J., van Amelsvoort, T. A., Becker, H. E., Nieman, D. H., van der Gaag, M. *et al*. (2009). Early intervention in patients at ultra high risk of psychosis: Benefits and risks. *Acta Psychiatrica Scandinavica*, *119*(6), 426–42.

Derryberry, D. and Reed, M. A. (2002). Anxiety-related attentional biases and their regulation by attentional control. *Journal of Abnormal Psychology, 111*(2), 225–36.

Derryberry, D. and Rothbart, M. K. (1988). Arousal, affect, and attention as components of temperament. *Journal of Personality and Social Psychology, 55*(6), 958–66.

Díez-Alegría, C., Vázquez, C. and Hernández-Lloreda, M. J. (2008). Covariation assessment for neutral and emotional verbal stimuli in paranoid delusions. *The British Journal of Clinical Psychology/The British Psychological Society, 47*(4), 427–37.

Dolan, R. J. and Vuilleumier, P. (2003). *Amygdala automaticity in emotional processing: A heterogeneous set of cognitive abilities (e.g. allocation of attention, inhibitory control, hypothesis generation) governed by the prefrontal cortex.* New York: Oxford University Press.

Drake, R., Haddock, G., Tarrier, N., Bentall, R. and Lewis, S. (2007). The psychotic symptom rating scales (PSYRATS): Their usefulness and properties in first episode psychosis. *Schizophrenia Research, 89*(1–3), 119–22.

Drake, R. J., Haley, C. J., Akhtar, S. and Lewis, S. W. (2000). Causes and consequences of duration of untreated psychosis in schizophrenia. *The British Journal of Psychiatry: The Journal of Mental Science, 177*, 511–15.

Dudley, R. E., J., C. H., Young, A. W. and Over, D. E. (1997a). The effect of self-referent material on the reasoning of people with delusions. *The British Journal of Clinical Psychology/The British Psychological Society, 36*(4), 575–84.

Dudley, R. E., J., C. H., Young, A. W. and Over, D. E. (1997b). Normal and abnormal reasoning in people with delusions. *The British Journal of Clinical Psychology/The British Psychological Society, 36*(2), 243–58.

Dudley, R. E. J. and Over, D. E. (2003). People with delusions jump to conclusions: A theoretical account of research findings on the reasoning of people with delusions. *Clinical Psychology and Psychotherapy, 10*, 263–74.

Eckersley, R. (2011). Troubled youth: An island of misery in an ocean of happiness, or the tip of an iceberg of suffering? *Early Intervention in Psychiatry, 5 Suppl 1*, 6–11.

Ehlers, A., Margraf, J., Davies, S. and Roth, W. T. (1988). Selective processing of threat cues in subjects with panic attack. *Cognition and Emotion, 2*, 201–19.

Eldar, S., Apter, A., Lotan, D., Edgar, K. P., Naim, R., Fox, N. A., Pine, D. S. and Bar-Haim, Y. (2012). Attention bias modification treatment for pediatric anxiety disorders: a randomized controlled trial. *American Journal of Psychiatry, 169*(2), 213–20.

Elstein, A. S. (1989). On the clinical significance of hindsight bias. *Medical Decision Making, 9*(1), 70.

Ensum, I. and Morrison, A. P. (2003). The effects of focus of attention on attributional bias in patients experiencing auditory hallucinations. *Behaviour Research and Therapy, 41*(8), 895–907.

Eysenck, M. W. (1992). *Anxiety: The cognitive perspective.* London: Lawrence Erlbaum Associates.

Eysenck, M. W. and Calvo, M. G. (1992). Anxiety and performance: The processing efficiency theory. *Cognition and Emotion, 6*(6), 409–34.

Fear, C., Sharp, H., and Healy, D. (1996). Cognitive processes in delusional disorders. *The British Journal of Psychiatry: The Journal of Mental Science, 168*(1), 61.

Fear, C. F. and Healy, D. (1997). Probabilistic reasoning in obsessive–compulsive and delusional disorders. *Psychological Medicine, 27*(1), 199–208.

Festinger, L. (1957). *A theory of cognitive dissonance.* Stanford, CA: Stanford University Press.

Fox, E. (1994). Attentional bias in anxiety: A defective inhibition hypothesis. *Cognition and Emotion, 8*(2), 165–95.

Frame, L. and Morrison, A. P. (2001). Causes of posttraumatic stress disorder in psychotic patients. *Archives of General Psychiatry, 58*(3), 305.

Freeman, D., Garety, P. A. and Kuipers, E. (2001). Persecutory delusions: Developing the understanding of belief maintenance and emotional distress. *Psychological Medicine, 31*(7), 1293–306.

Freeman, D., Garety, P. A., Fowler, D., Kuipers, E., Bebbington, P. E. and Dunn, G. (2004). Why do people with delusions fail to choose more realistic explanations for their experiences? An empirical investigation. *Journal of Consulting and Clinical Psychology*, *72*(4), 671–80.

Freeman, D., Garety, P. A., Bebbington, P., Slater, M., Kuipers, E., Fowler, D. et al. (2005). The psychology of persecutory ideation II: A virtual reality experimental study. *The Journal of Nervous and Mental Disease*, *193*(5), 309–15.

Freeman, D., Garety, P., Kuipers, E., Colbert, S., Jolley, S., Fowler, D. et al. (2006). Delusions and decision-making style: Use of the need for closure scale. *Behaviour Research and Therapy*, *44*(8), 1147–58.

Freeston, M. H., Rheaume, J., Letarte, H., Dugas, M. J. and Ladouceur, R. (1994). Why do people worry? *Personality and Individual Differences*, *17*, 791–802.

French, P. and Morrison, A. P. (2004). *Early detection and cognitive therapy for people at high risk of developing psychosis: A treatment approach.* Chichester: John Wiley & Sons.

Frenkel, E., Kugelmass, S., Nathan, M. and Ingraham, L. J. (1995). Locus of control and mental health in adolescence and adulthood. *Schizophrenia Bulletin*, *21*(2), 219–26.

Frijda, N. H. (1994). Emotions are functional, most of the time. In P. Ekman and R. J. Davidson (eds), *The nature of emotion: Fundamental questions.* (pp. 112–22). New York: Oxford University Press.

Fusar-Poli, P., Bonoldi, I., Yung, A. R., Borgwardt, S., Kempton, M., Barale, F., et al. (2012). Predicting psychosis: A meta-analysis of transition outcomes in individuals at high clinical risk. *Archives of General Psychiatry*, *69*(3), 220–29.

Gallup, G. H. and Newport, F. (1991). Belief in paranormal phenomena among adult Americans. *Skeptical Inquirer*, *15*(2), 137–46.

Garety, P. A. and Freeman, D. (1999). Cognitive approaches to delusions: A critical review of theories and evidence. *The British Journal of Clinical Psychology/The British Psychological Society*, *38*(2), 113–54.

Garety, P. A., Bebbington, P., Fowler, D., Freeman, D. and Kuipers, E. (2007). Implications for neurobiological research of cognitive models of psychosis: A theoretical paper. *Psychological Medicine*, *37*(10), 1377–91.

Garety, P. A., Freeman, D., Jolley, S., Dunn, G., Bebbington, P. E., Fowler, D. G. et al. (2005). Reasoning, emotions, and delusional conviction in psychosis. *Journal of Abnormal Psychology*, *114*(3), 373–84.

Garety, P. A., Hemsley, D. R. and Wessely, S. (1991). Reasoning in deluded schizophrenic and paranoid patients. Biases in performance on a probabilistic inference task. *The Journal of Nervous and Mental Disease*, *179*(4), 194–201.

Gee, D. G., Karlsgodt, K. H., van Erp, T. G., Bearden, C. E., Lieberman, M. D., Belger, A. et al. (2012). Altered age-related trajectories of amygdala-prefrontal circuitry in adolescents at clinical high risk for psychosis: A preliminary study. *Schizophrenia Research*, *134*(1), 1–9.

Glotzbach, E., Ewald, H., Andreatta, M., Pauli, P. and Muhlberger, A. (2012). Contextual fear conditioning predicts subsequent avoidance behaviour in a virtual reality environment. *Cognition and Emotion*, *26*(7), 1256–72.

Goldman, H. H., Skodol, A. E., and Lave, T. R. (1992). Revising axis V for DSM-IV: A review of measures of social functioning. *The American Journal of Psychiatry*, *149*(9), 1148–56.

Gorman, J. M., Kent, J. M., Sullivan, G. M. and Coplan, J. D. (2000). Neuroanatomical hypothesis of panic disorder, revised. *The American Journal of Psychiatry*, *157*(4), 493–505.

Gottesman, I. and Gould, T. (2003). The endophenotype concept in psychiatry: Etymology and strategic intentions. *The American Journal of Psychiatry*, *160*(4), 636–45.

Granholm, E., Ben-Zeev, D. and Link, P. C. (2009). Social disinterest attitudes and group cognitive-behavioral social skills training for functional disability in schizophrenia. *Schizophrenia Bulletin*, *35*(5), 874–83.

Grant, P. M. and Beck, A. T. (2009). Defeatist beliefs as a mediator of cognitive impairment, negative symptoms, and functioning in schizophrenia. *Schizophrenia Bulletin*, *35*(4), 798–806.

Grant, P. M., Huh, G. A., Perivoliotis, D., Stolar, N. M. and Beck, A. T. (2012). Randomized trial to evaluate the efficacy of cognitive therapy for low-functioning patients with schizophrenia. *Archives of General Psychiatry*, 69(2), 121–7.
Greenwood, C. M., Rangrej, J. and Sun, L. (2007). Optimal selection of markers for validation or replication from genome-wide association studies. *Genetic Epidemiology*, 31(5), 396–407.
Hall, P. L. and Tarrier, N. (2003). The cognitive-behavioural treatment of low self-esteem in psychotic patients: A pilot study. *Behaviour Research and Therapy*, 41(3), 317–32.
Hallion, L. S. and Ruscio, A. M. (2011). A meta-analysis of the effect of cognitive bias modification on anxiety and depression. *Psychological Bulletin*, 136(6), 940–58.
Hanssen, M., Bak, M., Bijl, R., Vollebergh, W. and van Os, J. (2005). The incidence and outcome of subclinical psychotic experiences in the general population. *The British Journal of Clinical Psychology/The British Psychological Society*, 44(2), 181–91.
Hariri, A. R., Bookheimer, S. Y. and Mazziotta, J. C. (2000). Modulating emotional responses: Effects of a neocortical network on the limbic system. *Neuroreport*, 11(1), 43–8.
Harrington, L., Siegert, R. J. and McClure, J. (2005). Theory of mind in schizophrenia: A critical review. *Cognitive Neuropsychiatry*, 10(4), 249–86.
Harvey, A. G., Watkins, E., Mansell, W. and Shafran, R. (2004). *Cognitive behavioural processes across psychological disorders: A transdiagnostic approach to research and treatment*. Oxford: Oxford University Press.
Heilbrun, A. B. J. (1980). Impaired recognition of self-expressed thought in patients with auditory hallucinations. *Journal of Abnormal Psychology*, 89(6), 728–36.
Henquet, C., Krabbendam, L., Dautzenberg, J., Jolles, J. and Merckelbach, H. (2005). Confusing thoughts and speech: Source monitoring and psychosis. *Psychiatry Research*, 133(1), 57–63.
Hickie, I. B. (2011). Youth mental health: We know where we are and we can now say where we need to go next. *Early Intervention in Psychiatry*, 5 Suppl 1, 63–9.
Hoffmann, H., Kupper, Z., and Kunz, B. (2000). Hopelessness and its impact on rehabilitation outcome in schizophrenia: An exploratory study. *Schizophrenia Research*, 43(2–3), 147–58.
Holton, B. and Pyszczynski, T. (1989). Biased information search in the interpersonal domain. *Personality and Social Psychology Bulletin*, 15, 42–51.
Hope, D. A., Rapee, R. M., Heimberg, R. G., and Dombeck, M. J. (1990). Representation of the self in social phobia: Vulnerability to social threat. *Cognitive Therapy and Research*, 14, 177–89.
Howes, O. D. and Kapur, S. (2009). The dopamine hypothesis of schizophrenia: Version iii–the final common pathway. *Schizophrenia Bulletin*, 35(3), 549–62.
Huq, S. F., Garety, P. A., and Hemsley, D. R. (1988). Probabilistic judgements in deluded and non-deluded subjects. *Quarterly Journal of Experimental Psychology*, 40(4), 801–12.
Hunter, E. C., Phillips, M. L., Chalder, T., Sierra, M. and David, A. S. (2003). Depersonalisation disorder: A cognitive-behavioural conceptualisation. *Behaviour Research and Therapy*, 41(12), 1451–67.
Insel, T. R. (2010). Rethinking schizophrenia. *Nature*, 468(7321), 187–93.
Ising, H. K., Veling, W., Loewy, R. L., Rietveld, M. W., Rietdijk, J., Dragt, S. et al. (2012). The validity of the 16-item version of the prodromal questionnaire (PQ-16) to screen for ultra high risk of developing psychosis in the general help-seeking population. *Schizophrenia Bulletin*, 38(6), 1288–96.
Jackson, C. and Iqbal, Z. (2000). Psychological adjustment to early psychosis. In M. Birchwood, D. Fowler and C. Jackson (eds), *Early intervention in psychosis*. London: John Wiley & Sons.
Janis, I. L. (1982). *Groupthink* (2nd edn., rev. edn.). Boston, MA: Houghton Mifflin.
Janssen, I., Versmissen, D., Campo, J. A., Myin-Germeys, I., van Os, J. and Krabbendam, L. (2006). Attribution style and psychosis: Evidence for an externalizing bias in patients but not in individuals at high risk. *Psychological Medicine*, 36(6), 771–8.
John, C. and Dodgson, G. (1994). Inductive reasoning in delusional thought. *Journal of Mental Health*, 3(1), 3–49.

Johns, L. C., Allen, P., Valli, I., Winton-Brown, T., Broome, M., Woolley, J. et al. (2010). Impaired verbal self-monitoring in individuals at high risk of psychosis. *Psychological Medicine, 40*, 1433–42.

Johns, L. C., Gregg, L., Allen, P. and McGuire, P. K. (2006). Impaired verbal self-monitoring in psychosis: Effects of state, trait and diagnosis. *Psychological Medicine, 36*(4), 465–74.

Johnston, L. (1996). Resisting change: Information-seeking and stereotype change. *European Journal of Social Psychology, 26*, 799–825.

Johnstone, E. C., Crow, T. J., Johnson, A. L. and MacMillan, J. F. (1986). The Northwick park study of first episodes of schizophrenia. I. Presentation of the illness and problems relating to admission. *The British Journal of Psychiatry: The Journal of Mental Science, 148*(2), 115–20.

Joiner, T. E. (2001). Negative attributional style hopelessness depression and endogeneous depression. *Behaviour Research and Therapy, 39*, 139–49.

Kaney, S. and Bentall, R. P. (1989). Persecutory delusions and attributional style. *The British Journal of Medical Psychology, 62*(2), 191–8.

Kaney, S., Bowen-Jones, K., Dewey, M. E. and Bentall, R. P. (1997). Two predictions about paranoid ideation: Deluded, depressed and normal participants' subjective frequency and consensus judgments for positive, neutral and negative events. *The British Journal of Clinical Psychology/The British Psychological Society, 36*(3), 349–64.

Kay, S. R., Fiszbein, A. and Opler, L. A. (1987). The positive and negative syndrome scale (PANSS) for schizophrenia. *Schizophrenia Bulletin, 13*(2), 261–76.

Keefe, R. S., Arnold, M. C., Bayen, U. J. and Harvey, P. D. (1999). Source monitoring deficits in patients with schizophrenia: A multinomial modelling analysis. *Psychological Medicine, 29*(4), 903–14.

Keefe, R. S., Poe, M. P., McEvoy, J. P. and Vaughan, A. (2003). Source monitoring improvement in patients with schizophrenia receiving antipsychotic medications. *Psychopharmacology (Berlin), 169*(3–4), 383–9.

Kendler, K. S., Gallagher, T. J., Abelson, J. M., and Kessler, R. C. (1996). Lifetime prevalence, demographic risk factors, and diagnostic validity of nonaffective psychosis as assessed in a US community sample. The national comorbidity survey. *Archives of General Psychiatry, 53*(11), 1022–31.

Kennedy, S. J., Rapee, R. M. and Mazurski, E. J. (1997). Covariation bias for phylogenetic versus ontogenetic fear-relevant stimuli. *Behaviour Research and Therapy, 35*(5), 415–22.

Kinderman, P. and Bentall, R. P. (1997). Causal attributions in paranoia and depression: Internal, personal, and situational attributions for negative events. *Journal of Abnormal Psychology, 106*(2), 341–5.

Kinderman, P. and Bentall, R. P. (2000). Self-discrepancies and causal attributions: Studies of hypothesized relationships. *The British Journal of Clinical Psychology/The British Psychological Society, 39*(3), 255–73.

Klosterkötter, J., Hellmich, M., Steinmeyer, E. M. and Schültze-Lutter, F. (2001). Diagnosing schizophrenia in the initial prodromal phase. *Archives of General Psychiatry, 58*(2), 158–64.

Krabbendam, L., Myin-Germeys, I., Hanssen, M., Bijl, R. V., de Graaf, R., Vollebergh, W. et al. (2004). Hallucinatory experiences and onset of psychotic disorder: Evidence that the risk is mediated by delusion formation. *Acta Psychiatrica Scandinavica, 110*(4), 264–72.

Lader, M. H. and Wing, L. (1966). *Physiological measures, sedative drugs and morbid anxiety.* New York: Oxford University Press.

Langdon, R., Corner, T., McLaren, J., Ward, P. B. and Coltheart, M. (2006). Externalizing and personalizing biases in persecutory delusions: The relationship with poor insight and theory-of-mind. *Behaviour Research and Therapy, 44*(5), 699–713.

Langdon, R., Ward, P. B. and Coltheart, M. (2010). Reasoning anomalies associated with delusions in schizophrenia. *Schizophrenia Bulletin, 36*(2), 321–30.

Large, M., Nielssen, O., Slade, T. and Harris, A. (2008). Measurement and reporting of the duration of untreated psychosis. *Early Intervention in Psychiatry, 2*(4), 201–11.

Laroi, F., Van der Linden, M. and Marczewski, P. (2004). The effects of emotional salience, cognitive effort and meta-cognitive beliefs on a reality monitoring task in hallucination-prone subjects. *The British Journal of Clinical Psychology/The British Psychological Society, 43*(Pt 3), 221–33.

Larsen, T. K., Melle, I., Auestad, B., Haahr, U., Joa, I., Johannessen, J. O. *et al.* (2011). Early detection of psychosis: Positive effects on 5-year outcome. *Psychological Medicine, 41*(7), 1461–9.

Laruelle, M. (2000). The role of endogenous sensitization in the pathophysiology of schizophrenia: Implications from recent brain imaging studies. *Brain Research Reviews, 31*(2–3), 371–84.

Lecomte, T., Leclerc, C., Corbière, M., Wykes, T., Wallace, C. J. and Spidel, A. (2008). Group cognitive behavior therapy or social skills training for individuals with a recent onset of psychosis? Results of a randomized controlled trial. *The Journal of Nervous and Mental Disease, 196*(12), 866–75.

LeDoux, J. E. (1996). *The emotional brain.* New York: Simon & Schuster.

LeDoux, J. E. (2000). Emotion circuits in the brain. *Annual Review of Neuroscience, 23*(1), 155–84.

Leucht, S. and Heres, S. (2006). Epidemiology, clinical consequences, and psychosocial treatment of nonadherence in schizophrenia. *The Journal of Clinical Psychiatry, 67 Suppl 5*, 3–8.

Levine, E., Jonas, H. and Serper, M. R. (2004). Interpersonal attributional biases in hallucinatory-prone individuals. *Schizophrenia Research, 69*(1), 23–8.

Lieberman, J. A., Stroup, T. S., McEvoy, J. P., Swartz, M. S., Rosenheck, R. A., Perkins, D. O. *et al.* (2005). Effectiveness of antipsychotic drugs in patients with chronic schizophrenia. *The New England Journal of Medicine, 353*(12), 1209–23.

Lincoln, T. M., Peter, N., Schäfer, M. and Moritz, S. (2010). From stress to paranoia: An experimental investigation of the moderating and mediating role of reasoning biases. *Psychological Medicine, 40*(1), 169–71.

Lincoln, T. M., Ziegler, M., Mehl, S. and Rief, W. (2010). The jumping to conclusions bias in delusions: Specificity and changeability. *Journal of Abnormal Psychology, 119*(1), 40–9.

Linney, Y. M., Peters, E. R. and Ayton, P. (1998). Reasoning biases in delusion-prone individuals. *The British Journal of Clinical Psychology/the British Psychological Society, 37* (3), 285–302.

Loewy, R. L., Bearden, C. E., Johnson, J. K., Raine, A. and Cannon, T. D. (2005). The prodromal questionnaire (PQ): Preliminary validation of a self-report screening measure for prodromal and psychotic syndromes. *Schizophrenia Research, 77*(2–3), 141–9.

Lovibond, P., Mitchell, C. J., Minard, E., Brady, A. and Menzies, R. G. (2009). Safety behaviours preserve threat beliefs: protection from extinction of human fear conditioning by an avoidance response. *Behaviour Research and Therapy, 47*(8), 716–20.

Lundgren, S. R. and Prislin, R. (1998). Motivated cognitive processing and attitude change. *Personality and Social Psychology Bulletin, 24*, 715–26.

Lyon, H. M., Kaney, S. and Bentall, R. P. (1994). The defensive function of persecutory delusions: Evidence from attribution tasks. *The British Journal of Psychiatry: The Journal of Mental Science, 164*(5), 637–46.

Lyon, H. M., Startup, M. and Bentall, R. P. (1999). Social cognition and the manic defense: Attributions, selective attention, and self-schema in bipolar affective disorder. *Journal of Abnormal Psychology, 108*(2), 273–82.

Maher, B. A. (1988). Anomalous experience and delusional thinking: The logic of explanations. In T. F. Oltmanns and B. A. Maher (eds), *Delusional beliefs.* (pp. 15–33). New York: John Wiley & Sons.

Marks, I. M. (1987). *Fears, phobias, and rituals.* New York: Oxford University Press.

Marshall, M., Lewis, S., Lockwood, A., Drake, R., Jones, P. and Croudace, T. (2005). Association between duration of untreated psychosis and outcome in cohorts of first-episode patients: A systematic review. *Archives of General Psychiatry, 62*(9), 975–83.

Marshall, W. L. (1988). Behaviour therapy. In C. G. Last and M. Hern (eds), *Handbook of anxiety disorders.* (pp. 338–61). Elmsford, NY: Pergamon Press.

Martin, D. J., Oren, Z. and Boone, K. (1991). Major depressives' and dysthymics' performance on the Wisconsin card sorting test. *Journal of Clinical Psychology*, *47*(5), 684–90.

Mateer, C. A. (1999). The rehabilitation of executive disorders. In D. T. Stuss and G. Winocor (eds), *Cognitive neurohabilitation.* (pp. 314–32). New York: Cambridge University Press.

Mathews, A. (1990). Why worry? The cognitive function of anxiety. *Behaviour Research and Therapy*, *28*(6), 455–68.

Mathews, A. and MacLeod, C. (1994). Cognitive approaches to emotion and emotional disorders. *Annual Review of Psychology*, *45*, 25–50.

Mathews, A. and MacLeod, C. (2002). Induced processing biases have causal effects on anxiety. *Cognition and Emotion*, *16*(3), 331–54.

Mathews, A., Mogg, K., Kentish, J. and Eysenck, M. (1995). Effect of psychological treatment on cognitive bias in generalized anxiety disorder. *Behaviour Research and Therapy*, *33*(3), 293–303.

Mattia, J. I., Heimberg, R. G. and Hope, D. A. (1993). The revised Stroop color-naming task in social phobics. *Behaviour Research and Therapy*, *31*(3), 305–13.

Mattick, R. P. and Clarke, J. C. (1998). Development and validation of measures of social phobia scrutiny fear and social interaction anxiety. *Behaviour Research and Therapy*, *36*(4), 455–70.

Mayberg, H. (2003). Modulating dysfunctional limbic–cortical circuits in depression: Towards development of brain-based algorithms for diagnosis and optimised treatment. *British Medical Bulletin*, *65*, 193–207.

McGlashan, T. H., Zipursky, R. B., Perkins, D., Addington, J., Miller, T. J., Woods, S. W., *et al.* (2003). The PRIME North America randomized double-blind clinical trial of olanzapine versus placebo in patients at risk of being prodromally symptomatic for psychosis. I. Study rationale and design. *Schizophrenia Research*, *61*(1), 7–18.

McGlashan, T. H., Zipursky, R. B., Perkins, D., Addington, J., Miller, T., Woods, S. W. *et al.* (2006). Randomized, double-blind trial of olanzapine versus placebo in patients prodromally symptomatic for psychosis. *The American Journal of Psychiatry*, *163*(5), 790–9.

McGorry, P. D. (n.d.). The NEURAPRO-E study: A multicenter randomized controlled trial (RCT) of omega-3 fatty acids and cognitive-behavioural case management for symptomatic patients at ultra-high risk for early progression to schizophrenia and other psychotic disorders to assess the 6-month transition rate to first episode psychosis. Online at: www.anzctr.org.au/Trial/Registration/TrialReview.aspx?ACTRN=12608000475347.

McGorry, P. D. (2010). Risk syndromes, clinical staging and DSM V: New diagnostic infrastructure for early intervention in psychiatry. *Schizophrenia Research*, *120*, 49–53.

McGorry, P. D. (2011). Transition to adulthood: the critical period for pre-emptive, disease-modifying care for schizophrenia and related disorders. *Schizophrenia Bulletin*, *37*(3), 524–30.

McGorry, P. D., Chanen, A., McCarthy, E., Van Riel, R., McKenzie, D. and Singh, B. S. (1991). Posttraumatic stress disorder following recent-onset psychosis. An unrecognized postpsychotic syndrome. *The Journal of Nervous and Mental Disease*, *179*(5), 253–8.

McGorry, P. D., Hickie, I. B., Yung, A. R., Pantelis, C. and Jackson, H. J. (2006). Clinical staging of psychiatric disorders: A heuristic framework for choosing earlier, safer and more effective interventions. *The Australian and New Zealand Journal of Psychiatry*, *40*(8), 616–22.

McGorry, P. D., Nelson, B., Amminger, G. P., Bechdolf, A., Francey, S. M., Berger, G. *et al.* (2009). Intervention in individuals at ultra high risk for psychosis: A review and future directions. *The Journal of Clinical Psychiatry*, *70*(9), 1206–12.

McGorry, P. D., Yung, A. R. and Phillips, L. J. (2003). The 'close-in' or ultra high-risk model: A safe and effective strategy for research and clinical intervention in prepsychotic mental disorder. *Schizophrenia Bulletin*, *29*(4), 771–90.

McGorry, P. D., Yung, A. R., Phillips, L. J., Yuen, H. P., Francey, S., Cosgrave, E. M. *et al.* (2002). Randomized controlled trial of interventions designed to reduce the risk of progression to first-episode psychosis in a clinical sample with subthreshold symptoms. *Archives of General Psychiatry*, *59*(10), 921–8.

McKay, R., Langdon, R. and Coltheart, M. (2006). Need for closure, jumping to conclusions, and decisiveness in delusion-prone individuals. *The Journal of Nervous and Mental Disease, 194*(6), 422–6.

Melle, I., Larsen, T. K., Haahr, U., Friis, S., Johannesen, J. O., Opjordsmoen, S., et al. (2008). Prevention of negative symptom psychopathologies in first-episode schizophrenia: Two-year effects of reducing the duration of untreated psychosis. *Archives of General Psychiatry, 65*(6), 634–40.

Menon, M., Mizrahi, R. and Kapur, S. (2008). 'Jumping to conclusions' and delusions in psychosis: Relationship and response to treatment. *Schizophrenia Research, 98*(1–3), 225–31.

Menon, M., Pomarol-Clotet, E., McKenna, P. J. and McCarthy, R. A. (2006). Probabilistic reasoning in schizophrenia: A comparison of the performance of deluded and nondeluded schizophrenic patients and exploration of possible cognitive underpinnings. *Cognitive Neuropsychiatry, 11*(6), 521–36.

Merrin, J., Kinderman, P. and Bentall, R. P. (2007). 'Jumping to conclusions' and attributional style in persecutory delusions. *Cognitive Therapy Research, 31*(6), 741–58.

Miller, G. (2010). Beyond DSM: Seeking a brain-based classification of mental illness. *Science, 327*(5972), 1437.

Miller, G. and Holden, C. (2010). Proposed revisions to psychiatry's canon unveiled. *Science, 327*(5967), 770.

Miller, T. J., McGlashan, T. H., Rosen, J. L., Cadenhead, K., Cannon, T., Ventura, J. et al. (2003). Prodromal assessment with the structured interview for prodromal syndromes and the scale of prodromal symptoms: Predictive validity, interrater reliability, and training to reliability. *Schizophrenia Bulletin, 29*(4), 703–15.

Miller, T. J., McGlashan, T. H., Rosen, J. L., Somjee, L., Markovich, P. J., Stein, K. et al. (2002). Prospective diagnosis of the initial prodrome for schizophrenia based on the structured interview for prodromal syndromes: Preliminary evidence of interrater reliability and predictive validity. *The American Journal of Psychiatry, 159*(5), 863–5.

Mineka, S. and Sutton, S. K. (1992). Cognitive biases and the emotional disorders. *Psychological Science, 3*(1), 65.

Mogg, K. and Bradley, B. P. (1998). A cognitive–motivational analysis of anxiety. *Behaviour Research and Therapy, 36*(9), 809–48.

Mohlman, J. and Gorman, J. M. (2005). The role of executive functioning in CBT: A pilot study with anxious older adults. *Behaviour Research and Therapy, 43*(4), 447–65.

Moore, M. T. and Fresco, D. M. (2007). The relationship of explanatory flexibility to explanatory style. *Behavior Therapy, 38*(4), 325–32.

Moritz, S. and Woodward, T. S. (2005). Jumping to conclusions in delusional and non-delusional schizophrenic patients. *The British Journal of Clinical Psychology/The British Psychological Society, 44*(Pt 2), 193–207.

Moritz, S. and Woodward, T. S. (2006). A generalized bias against disconfirmatory evidence in schizophrenia. *Psychiatry Research, 142*(2–3), 157–65.

Moritz, S. and Woodward, T. S. (2007a). Metacognitive training for schizophrenia patients (MCT): A pilot study on feasibility, treatment adherence, and subjective efficacy. *German Journal of Psychiatry, 10*, 69–78.

Moritz, S. and Woodward, T. S. (2007b). Metacognitive training in schizophrenia: From basic research to knowledge translation and intervention. *Current Opinion in Psychiatry, 20*(6), 619–25.

Moritz, S., Kerstan, A., Veckenstedt, R., Randjbar, S., Vitzthum, F., Schmidt, C. et al. (2011). Further evidence for the efficacy of a metacognitive group training in schizophrenia. *Behaviour Research and Therapy, 49*(3), 151–7.

Moritz, S., Veckenstedt, R., Randjbar, S., Hottenrott, B., Woodward, T. S., von Eckstaedt, F. V. et al. (2009). Decision making under uncertainty and mood induction: Further evidence for liberal acceptance in schizophrenia. *Psychological Medicine, 39*(11), 1821–9.

Moritz, S., Vitzthum, F., Randjbar, S., Veckenstedt, R. and Woodward, T. S. (2010). Detecting and defusing cognitive traps: Metacognitive intervention in schizophrenia. *Current Opinion in Psychiatry*, *23*(6), 561–9.

Moritz, S., Woodward, T. S. and Ruff, C. C. (2003). Source monitoring and memory confidence in schizophrenia. *Psychological Medicine*, *33*(1), 131–9.

Morrison, A. P. and Haddock, G. (1997). Cognitive factors in source monitoring and auditory hallucinations. *Psychological Medicine*, *27*(03), 669–79.

Morrison, A. P., French, P., Parker, S., Roberts, M., Stevens, H., Bentall, R. P. et al. (2007). Three-year follow-up of a randomized controlled trial of cognitive therapy for the prevention of psychosis in people at ultrahigh risk. *Schizophrenia Bulletin*, *33*(3), 682–7.

Morrison, A. P., French, P., Stewart, S. L. K., Birchwood, M., Fowler, D., Gumley, I. et al. (2012). Early detection and intervention evaluation for people at risk of psychosis: Multisite randomised controlled trial. *British Medical Journal (Clinical Research Ed.)*, *344*(apr05 1), e2233.

Morrison, A. P., French, P., Walford, L., Lewis, S. W., Kilcommons, A., Green, J. et al. (2004). Cognitive therapy for the prevention of psychosis in people at ultra-high risk: Randomised controlled trial. *The British Journal of Psychiatry: The Journal of Mental Science*, *185*, 291–7.

Morrison, A. P., Gumley, A. I., Ashcroft, K., Manousos, I. R., White, R., Gillan, K. et al. (2011a). Metacognition and persecutory delusions: Tests of a metacognitive model in a clinical population and comparisons with non-patients. *The British Journal of Clinical Psychology/The British Psychological Society*, *50*, 223–33.

Morrison, A. P., Stewart, S. L., French, P., Bentall, R. P., Birchwood, M., Byrne, R. et al. (2011b). Early detection and intervention evaluation for people at high-risk of psychosis-2 (EDIE-2): Trial rationale, design and baseline characteristics. *Early Intervention in Psychiatry*, *5*(1), 24–32.

Mortimer, A. M., Bentham, P., McKay, A. P., Quemada, I., Clare, L., Eastwood, N. et al. (1996). Delusions in schizophrenia: A phenomenological and psychological exploration. *Cognitive Neuropsychiatry*, *1*(4), 289–304.

Moutoussis, M., Bentall, R. P., Williams, J. and Dayan, P. (2008). A temporal difference account of avoidance learning. *Network (Bristol, England)*, *19*(2), 137–60.

Moutoussis, M., Williams, J., Dayan, P. and Bentall, R. P. (2007). Persecutory delusions and the conditioned avoidance paradigm: Towards an integration of the psychology and biology of paranoia. *Cognitive Neuropsychiatry*, *12*(6), 495–510.

Mowrer, O. H. (1960). *Learning theory and behaviour*. Oxford: John Wiley & Sons.

Muris, P., Merckelbach, H. and van Spauwen, I. (2003). The emotional reasoning heuristic in children. *Behaviour Research and Therapy*, *41*(3), 261–72.

Muris, P., Merkelbach, H., Schepers, S. and Meesters, C. (2003). Anxiety, threat perception abnormalities, and emotional reasoning in nonclinical Dutch children. *Journal of Clinical Child Adolescent Psychology*, *32*(3), 453–59.

Nelson, B. and Yung, A. R. (2007). When things are not as they seem: Detecting first-episode psychosis upon referral to ultra high risk ('prodromal') clinics. *Early Intervention in Psychiatry*, *1*(2), 208–11.

Nelson, B., Thompson, A. and Yung, A. R. (2012). Basic self-disturbance predicts psychosis onset in the ultra high risk for psychosis 'prodromal' population. *Schizophrenia Bulletin*, *37*(1), 61–72.

Nelson, B., Yung, A. R., Bechdolf, A. and McGorry, P. D. (2008). The phenomenological critique and self-disturbance: Implications for ultra-high risk ('prodrome') research. *Schizophrenia Bulletin*, *34*(2), 381–92.

Nemeth, C. J. and Rogers, J. (1996). Dissent and the search for information. *British Journal of Social Psychology*, *35*, 67–76.

NICE (2009, March). *Schizophrenia: Core interventions in the treatment and management of schizophrenia in primary and secondary care (update)*. London: National Institute of Clinical Excellence.

Nieman, D. H., Rike, W. H., Becker, H. E., Dingemans, P. M., van Amelsvoort, T. A., de Haan, L. et al. (2009). Prescription of antipsychotic medication to patients at ultra high risk of developing psychosis. *International Clinical Psychopharmacology, 24*(4), 223–8.

Nienow, T. M. and Docherty, N. M. (2004). Internal source monitoring and thought disorder in schizophrenia. *The Journal of Nervous and Mental Disease, 192*(10), 696–700.

Nordentoft, M., Thorup, A., Petersen, L., Ohlenschlaeger, J., Melau, M., Christensen, T. O. et al. (2006). Transition rates from schizotypal disorder to psychotic disorder for first-contact patients included in the OPUS trial. A randomized clinical trial of integrated treatment and standard treatment. *Schizophrenia Research, 83*(1), 29–40.

Norman, D. A. and Shallice, T. (1986). Attention to action: Willed and automatic control of behavior. In R. J. Davidson, G. E. Schwarts and D. Shapiro (eds), *Consciousness and self-regulation.* (pp. 1–18). New York: Plenum Press.

Ohayon, M. M. (2000). Prevalence of hallucinations and their pathological associations in the general population. *Psychiatry Research, 97*(2–3), 153–64.

Palaniyappan, L., Mallikarjun, P., Joseph, V., White, T. P. and Liddle, P. F. (2010). Reality distortion is related to the structure of the salience network in schizophrenia. *Psychological Medicine, 41*(8), 1701–8.

Pelletier, M., Bouthillier, A., Levesque, J., Carrier, S., Breault, C., Paquette, V. et al. (2003). Separate neural circuits for primary emotions? Brain activity during self-induced sadness and happiness in professional actors. *Neuroreport, 14*(8), 1111–16.

Perivoliotis, D., Morrison, A. P., Grant, P. M., French, P. and Beck, A. T. (2009). Negative performance beliefs and negative symptoms in individuals at ultra-high risk of psychosis: A preliminary study. *Psychopathology, 42*(6), 375–9.

Perkins, D. O., Gu, H., Boteva, K. and Lieberman, J. A. (2005). Relationship between duration of untreated psychosis and outcome in first-episode schizophrenia: A critical review and meta-analysis. *The American Journal of Psychiatry, 162*(10), 1785–804.

Pessoa, L., Padmala, S. and Morland, T. (2005). Fate of unattended fearful faces in the amygdala is determined by both attentional resources and cognitive modulation. *NeuroImage, 28*(1), 249–55.

Peters, E. and Garety, P. (2006). Cognitive functioning in delusions: A longitudinal analysis. *Behaviour Research and Therapy, 44*(4), 481–514.

Peters, E., Colbert, S., Linney, Y., Lawrence, E. and Garety, P. (2003). Cognitive biases involved in the formation of delusional beliefs. *International Congress on Schizophrenia Research*, 178.

Peters, E. R., Thornton, P., Siksou, L., Linney, Y. and MacCabe, J. H. (2008). Specificity of the jump-to-conclusions bias in deluded patients. *The British Journal of Clinical Psychology/The British Psychological Society, 47*(Pt 2), 239–44.

Phillips, L. J., McGorry, P. D., Yuen, H. P., Ward, J., Donovan, K., Kelly, D. et al. (2007). Medium term follow-up of a randomized controlled trial of interventions for young people at ultra high risk of psychosis. *Schizophrenia Research, 96*(1–3), 25–33.

Pinkley, R. L., Griffith, T. L. and Northcraft, G. B. (1995). 'Fixed pie' a la mode: Information availability, information processing, and the negotiation of suboptimal agreements. *Organizational Behaviour and Human Decision Porcesses, 62*, 101–12.

Posner, M. I. and Rothbart, M. K. (1998). Attention, self-regulation, and consciousness. *Philosophical Transcripts of the Royal Society of London, B353*, 1915–27.

Poulton, R., Caspi, A., Moffitt, T. E., Cannon, M., Murray, R. and Harrington, H. (2000). Children's self-reported psychotic symptoms and adult schizophreniform disorder: A 15-year longitudinal study. *Archives of General Psychiatry, 57*(11), 1053–8.

Priebe, S., Huxley, P., Knight, S. and Evans, S. (1999). Application and results of the Manchester short assessment of quality of life (MANSA). *The International Journal of Social Psychiatry, 45*(1), 7–12.

Rachman, S. (2004). Fear of contamination. *Behaviour Research and Therapy, 42*(11), 1227–55.

Rasmussen, S. and Eisen, J. (1989). The epidemiology and clinical features of obsessive compulsive disorder. *Psychiatric Clinics of North America, 98*, 743–58.

Rietdijk, J., Klaassen, R., Ising, H., Dragt, S., Nieman, D. H., van de Kamp, J. *et al.* (2012). Detection of people at risk of developing a first psychosis: Comparison of two recruitment strategies. *Acta Psychiatrica Scandinavica*, 126, 21–30.

Rietdijk, J., Linszen, D. and van der Gaag, M. (2011). Field testing attenuated psychosis syndrome criteria. *The American Journal of Psychiatry*, *168*(11), 1221.

Rosenthal, R. and Rubin, D. B. (1982). A simple, general purpose display of magnitude of experimental effect. *Journal of Educational Psychology*, *74*(2), 166.

Ross, K., Freeman, D., Dunn, G. and Garety, P. (2011). A randomized experimental investigation of reasoning training for people with delusions. *Schizophrenia Bulletin*, *37*(2), 324–33.

Rössler, W., Hengartner, M. P., Ajdacic-Gross, V., Haker, H., Gamma, A. and Angst, J. (2011). Sub-clinical psychosis symptoms in young adults are risk factors for subsequent common mental disorders. *Schizophrenia Research*, *131*(1–3), 18–23.

Rudnick, A. (2003). Paranoia and reinforced dogmatism. *Philosophy of the Social Sciences*, *33*(3), 339.

Rudski, J. M. (2002). Hindsight and confirmation biases in an exercise in telepathy. *Psychological Reports*, *91*(3 Pt 1), 899–906.

Ruhrmann, S., Schultze-Lutter, F., Salokangas, R. K., Heinimaa, M., Linszen, D., Dingemans, P. *et al.* (2010). Prediction of psychosis in adolescents and young adults at high risk: Results from the prospective European prediction of psychosis study. *Archives of General Psychiatry*, *67*(3), 241–51.

Salkovskis, P. M. (1991). The importance of behaviour in the maintenance of anxiety and panic: A cognitive account. *Behavioural Psychotherapy*, 19, 6–19.

Sass, L. A. and Parnas, J. (2003). Schizophrenia, consciousness, and the self. *Schizophrenia Bulletin*, *29*(3), 427–44.

Schienle, A., Vaitl, D. and Stark, R. (1996). Covariation bias and paranormal belief. *Psychological Reports*, *78*(1), 291–95.

Schültze-Lutter, F. and Klosterkötter, J. (2002). *Bonn scale for the assessment of basic symptoms: Prediction list (BSABS-P)*. Cologne: University of Cologne.

Schwarz, N. and Clore, G. L. (1983). Mood, misattribution and judgments of well being: Informative and directive functions of affective states. *Journal of Personality and Social Psychology*, 45, 513–23.

Schwarz, N. and Clore, G. L. (1988). How do I feel about it? The informative function of affective states. In K. Fiedler and J. P. Forgas (eds), *Affect, cognition and social behaviour.* (pp. 44–62). Toronto: Hogrefe.

Sharp, H., Fear, C. and Healy, D. (1997). Attributional style and delusions: An investigation based on delusional content. *European Psychiatry: The Journal of the Association of European Psychiatrists*, *12*(1), 1–7.

Shin, L. M., Rauch, S. L. and Pitman, R. K. (2006). Amygdala, medial prefrontal cortex, and hippocampal function in PTSD. *Annals of the New York Academy of Sciences*, 1071, 67–79.

Silverman, R. J. and Peterson, C. (1993). Explanatory style in schizophrenic and depressed outpatients. *Cognitive Therapy and Research*, 17, 457–70.

Simon, A. E., Cattapan-Ludewig, K., Gruber, K., Ouertani, J., Zimmer, A., Roth, B. *et al.* (2009). Subclinical hallucinations in adolescent outpatients: An outcome study. *Schizophrenia Research*, *108*(1–3), 265–71.

So, S. H., Freeman, D. and Garety, P. (2008). Impact of state anxiety on the jumping to conclusions delusion bias. *The Australian and New Zealand Journal of Psychiatry*, *42*(10), 879–86.

Spauwen, J., Krabbendam, L., Lieb, R., Wittchen, H. U. and van Os, J. (2003). Sex differences in psychosis: Normal or pathological? *Schizophrenia Research*, *62*(1–2), 45–9.

Startup, H., Freeman, D. and Garety, P. A. (2008). Jumping to conclusions and persecutory delusions. *European Psychiatry: The Journal of the Association of European Psychiatrists*, *23*(6), 457–9.

Startup, M., Startup, S. and Sedgman, A. (2008). Immediate source-monitoring, self-focused attention and the positive symptoms of schizophrenia. *Behaviour Research and Therapy*, *46*(10), 1176–80.

Stein, D. J., Westenberg, H. G. and Liebowitz, M. R. (2002). Social anxiety disorder and generalized anxiety disorder: Serotonergic and dopaminergic neurocircuitry. *The Journal of Clinical Psychiatry*, *63 Suppl 6*, 12–9.

Strunk, D. R. and Adler, A. D. (2009). Cognitive biases in three prediction tasks: A test of the cognitive model of depression. *Behaviour Research and Therapy*, *47*(1), 34–40.

Taylor, K. N., Graves, A. and Stopa, L. (2009). Strategic cognition in paranoia: The use of thought control strategies in a non-clinical population. *Behavioural and Cognitive Psychotherapy*, *37*(1), 25–38.

Tomarken, A. J., Mineka, S. and Cook, M. (1989). Fear-relevant selective associations and covariation bias. *Journal of Abnormal Psychology*, *98*(4), 381–94.

van Dael, F., Versmissen, D., Janssen, I., Myin-Germeys, I., van Os, J. and Krabbendam, L. (2006). Data gathering: Biased in psychosis? *Schizophrenia Bulletin*, *32*(2), 341–51.

van der Gaag, M., Nieman, D. H., Rietdijk, J., Dragt, S., Ising, H. K., Klaassen, R. M. *et al.* (2012). Cognitive behavioral therapy for subjects at ultrahigh risk for developing psychosis: A randomized controlled clinical trial. *Schizophrenia Bulletin*, *38*(6), 1180–8.

van der Gaag, M., van Oosterhout, B., Daalman, K., Sommer, I. E. and Korrelboom, K. (2012). Initial evaluation of the effects of competitive memory training (COMET) on depression in schizophrenia-spectrum patients with persistent auditory verbal hallucinations: A randomized controlled trial. *The British Journal of Clinical Psychology/The British Psychological Society*, *51*(2), 158–71.

van der Gaag, M., Schütz, C., Ten Napel, A., Landa, Y., Delespaul, P., Bak, M., *et al.* (2013). Development of the Davos Assessment of Cognitive Biases Scale (DACOBS). *Schizophrenia Research 144*(1–3), 63–71

van Os, J. and Delespaul, P. (2005). Toward a world consensus on prevention of schizophrenia. *Dialogues in Clinical Neuroscience*, *7*(1), 53–67.

van Os, J., Hanssen, M., Bijl, R. V. and Vollebergh, W. (2001). Prevalence of psychotic disorder and community level of psychotic symptoms: An urban-rural comparison. *Archives of General Psychiatry*, *58*(7), 663–8.

Vuilleumier, P., Armony, J. L., Driver, J. and Dolan, R. J. (2001). Effects of attention and emotion on face processing in the human brain: An event-related fMRI study. *Neuron*, *30*(3), 829–41.

Warman, D. M. and Martin, J. M. (2006a). Cognitive insight and delusion proneness: An investigation using the beck cognitive insight scale. *Schizophrenia Research*, *84*(2–3), 297–304.

Warman, D. M. and Martin, J. M. (2006b). Jumping to conclusions and delusion proneness: The impact of emotionally salient stimuli. *The Journal of Nervous and Mental Disease*, *194*(10), 760–5.

Warman, D. M., Lysaker, P. H., Martin, J. M., Davis, L. and Haudenschield, S. L. (2007). Jumping to conclusions and the continuum of delusional beliefs. *Behaviour Research and Therapy*, *45*(6), 1255–69.

Waters, F. A. and Badcock, J. C. (2010). First-Rank symptoms in schizophrenia: Reexamining mechanisms of self-recognition. *Schizophrenia Bulletin*, *36*(3), 510–17.

Wells, A. and Matthews, G. (1996). Modelling cognition in emotional disorder: The S-REF model. *Behaviour Research and Therapy*, *34*(11–12), 881–8.

White, L. O. and Mansell, W. (2009). Failing to ponder? Delusion-prone individuals rush to conclusions. *Clinical Psychology and Psychotherapy*, *16*(2), 111–24.

Wiersma, D., Nienhuis, F. J., Slooff, C. J. and Giel, R. (1998). Natural course of schizophrenic disorders: A 15-year followup of a Dutch incidence cohort. *Schizophrenia Bulletin*, *24*(1), 75–85.

Williams, J. M. G., Watts, F., MacLeod, C. and Mathews, A. (1988). *Cognitive psychology and emotional disorders* (1st edn.). Chichester: John Wiley & Sons.

Williams, J. M. G., Watts, F. N., MacLeod, C. and Matthews, A. (1997). *Cognitive psychology and emotional disorders* (2nd edn.). Chichester: John Wiley & Sons.
Woodward, T. S., Buchy, L., Moritz, S. and Liotti, M. (2007). A bias against disconfirmatory evidence is associated with delusion proneness in a nonclinical sample. *Schizophrenia Bulletin, 33*(4), 1023–8.
Woodward, T. S., Menon, M. and Whitman, J. C. (2007). Source monitoring biases and auditory hallucinations. *Cognitive Neuropsychiatry, 12*(6), 477–94.
Woodward, T. S., Moritz, S., Arnold, M. M., Cuttler, C., Whitman, J. C. and Lindsay, D. S. (2006a). Increased hindsight bias in schizophrenia. *Neuropsychology, 20*(4), 461–7.
Woodward, T. S., Moritz, S., Cuttler, C. and Whitman, J. C. (2006b). The contribution of a cognitive bias against disconfirmatory evidence (BADE) to delusions in schizophrenia. *Journal of Clinical and Experimental Neuropsychology, 28*(4), 605–17.
Woodward, T. S., Moritz, S., Menon, M. and Klinge, R. (2008). Belief inflexibility in schizophrenia. *Cognitive Neuropsychiatry, 13*(3), 267–77.
Woodward, T. S., Munz, M., Leclerc, C. and Lecomte, T. (2009). Change in delusions is associated with change in 'jumping to conclusions'. *Psychiatry Research, 170*, 124–7.
World Health Organization (1999). *Schedules for clinical assessment in neuropsychiatry* (Version 2.1 edn.). Geneva, Switzerland.
Wunderink, A., Nienhuis, F. J., Sytema, S. and Wiersma, D. (2006). Treatment delay and response rate in first episode psychosis. *Acta Psychiatrica Scandinavica, 113*(4), 332–9.
Young, H. F. and Bentall, R. P. (1997). Probabilistic reasoning in deluded, depressed and normal subjects: Effects of task difficulty and meaningful versus non-meaningful material. *Psychological Medicine, 27*(2), 455–65.
Yung, A. R. and McGorry, P. D. (1996). The prodromal phase of first-episode psychosis: Past and current conceptualizations. *Schizophrenia Bulletin, 22*(2), 353–70.
Yung, A. R. and Nelson, B. (2011). Young people at ultra high risk for psychosis: A research update. *Early Intervention in Psychiatry, 5 Suppl 1*, 52–7.
Yung, A. R., Nelson, B., Stanford, C., Simmons, M. B., Cosgrave, E. M., Killackey, E. *et al.* (2008). Validation of 'prodromal' criteria to detect individuals at ultra high risk of psychosis: 2 year follow-up. *Schizophrenia Research, 105*(1–3), 10–17.
Yung, A. R., Phillips, L. J., McGorry, P. D., McFarlane, C. A., Francey, S., Harrigan, S. *et al.* (1998). Prediction of psychosis. A step towards indicated prevention of schizophrenia. *The British Journal of Psychiatry. Suppl. 172*(33), 14–20.
Yung, A. R., Phillips, L. J., Nelson, B., Francey, S. M., Panyuen, H., Simmons, M. B. *et al.* (2011). Randomized controlled trial of interventions for young people at ultra high risk for psychosis: 6-month analysis. *The Journal of Clinical Psychiatry, 72*(4), 430–40.
Yung, A. R., Phillips, L. J., Yuen, H. P. and McGorry, P. D. (2004). Risk factors for psychosis in an ultra high-risk group: Psychopathology and clinical features. *Schizophrenia Research, 67*(2–3), 131–42.
Yung, A. R., Phillips, L. J., Yuen, H. P., Francey, S. M., McFarlane, C. A., Hallgren, M. *et al.* (2003). Psychosis prediction: 12-month follow up of a high-risk ('prodromal') group. *Schizophrenia Research, 60*(1), 21–32.
Yung, A. R., Yuen, H. P., Berger, G., Francey, S., Hung, T. C., Nelson, B. *et al.* (2007). Declining transition rate in ultra high risk (prodromal) services: Dilution or reduction of risk? *Schizophrenia Bulletin, 33*(3), 673–81.
Yung, A. R., Yuen, H. P., McGorry, P. D., Phillips, L. J., Kelly, D., Dell'Olio, M. *et al.* (2005). Mapping the onset of psychosis: The comprehensive assessment of at-risk mental states. *The Australian and New Zealand Journal of Psychiatry, 39*(11–12), 964–71.
Zawadzki, J. A., Woodward, T. S., Sokolowski, H. M., Boon, H. S., Wong, A. H., and Menon, M. (2012). Cognitive factors associated with subclinical delusional ideation in the general population. *Psychiatry Research, 197*(3), 345–9.

Index

Page references to figures or tables will be in *italics*.

ABC (Activating event, Beliefs, Consequences) model 62, 82, 162–3, 171–4; extended form 89, *91*; extraordinary experiences *84*, *91–3*; introduction 79; rationale 149; registration of extraordinary experiences 80–1; suspiciousness 144–5; *see also* treatment protocol for ARMS subjects ('Coping with Extraordinary and Remarkable Experiences' manual)
Abercrombie, H. 22
abnormal reasoning styles 28, 33
Abrahamson, L. Y. 26
activity scheduling 38
Addington, J. 54
Adler, A. D. 36, 49
adolescents, genetic risk of psychosis 27
age factors 51, 52
Aghotor, J. 50
Alden, L. E. 44
alienating experiences 69, 110–11
Allen, P. P. 23
Alloy, L. B. 26, 29
alternative explanations 47; coincidence, underestimation of likelihood of 149; derealisation/depersonalisation 159; extraordinary experiences *91–3*; intrusive experiences/thoughts 152; magical thinking 162–3; supernatural, fear of 155–6; suspiciousness 144–5
Alvarez-Jiménez, M. 52

Amaral, D. 22
American Psychiatric Association (APA) 43
Amminger, G. P. 54
amygdala, brain 20, 21, 22, 101
analogue studies 49
Anderson, K. K. 9
anger, voices feeding on 114–17
anterior cingulate cortex (ACC) 22, 48, 114, 115, 116
anterior insula 48
anti-anxiety drugs 22
antipsychotic medication 9, 34, 53–55, 73
anxiety disorders: and attribution bias 28; avoidance behaviour (evading threat) 43–4, 47, 114; case studies 15, 16, 41, 143–4, 155; cognitive bias modification 49; cognitive model 28; and emotional reasoning 40; fear versus anxiety 43; and paranoia 49; and perceptual bias 20; transdiagnostic biases 47
APA (American Psychiatric Association) 43
Armony, J. 20
ARMS (At Risk Mental State): ARMS period 9–10; avoidance behaviour in subjects 43–4, 47; closing-in strategy 7–8, 10, 11; and cognitive biases 19–44, *46*; cognitive biases associated with *see* cognitive biases 19–44; definition/features 5–8; ethical issues 8; identifying subjects with *see* ARMS; incidence of psychosis in 6–7; jumping to conclusions reasoning style 33, 35;

prevalence and incidence 7; psychosis risk in help-seeking subjects 8; referral of subjects 11; transition rates into psychosis 6, 7, 8, 52, 53, 56, 57; treatment protocol for patients with *see* treatment protocol for ARMS subjects ('Coping with Extraordinary and Remarkable Experiences' manual);
ARMS, identifying subjects with 9–16; fulfilment of criteria 13–16; importance of identification 9–10; instruments 10–11; interviews with patients/parents 12; procedure 11–13
Arntz, A. 30, 40
At Risk Mental State (ARMS) *see* ARMS
Attention Deficit and Hyperactivity Disorder (ADHD) 39
attenuated psychotic symptoms 11, 48, 51, 55
attribution bias 26–31
attribution style, and cognitive biases 19
auditory hallucinations 24
Avery, R. 37
avoidance behaviour (evading threat) 43–4, 47, 114
Ayton, P. 32

Babcock, J. C. 23
BAI *see* Beck Anxiety Inventory
Bak, M. 7
Baker, G. A. 23
Bar-Haim, Y. 20
basic assumptions 94, 137
Beck Depression Inventory-2 (BDI2) 56, 63, 66, 75, 86
'beads' reasoning test 19, 32–3, 34
Beard, C. 49
Beauregard, M. 22
Bechdolf, A. 54
Beck, A. T. 20, 27, 28, 36, 36–7, 38, 40, 56, 63, 66
Beck Anxiety Inventory (BAI) 63, 66, 75, 86, 140
Beck Cognitive Insight Scale 19
behavioural bias 43–4
behavioural experiment form 129, 183–4
behavioural experiments 128, 185–6; examples *134–5*
beliefs 19, 79, 82; defeatist 36, 37; persistence after evidential discrediting 39; *see also* paranormal, belief in
Bell, V. 19, 31
Bennett, K. 50

Bentall, R. P. 23, 26, 27, 31, 32, 36
Ben-Zeev, D. 37
bias against disconfirmatory evidence (BADE) 34, 42–3, 105
Bieling, P. 44
biological markers 45
Birchwood, M. 56
Bishop, S. J. 20, 21
Blackmore, S. J. 30
Blackwood, N. 19
Bleuler, E. 11
BLIPS (brief limited intermittent psychotic symptoms) 5, 14, 55
Bonn Scale for the Assessment of Basic Symptoms (BSABS/BSABS-P) 11
Bookheimer, S. Y. 21, 22
Boone, K. 21
Boonstra, N. 11, 52, 167
booster sessions 141
bottom-up sensory control processes 21
Bourgouin, P. 22
Bradley, B. P. 20
brain: amygdala 20, 21, 22, 101; anterior cingulate cortex 22, 48, 114–16; Broca's area 115; dopamine released in 71, 72, 76, 149; feed-forward and feed-backward systems 21, 112, *113*; motor cortex 114; prefrontal cortex 20, 21–2, 101–2, 114, 115; sensory cortex 114; supplemental motor areas 114; and threat-related stimuli 20, 21; Wernicke's area 115; *see also* dopamine
brain scanning techniques 78
Brakoulias, V. 27, 28, 50
brief limited intermittent psychotic symptoms (BLIPS) 5, 14, 55
Broca's area, brain 115
Brockner, J. 42
Broome, M. R. 11, 19, 32, 35
Brown, G. K. 56
Brüne, M. 26
Brunelin, J. 24
Brunet, K. 52
Buchy, L. 42

CAARMS (Comprehensive Assessment of At Risk Mental States) 11, 13, 55–57, 140, 167; case example (Agnes) 15–16; case example (Ben) 14–15; case example (Ibrahim) 13–14; composition 10; 'gold standard' interview 8; scoring 12; and treatment protocol for ARMS subjects ('Coping with Extraordinary

and Remarkable Experiences' manual) 61, 62–3
Calabria, K. 37
Candido, C. L. 26
Cannistraro, P. A. 21
Cannon, T. D. 51
Carpenter, W. T. 1
case formulation: coincidence, underestimation of likelihood of 149–50; completed form *121*, 175; derealisation/depersonalisation 160; direct influence of life experiences 120; indirect influence of life experiences 120–1; intrusive experiences/thoughts 153; life experiences included in 119; magical thinking *163*; supernatural, fear of 156; suspiciousness, impeding of functioning 146; treatment goals, setting 121; treatment protocol for ARMS subjects 89, 118–21
catastrophic thoughts, challenging 22
causality, overestimation of (covariation bias) 29–31, 108–9
CBM (cognitive bias modification) 49
CBT *see* cognitive behavioural therapy
chance, underestimation of 109, 148; covariation bias 29–31, 108–9
Chapman, J. P. 29
Chapman, L. J. 29
children, emotional reasoning bias 40–1
chi-square linear-by-linear analysis 58
Christensen-Szalanski, J. J. J. 25
Chudleigh, C. 52
Clarke, J. C. 56
Clore, G. L. 40
closing-in strategy 7–8, 10, 11
cognitive behavioural therapy (CBT) 53, 122–40; and abnormal reasoning styles 28; assessment and metacognitive training (treatment protocol) 85–118; avoidance behaviour, tackling 43; booster sessions 141; coincidence, underestimation of likelihood of 150–1; defeatist beliefs, challenging 37; derealisation/depersonalisation 161; evaluation and relapse prevention 141; and intact executive functioning 21; intrusive experiences/thoughts 153–4; and jumping to conclusions 34; magical thinking 164–5; post-assessment 140–1; and prefrontal cortex 22; protocol 119; supernatural, fear of 157–8; suspiciousness, impeding of functioning 146–7; treatment plan 122–40; *see also* treatment protocol for ARMS

subjects ('Coping with Extraordinary and Remarkable Experiences' manual) 67–118
cognitive bias modification (CBM) 49
cognitive biases: associated with ARMS 19–44; attribution 26–31; awareness of 56; 'beads' reasoning test 19, 32–3, 34; behavioural bias 43–4; case examples 24–40; confirmation 42–3, 105; covariation 29–31, 47, 108–9; and delusions *see* delusions, and cognitive biases; dopamine sensitisation 47–8; emotional reasoning 40–2, 106, *107*; endophenotypes 45, 47; hindsight 24–6; memory 23–4, 83, 98–100; modification in anxiety and mood disorders 49; nature of 45–50; negative expectation 36–8; whether open to change 49–50; perceptual 20–3, 96–7; reasoning 31–43, 100–10; and schizophrenia 19, 23, *46*; transdiagnostic 47; treatment protocol for ARMS patients ('Coping with Extraordinary and Remarkable Experiences' manual) 83, *84–5*
cognitive challenging 22, 123–8, 137, 157–8
cognitive restructuring 21, 22
COGPACK (cognitive remediation package) 50
coincidence, underestimation of likelihood of 30, 108–9, 148–51; *see also* covariation bias; case formulation 149–50; cognitive behavioural therapy 150–1; introduction/assessment 148–9; metacognitive training 149; normalising information/alternative explanations 149; relapse prevention/end of therapy 151
Colbert, S. M. 32, 33, 35
'common sense,' loss of 18
confirmation bias (bias against disconfirmatory evidence) 34, 42–3, 47, 105
Connolly, K. M. 30
consonant information 42
contamination fear, covariation biases in 30
control, feelings of loss 112, *113*
convictions and habits, helpful 117–18
Conway, C. R. 32
Cook, M. 30
'Coping with Extraordinary and Remarkable Experiences' manual *see* treatment protocol for ARMS subjects
Corcoran, R. 35, 50
covariation bias 29–31, 47; treatment protocol 108–9
Cuijpers, P. 51
cumulative probability, calculating 125, 181–2

D2 receptor blockade 48
DACOBS documentation 63, 66, 75, 86
danger: and emotional reasoning 40–2, 106, *107*; extraordinary experiences, following 73–4; overestimation of 96–7; seeing anywhere 20–3; *see also* threat
data-gathering bias 19, 31–6, 45
Davidson, R. J. 22
Davies, M. F. 31, 39
decision-making, and cognitive biases 19, 42
defeatist beliefs 36, 37
déjà vu 16, 76
Delespaul, P. 8
delusions 7, 18; and cognitive biases *see* delusions, and cognitive biases; defined 31; and dogmatism bias 39; and dopamine sensitisation 48; versus hallucinations 23; jumping to conclusions bias 32; in schizophrenia 31
delusions, and cognitive biases 19; attribution bias 26, 27; hindsight bias 24; jumping to conclusions 33–4; memory biases 23
depression 5, 71, 159; attribution bias 26; case studies 13–14; cognitive model 49; and paranoia 50; and pessimistic reasoning style 36
derealisation/depersonalisation 18, 110–11, 158–61; case formulation 160; cognitive behavioural therapy 161; introduction/assessment 158–9; metacognitive training 159–60; normalising information/alternative explanations 159; relapse prevention/end of therapy 161
deregulation, dopamine 48, 109–10, 116
Derryberry, D. 20, 21
detection, early 52–3
devil, fear of 14, 44, 74, 154
Dewey, M. E. 26
Diagnostic and Statistical Manual of Mental Disorders (DSM) IV criteria 12, 43, 47, 161, 167
dimensional approach, in psychiatry 47, 167
disconfirmatory evidence, bias against *see* bias against disconfirmatory evidence (BADE)
disease awareness 61, 65, 67, 89
disengagement, as protective safety behaviour 37
dissonant information 42
distancing 132–3
distorted self-experiences 17–18
dog phobia 47, 79, 83, 114

dogmatism bias/belief inflexibility 39–40, 89, 104
Dolan, R. J. 20
dopamine 76–7, 102, 107; brain, released in 71, 72, 76, 149; deregulation 48, 109–10, 116; disruption of and recommended actions 72–3; as misleader 71–2; sensitisation 47–8, 72; striatal dopamine neurons 28
downward arrow technique 121
Dragt, S. 51
Drake, R. 9, 50
Dudley, R. E. J. 32, 34
DUP (duration of untreated psychosis) 9, 10, 51, 52

Early Detection and Intervention Evaluation study, Manchester 54
Early Detection and Intervention Team (EDIT) 14, 152
Early Detection and Intervention Evaluation trial (EDIE-NL), Dutch: interventions 56; participants 55; protocol, evidence for 58; remission status at 18-months follow-up 58; results 57–8
early experiences, influence 80
eating disorders 47
Eckersley, R. 52
egocentric perspective 27
Ehlers, A. 28
El Niño 108
Eldar, S. 20, 49
Elstein, A. S. 25
Emery, G. D. 28
emotion regulation skills 50
emotional reasoning bias 40–2; treatment protocol 106, *107*
endophenotypes, and cognitive biases 45
enrichment 8
Ensum, I. 23
ethical issues 8
executive functioning (EF) 21, 22
experiences, intrusive *see* intrusive experiences/thoughts
exposure assignments 128
external locus of control 27
externalising bias 26
extraordinary experiences 17–18; alienating 110–11; with alternative explanations 89–90, *91–3*; assessment 86–8; 'Coping with Extraordinary and Remarkable Experiences' manual *see* treatment protocol for ARMS

subjects ('Coping with Extraordinary and Remarkable Experiences' manual); defined 68; entering danger zone following 73–4; frequently occurring, examples 67, *69*; intrusive or dominant, becoming 110–17; judging *85*; normal and abnormal 67–8; registration of 80–1, *84*
extrasensory perception (ESP) 29
Eysenck, M. W. 20, 21, 28

facts, versus interpretations 99
failure, blaming others for 26–9
false positive subjects 6, 7–8
fear: versus anxiety 43; automatic responses 22, 107; voices feeding on 114–17
Fear, C. F. 26, 32
feed-forward and feed-backward systems, brain 21, 112, *113*
FEP (first-episode psychosis): Dutch Early Detection and Intervention Evaluation trial (EDIE-NL) 55–8; early detection, goals 52–3; early intervention, evidence 53–5; evidence for preventing/postponing 51–8; treatment protocol for ARMS patients *see* treatment protocol for ARMS subjects ('Coping with Extraordinary and Remarkable Experiences' manual)
Fernyhough, C. 27
Festinger, L. 42
first-episode psychosis (FEP) *see* FEP
first-person perspective, distorted 18
Fiszbein, A. 50
Fox, E. 21
Frame, L. 9
Freeman, D. 19, 31, 32, 34, 35, 44
Freeston, M. H. 33
Freeston Intolerance of Uncertainty scale 33
French, P. 2, 37, 56
Frenkel, E. 27
Fresco, D. M. 26
Frijda, N. H. 21
Fuhrer, R. 9
functional magnetic resonance imaging (fMRI) 22

Gallup, G. H. 30
Garety, P. A. 19, 31, 32, 33, 34, 35, 44, 50
Gee, D. G. 21
general practitioners (GPs) 51
generalised anxiety disorder (GAD) 21, 28
genes 45

genetic factors 45; at-risk groups 5, 27
German Research Network on Schizophrenia 54–5
ghosts, fear of *see* supernatural, fear of
Global Assessment of Functioning (GAF) scale 12
Glotzbach, E. 43
God, existence of 39
Goldman, H. H. 5, 12, 55, 56
Gorman, J. M. 22
Gottesman, I. 45
Gould, T. 45
Granholm, E. 37
Grant, P. M. 27, 36, 37, 38
Graves, A. 50
Greenberg, R. L. 28
Greenwood, C. M. 45
Griffith, T. L. 42
Gross, G. 11

habits 117–18
Haddock, G. 24
Hall, P. L. 139
Hallion, L. S. 49
hallucinations 16, 68, 78; auditory 24; case studies 14, 16; versus delusions 23; and dopamine sensitisation 48; hypnagogic 7, 16; hypnopompic 7; sensory experiences 17; and source monitoring 23–4
haloperidol 55
Hanssen, M. 7, 52
Hariri, A. R. 21, 22
Harrington, L. 26
Harvey, A. G. 29, 43
hasty conclusions 31–6
Havers, S. 23
Healy, D. 26, 32
Heilbrun, A. B. J. 23
Heimberg, R. G. 28
Hemsley, D. R. 32
Heres, S. 52
Hickie, I. B. 51
hindsight bias (knowing it all along) 24–6
Hoffmann, H. 37
Holden, C. 167
Holton, B. 42
Hope, D. A. 28
hot cognitions 94
Howes, O. D. 48
Huber, G. 11
Hunter, E. C. *111*

Huq, S. F. 32
hypnagogic hallucinations 7, 16
hypnopompic hallucinations 7

ideas of reference 18
information processing biases 28
insight, poor 27
integrated therapy 54
intermediate assumptions, assessing 94
internal dialogues 153
interpretations, versus facts 99
intrusive experiences/thoughts 98, 149, 151–4; case formulation 153; case studies 24, 31; cognitive behavioural therapy 153–4; introduction/assessment 152; metacognitive training 152–3; normalising information/ alternative explanations 152; relapse prevention/end of therapy 154; *see also* voices, hearing
Iqbal, Z. 140
Ising, H. K. 11, 51, 167

Jackson, C. 140
Janis, I. L. 42
Janssen, I. 26
Jenkins, R. 20
Johnston, L. 42
Johnstone, E. C. 9
Joiner, T. E. 26
Jong, P. de 29, 30
jumping to conclusions (JTC) 19, 31–6; and delusions 33–4; disadvantages of 101; and efficacy of CBT 34; and psychosis 35; suspiciousness 145; and symptom severity 35; treatment protocol for ARMS subjects 100–3

Kaney, S. 26, 27
Kaplan-Meyer curves, Dutch Early Detection and Intervention Evaluation trial 57
Kapur, S. 32, 48
Kay, S. R. 50
Kendler, K. S. 7
Kennedy, S. J. 30
Kinderman, P. 26, 27
Klaassen, R. M. 51
Klosterkötter, J. 11
Koning, M. B. de 53
Krabbendam, L. 7
Kuipers, E. 44
Kunz, B. 37
Kupper, Z. 37

Lader, M. H. 43
Langdon, R. 27, 28
Large, M. 9
Larsen, T. K. 9
Laruelle, M. 47–8
Lave, T. R. 5, 12, 55, 56
Lawrence, A. D. 20
Lecomte, T. 34
LeDoux, J. 22
Ledoux, J. 20
Leucht, S. 52
Lévesque, J. 22
Lieberman, J. A. 1
Liebowitz, M. R. 21–2
life experiences: direct influence 120; included in case formulation 119; indirect influence 120–1
lifestyle recommendations 82
Likert scale 10, 33
Lincoln, T. M. 49
Link, P. C. 37
Linney, Y. M. 32
Linszen, D. H. 11, 51
Liotti, M. 42
Loewy, R. L. 11, 57, 167
Lovibond, P. 43
Lundgren, S. R. 42
Lyon, H. M. 26

MacLeod, C. 20
magical thinking 161–5; case formulation *163*; cognitive behavioural therapy 164–5; introduction/assessment 162; metacognitive training 163; normalising information/alternative explanations 162–3; relapse prevention/end of therapy 165
Maher, B. A. 31
Malla, A. K. 9
Mansell, W. 33–4
Marks, I. M. 43
Marshall, M. 9, 11
Marshall, W. L. 43
Martin, D. J. 21
Martin, J. M. 19, 32
Mateer, C. A. 22
Mathews, A. 20, 28
Matthews, G. 22
Mattia, J. I. 28
Mattick, R. P. 56
Mayberg, H. 22
Mazurski, E. J. 30

Mazziotta, J. C. 21, 22
McClure, J. 26
McGlashan, T. H. 10
McGorry, P. D. 5, 6, 9, 53, 54, 61, 167, 168
McKay, R. 19
medial prefrontal cortex 22
Melle, I. 9
memory biases 23–4, 83; treatment protocol for ARMS subjects 98–100
Menon, M. 32, 34–5
Merckelbach, H. 29, 30, 40–1
metacognitive training (MCT): coincidence underestimation of likelihood of 149; derealisation/depersonalisation 159–60; introducing 95–6; intrusive experiences/thoughts 152–3; magical thinking 163; psychosis 50; reasoning biases 50; schizophrenia patients 19; suspiciousness, impeding of functioning 145; treatment protocol for ARMS subjects 95–6
Miller, G. 167
Miller, T. J. 5, 6, 10, 47, 61
Mineka, S. 30
Mizrahi, R. 32
Mogg, K. 20
Mohlman, J. 22
mood disorders: cognitive bias modification 49; see also anxiety disorders; depression
Moore, M. T. 26
Moritz, S. 2, 19, 32, 33, 34, 42, 50, 103
Morland, T. 21
Morrison, A. P. 2, 9, 23, 24, 49, 54, 55, 56
Mortimer, A. M. 32
motivation, and dopamine 72
motor cortex (MC), brain 114
Moutoussis, M. 28
Mowrer, O. H. 43
multidimensional evaluation 137, 140, 151; form 187–8
Muris, P. 40–1

needs-based therapy 53
negative expectation bias (pessimism) 36–8; treatment protocol for ARMS subjects 99–100
negative interpretation bias 49
Nelson, B. 11, 17, 53
NEMESIS study 7
Nemeth, C. J. 42
neurocognitive impairment, and pessimism 37, 38

neuroimaging 20
neurons 28, 48
neurotransmitters 71, 118
Newport, F. 30
NICE 140
Nieman, D. H. 6, 11, 51, 167
Nordentoft, M. 54
normalising: coincidence, underestimation of likelihood of 149; derealisation/depersonalisation 159; magical thinking 162–3; and psycho-education 63–6, 74–85; supernatural, fear of 155–6; suspiciousness, impeding of functioning 144–5
Norman, D. A. 22
Northcraft, G. B. 42
Northwick Park Study 9
nucleus accumbens (NAcc) 102

obsessive thoughts 98; see also intrusive experiences/thoughts
obsessive-compulsive disorder (OCD) 42, 151, 155, 161
obsessive-compulsive symptoms (OCS) 30, 31 44, 162–5
Ohayon, M. M. 7
olanzapine 54
omega-3 fish oil 53, 54
Opler, L. A. 50
OPUS trial, Denmark 54
Oren, Z. 21
Over, D. E. 34

PACE clinic, Melbourne 53
Padmala, S. 21
Palaniyappan, L. 48
panic disorder 28, 41, 148
paranoia: and anxiety 49; being threatened 114; and depression 50; and dogmatism/belief inflexibility bias 39; personalisation bias 26, 27; and pessimistic reasoning style 36; subclinical 50; transdiagnostic biases 47; see also suspiciousness
paranormal, belief in 25, 29, 30, 73
Parnas, J. 17
Pelletier, M. 22
perceptual abnormalities subscale, ARMS criteria 14, 15
perceptual bias 20–3; ARMS treatment protocol 96–7
perceptual load, high or low 21

Perivoliotis, D. 27, 37
Perkins, D. O. 9
personalisation bias 26–9, 48
pessimism 36–8, 99–100
Pessoa, L. 21
Peters, E. 32, 33, 34, 35
Peterson, C. 26
Phillips, L. J. 5, 6, 53
phobias 29, 154; dog phobia 47, 79, 83, 114; social phobia 28, 43, 44
pie chart technique 123, 124, form 179–80
Pinkley, R. L. 42
Pitman, R. K. 21
plague 108
Posner, M. I. 21
post-assessment 140–1
post-traumatic stress disorder (PTSD) 9, 151, 152
Poulton, R. 7
PQ-16 (16-item Prodromal Questionnaire) 11
prefrontal cortex (PFC), brain 20, 21–2, 48, 101–2, 114, 115
preventive medicine 8
Priebe, S. 56
PRIME (Prevention through Risk Identification, Management and Education), US 54
Prislin, R. 42
probabilistic reasoning/probability judgement 27, 30, 34
prodromal period 5, 9, 27, 54–5
Prodromal Questionnaire (PQ) 11, 57, 167
proteins, and genes 45
psychiatric diseases, costs to society 51–2
psychic abilities, belief in 26, 73
psycho-education 10, 86; idiosyncratic 78–9; intervening with 123; and normalising 63–6, 74–85
psychological appraisal processes 7
psychosis: as aberrant salience driven by dopamine 48; attenuated symptoms 48; duration of untreated psychosis 9, 10, 51; Dutch Early Detection and Intervention Evaluation trial 55–8; early detection, goals 52–3; early intervention, evidence 53–5; evidence for preventing/postponing first episode 51–8; first episode in patients with an ARMS, treatment protocol *see* treatment protocol for ARMS subjects; first-degree relatives of patients, cognitive biases in *46*; first-episode *see* FEP (first-episode psychosis); genetic factors 45; and jumping to conclusions 35; longitudinal studies 34–5; metacognitive training, effects in 50; and OCD 161; persistent symptoms 7; prodromal symptoms 5, 9, 27; psychotic features in general population 7; risk of in help-seeking ARMS subjects 8; subclinical symptoms 5, 7, 8, 50; transition rates from ARMS into 6, 7, 8, 52, 53, 56, 57; ultra-high risk of developing 5, *6*, 11
Psychotic Symptoms Rating Scales (PSYRATS) 50, 58
punishment 49
Pyszczynski, T. 42

questionnaires 86

Rachman, S. 30
randomised controlled trials (RCTs) 34, 53
Rangrej, J. 45
Rapee, R. M. 30
Rauch, S. L. 21
Rauner, M. 40
reality, losing touch with *see* derealisation/depersonalisation; psychosis
reasoning biases 31–43; confirmation bias (bias against disconfirmatory evidence) 34, 42–3, 47, 105; covariation bias 29–31, 108–9; dogmatism/belief inflexibility 39–40, 89, 104; emotional reasoning 40–2, 106, *107*; jumping to conclusions 31–6, 100–3; longitudinal studies 34–5; metacognitive training 50; and paranoia 49; treatment protocol for ARMS subjects 100–10
Reed, M. A. 20
reference, ideas of 18
reflectivity, intense 18
rehabilitation 37
rejection, fear of 16
relapse prevention 141; coincidence, underestimation of likelihood of 151; derealisation/depersonalisation 161; intrusive experiences/thoughts 154; magical thinking 165; supernatural, fear of 158; suspiciousness, impeding of functioning 147–8
religious dogmatism 39
Revised Paranormal Belief Scale (Tobacyk) 25
Rietdijk, J. 11, 51, 53
risperidone 53
Rogers, J. 42
Romney, D. M. 26
Rosenthal, R. 25

Ross, K. 50
Rössler, W. 167
Rothbart, M. K. 21
Rubin, D. B. 25
Rubin, J. Z. 42
Rudnick, A. 39
Rudski, J. M. 25
Ruhrmann, S. 6
Ruscio, A. M. 49

Salkovskis, P. M. 43
Sass, L. A. 17
Scale of Prodromal Symptoms (SOPS) 10
Schedules for Clinical Assessment in Neuropsychiatry (SCAN), WHO 56, 58
Schienle, A. 29
schizophrenia 5, 8, 11; and cognitive biases 19, 23, 46; delusions in 31; Dutch Early Detection and Intervention Evaluation trial (EDIE-NL) 58; endophenotypes 45; German Research Network on Schizophrenia 54–5; longitudinal studies 34; metacognitive training for patients 19; as neurodevelopmental disorder 1; personalisation 26, 27; stigmatisation 52–3; theory-of-mind dysfunction 26; voices, hearing 43
Schültze-Lutter, F. 11
Schwarz, N. 40
selective attention 20–3, 47, 96–7, 109
self-blame 26
self-esteem: negative 16, 154; reinforcing 139, 189
self-experiences, distorted 17–18
self-referential bias *see* personalisation bias
self-serving bias 26–9
sensitisation, dopamine 47–8, 72
sensory cortex (SC), brain 114
sensory experiences 17
serotonin 71
session forms 63, 169–70
Shalice, T. 22
Sharp, H. 26
Shin, L. M. 21
shyness 83
Siegert, R. J. 26
Silverman, R. J. 26
Simon, A. E. 8
SIPS (Structured Interview of Prodromal Syndromes) 12; Likert scale 10–11; Scale of Prodromal Symptoms 10; and treatment protocol for ARMS subjects ('Coping with Extraordinary and Remarkable Experiences' manual) 61, 62–3
Skodol, A. E. 5, 12, 55, 56
smoking, and cancer 108
Social and Occupational Functioning Assessment Scale (SOFAS) 5, 12, 55
Social Comparison Rating Scale 153
social phobia 28, 43, 44
Socratic interviewing 127
SOFAS *see* Social and Occupational Functioning Assessment Scale
sounds, alarming 16
source monitoring bias 23–4, 98
Spauwen, J. 7
speech 115
speech/motor derailment 18
Stark, R. 29
Startup, M. 26, 37
Steer, R. A. 56, 63, 66
Stein, D. J. 21–2
stigmatisation 10, 52–3
Stopa, L. 50
Strauss, J. S. 1
stress, and neurotransmitter imbalance 71
striatal dopamine neurons 28
structured day, importance of 14
Structured Interview of Prodromal Syndromes *see* SIPS
Strunk, D. R. 36, 49
subclinical symptoms, psychosis 5, 7, 8, 50
subcortical thalamo-amygdala pathway 20
subthreshold frequency group/subthreshold intensity group 5
success, taking credit for 26
Sun, L. 45
supernatural, fear of 154–8; case formulation 156; case studies 15; cognitive behavioural therapy 157–8; devil 14, 44, 74, 154; introduction/assessment 155; normalising information/alternative explanations 155–6; relapse prevention/end of therapy 158
supplemental motor areas (SMAs), brain 114
suspiciousness: case formulation 146; case studies 39–40; cognitive behavioural therapy 146–7; advantage of 67; impeding of functioning 143–8; introduction/assessment 143–4; metacognitive training 145; normalising information/alternative explanations 144–5; relapse prevention/end of therapy 147–8; *see also* paranoia

Sutton, S. K. 30
symptom severity, and jumping to conclusions 35

Tabachnik, N. 29
Tarrier, N. 139
Taylor, K. N. 50
telepathy 67
temporal contiguity, versus covariation 29
theory-of-mind dysfunction 26, 27
there-you-go reasoning (confirmation bias) 42–3, 47, 105
Thompson, A. 17
thought–event fusion 155
thoughts: attributing to others 23–4, 71, 98, 112, 148; catastrophic, challenging 22; hearing out loud of own 98; influenced more frequently, seeming 112, *113*; intrusive 24, 31, 98, 149, 151–4; restructuring 21, 22; suppressing 24; unpleasant, coping with 49–50, 112; unusual content, psychotic disorder criteria 14, 15
threat: attribution bias 28; cognitive biases as *85*; emotional reasoning bias 106, *107*; evading (avoidance behaviour) 43–4, 47, 114; and paranoia 114; selective attention for 20–3, 47, 96–7, 109; *see also* danger
Tobacyk, J. J. 25
Tomarken, A. J. 30
top-down attentional control 20, 21
transdiagnostic biases 47
transition to psychosis 6, 7, 8; Dutch Early Detection and Intervention Evaluation trial (EDIE-NL) 56, 57; prevention 52, 53
trauma-focused interventions 139
treatment goals, setting 121, 177
treatment plans, CBT 122–40; behavioural experiments 128, *134–5*; cognitive challenging 22, 123–8, 137, 157–8; distancing 132–3; negative basic assumptions 137; psycho-education 123; self-esteem, reinforcing 139; trauma-focused interventions 139
treatment protocol for ARMS subjects ('Coping with Extraordinary and Remarkable Experiences' manual) 61–142; ABC model, introduction 79; alienating experiences 110–11; alternative explanations 89–90, *91–3*; anger and fear, voices feeding on 114–17; assessment of extraordinary experiences 86–8; assumptions, assessing 94–5; basic information 66; beliefs, influence of 79, 82; booster sessions 141; case formulation 89, 118–19, *121*; CBT assessment 85–118; cognitive biases 83, *85*; components of protocol 61; confirmation bias 105; consolidation 141; convictions and habits, helpful 117–18; covariation bias 108–9; disease awareness 61, 65, 67, 89; dogmatism/belief inflexibility 104; and dopamine *see* dopamine; emotional reasoning bias 106, *107*; entering danger zone following extraordinary experiences 73–4; extraordinary experiences becoming intrusive or dominant 110–17; homework 22, 66–7, 83, 90, 141; idiosyncratic psycho-education 78–9; intermediate assumptions, assessing 94; introduction and pre-assessment (one session) 62–74; introduction of module 67–8; jumping to conclusions 100–3; lifestyle recommendations 82; measurements, administering 66, 75; memory biases 98–100; metacognitive training 95–6; method of module 68–71, 75; negative expectation bias (pessimism) 99–100; normal and abnormal extraordinary experiences 67–8; normalising 63–6, 74–85; outline of stages 62; paranoia 114; perceptual bias 96–7; preparation 62–7; psycho-education 10, 63–6, 74–85, 78–9, 86; questionnaires 86; rationale of treatment 61–2; reasoning biases 100–10; registration of extraordinary experiences 80–1, *84*; session forms 63, 169–70; vignettes 129–32, 137–8, 139; withdrawal from social contacts 117; *see also* cognitive biases
Troscianko, A. 30

ultra-high risk groups 5, 6, 11
uncertainty, intolerance of 19, 33
unnecessary treatment, avoiding 8

Vaitl, D. 29
van Dael, F. 32, 33, 35
van den Hout, M. 29, 30, 40
van der Gaag, M. 6, 51, 139
van Os, J. 7, 8
van Spauwen, I. 40–1
ventral pallidus (VP) 102
ventral tegmental area (VTA) 102
ventrolateral prefrontal cortex activation 21
vignettes 129–32, 137–8, 139, 143–65

visions 68
Voice Power Differential Scale 153
voices, hearing 43, 71, 73–4; anger and fear, feeding on 114–17; case studies 14, 15, 24; own thoughts 98; *see also* intrusive experiences/thoughts
Vuilleumier, P. 20
vulnerability markers 45

Warman, D. M. 19, 32
Waters, F. A. 23
Wells, A. 22
Wernicke's area, brain 115
Wessely, S. 32
Westenberg, H. G. 21–2
Whistehouse, W. G. 26

White, L. O. 33–4
whiteboards 38
Wiersma, D. 52
Willham, C. F. 25
Williams, J. M. G. 20, 28
Wing, L. 43
withdrawal from social contacts 53, 117, 147
Woodward, T. S. 2, 19, 24, 32, 33, 34, 42, 50, 103
World Health Organization (WHO) 56
Wunderink, A. 51, 53, 167

Young, H. F. 31, 32
Yung, A. R. 5, 6, 10, 11, 12, 17, 48, 51, 53, 54, 55, 56, 61

Zawadzki, J. A. 43

Taylor & Francis
eBooks
FOR LIBRARIES

ORDER YOUR FREE 30 DAY INSTITUTIONAL TRIAL TODAY!

Over 23,000 eBook titles in the Humanities, Social Sciences, STM and Law from some of the world's leading imprints.

Choose from a range of subject packages or create your own!

- ▶ Free MARC records
- ▶ COUNTER-compliant usage statistics
- ▶ Flexible purchase and pricing options

- ▶ Off-site, anytime access via Athens or referring URL
- ▶ Print or copy pages or chapters
- ▶ Full content search
- ▶ Bookmark, highlight and annotate text
- ▶ Access to thousands of pages of quality research at the click of a button

For more information, pricing enquiries or to order a free trial, contact your local online sales team.

UK and Rest of World: **online.sales@tandf.co.uk**
US, Canada and Latin America:
e-reference@taylorandfrancis.com

www.ebooksubscriptions.com

A flexible and dynamic resource for teaching, learning and research.